An Introduction to Metaphysics

An Introduction to Metaphysics

The Creative Mind

by HENRI BERGSON

of the Académie Francaise and the
Académie des Sciences morales et politiques

ROWMAN & LITTLEFIELD PUBLISHERS, INC.

Contents

	PAGE
Preface	7
I.—Introduction (Part I). Retrograde movement of the true growth of truth	11
II.—Introduction (Part II). Stating the problems	30
III.—The possible and the real	91
IV.—Philosophical intuition	107
V.—The perception of change	130
VI.—Introduction to Metaphysics	159
VII.—The philosophy of Claude Bernard	201
VIII.—On the pragmatism of William James. Truth and reality	209
IX.—The life and work of Ravaisson	220

Preface

This collection comprises first of all, two introductory essays written especially for it, and consequently heretofore unpublished. They make up a third of the volume. The rest are articles or lectures, mostly out of print, which appeared in France or in other countries. Taken as a whole, they date from the period between 1903 and 1923. They bear mainly upon the method I believe should be recommended to the philosopher. To go back to the origin of this method, to trace the direction it impresses upon research, is the particular object of the two essays which make up the introduction.

In a book which appeared in 1919 under the title *L'Energie spirituelle,* I collected some "essays and lectures" dealing with the results of some of my work. The present collection, in which are grouped "essays and lectures," is a sequel to the first, relating this time to the task of research.

The "Delegates of the Clarendon Press" of Oxford have very kindly authorized the re-printing in this volume of the two lectures, so carefully edited by them, which I gave in 1911 at Oxford University. I extend to them my cordial thanks.

H. B.

An Introduction to Metaphysics

I *Introduction*

RETROGRADE MOVEMENT OF THE TRUE GROWTH OF TRUTH

What philosophy has lacked most of all is precision. Philosophical systems are not cut to the measure of the reality in which we live; they are too wide for reality. Examine any one of them, chosen as you see fit, and you will see that it could apply equally well to a world in which neither plants nor animals have existence, only men, and in which men would quite possibly do without eating and drinking, where they would neither sleep nor dream nor let their minds wander; where, born decrepit, they would end as babes-in-arms; where energy would return up the slope of its dispersion, and where everything might just as easily go backwards and be upside down. The fact is that a self-contained (vrai) system is an assemblage of conceptions so abstract, and consequently so vast, that it might contain, aside from the real, all that is possible and even impossible. The only explanation we should accept as satisfactory is one which fits tightly to its object, with no space between them, no crevice in which any other explanation might equally well be lodged; one which fits the object only and to which alone the object lends itself. Scientific explanation can be of such a kind; it involves absolute precision and complete or mounting evidence. Can one say as much for philosophical theories?

There was one doctrine, however, which seemed to me as a youth to be an exception, and that is probably why I was drawn to it. The philosophy of Spencer aimed at taking the impression of things and modeling itself on the facts in every detail. To be sure it still sought its basis in vague generalities, and I was quite conscious

11

of the weak points in his *First Principles*. But these weaknesses seemed to me to be due to the author's insufficient preparation and his inability to grasp the significance of the "latest ideas" of mechanics; I should have liked to take up this part of his work, complete and consolidate it, and I set to work on this task to the best of my ability. That was what led me to consider the idea of Time; and there a surprise awaited me.

I was indeed very much struck to see how real time, which plays the leading part in any philosophy of evolution, eludes mathematical treatment. Its essence being to flow, not one of its parts is still there when another part comes along. Superposition of one part on another with measurement in view is therefore impossible, unimaginable, inconceivable. There is no doubt but that an element of convention enters into any measurement, and it is seldom that two magnitudes, considered equal, are directly superposable one upon the other. Even then, this superposition must be possible for one of their aspects or effects which preserves something of them: this effect, this aspect then, is what we measure. But in the case of time, the idea of superposition would imply absurdity, for any effect of duration which will be superposable upon itself and consequently measurable, will have as its essence non-duration. Ever since my university days I had been aware that duration is measured by the trajectory of a body in motion and that mathematical time is a line; but I had not yet observed that this operation contrasts radically with all other processes of measurement, for it is not carried out on an aspect or an effect representative of what one wishes to measure, but on something which excludes it. The line one measures is immobile, time is mobility. The line is made, it is complete; time is what is happening, and more than that, it is what causes everything to happen. The measuring of time never deals with duration as duration; what is counted is only a certain number of extremities of intervals, or *moments,* in short, virtual halts in time. To state that an incident will occur at the end of a certain time *t,* is simply to say that one will have counted, from now until then, a number *t* of simultaneities of a certain kind. In between these simultaneities anything you like may happen. Time could be enormously and even infinitely accelerated; nothing would be changed for the mathematician, for the physicist or for the astronomer. And yet the difference with regard to consciousness would be profound (I am speaking naturally of a consciousness which would not be integrated with intra-cerebral movement); the wait from one day to another, from one hour to the next would no longer cause it the same fatigue. Science cannot concern itself with this specific wait (or interval), and its exterior cause: even when it is dealing with time which is passing or which will pass, it treats it as though it had passed. This is, in fact, quite natural; the role of science is to foresee. It extracts and retains from the material world that which can be repeated and calculated, and consequently that which is not in a state of flow. Thus it does nothing but lean in the direction of common sense, which is a beginning of science: usually when we speak of time we think of the measurement of duration, and not of duration itself. But this duration which science eliminates, and which is so difficult to conceive and express, is what one feels and lives. Suppose we try to find out what it is?—How would it appear to a consciousness which desired only to see it without measuring it, which would then grasp it without stopping it, which in short, would take itself as object, and which, spectator and actor alike, at once spontaneous and reflective, would bring ever closer together—to the point where they would coincide—the attention which is fixed, and time which passes?

Such was the question; and through it I delved deep into the domain of the inner life, which until then had held no interest for me. I very quickly spotted the inadequacy of the associationist conception of the mind; this conception, then common to most psychologists and philosophers, was the result of an artificial re-grouping of conscious life. What would direct vision give—immediate vision, with no interposed prejudices? A long series of reflections and analyses made me brush aside one prejudice after another, and abandon many ideas I had accepted without question; finally, I believed I had found pure, unadulterated inner continuity (duration), continuity which was neither unity nor multiplicity, and which did not fit into any of our categories of thought (*cadres*). That positive science had not been concerned with this duration was, I thought, quite natural: its function after all is to compose a world for us in which we can, for the convenience of action, ignore the effects of time. But how had Spencer's philosophy, a doctrine of evolution constructed to follow reality in its mobility, its progress, its inner maturing, been able to close its eyes to what is change itself?

This question was later to lead me to tackle once again the problem of the evolution of life, taking real time into account; I was to find then that Spencerian "evolutionism" had to be almost completely recast. For the moment, I was absorbed by the vision of duration. In reviewing the different systems, I noticed that philosophers had paid almost no attention to it. All through the history of philosophy time and space have been placed on the same level and treated as things of a kind; the procedure has been to study space, to determine its nature and function, and then to apply to time the conclusions thus reached. The theories of space and time thus become counterparts of one another. To pass from one to the other one had only to change a single word: "juxtaposition" was replaced by "succession." Real duration was systematically avoided. Why? Science has its own reasons for avoiding it, but metaphysics, which preceded science, was already doing so without having the same excuses. As I examined the various doctrines it struck me that language was largely responsible for this confusion; duration is always expressed in terms of extension; the terms which designate time are borrowed from the language of space. When we evoke time, it is space which answers our call. Metaphysics must have conformed to the habits of language, which in turn are governed by the habits of common sense.

But if science and common sense are in agreement on this point, if the intelligence, either spontaneous or reflective, rules out real time, might it not be because the goal of our understanding demands it? That is what I thought I observed in studying the structure of the human understanding. It seemed to me that one of its functions was precisely to mask duration, either in movement or in change.

If it is a question of movement, all the intelligence retains is a series of positions: first one point reached, then another, then still another. But should something happen between these points, immediately the understanding intercalates new positions, and so on indefinitely. It refuses to consider *transition;* if we insist, it so manages that mobility, pushed back into more and more narrow intervals as the number of considered positions increases—recedes, withdraws and finally disappears into the infinitely small. This is perfectly natural, if the intellect is destined first of all to prepare and bear upon our action on things. Our action exerts itself conveniently only on fixed points; fixity is therefore what our intelligence seeks; it asks itself where the mobile is to be found, where it will be, where it will *pass.* Even if it takes note of the moment of passing, even if it seems then to be concerned with duration, it restricts itself in that direction to verifying the simultaneity of two virtual halts: the halt of the mobility it is considering and the halt of another mobile whose course is presumed to be that of time. But it is always with immobilities, real or possible, that it seeks to deal. Suppose we skip this intellectual representation of movement, which shows it as a series of positions. Let us go directly to movement and examine it without any interposed concept: we shall find it simple and all-of-a-piece. Let us go further; suppose we get it to coincide with one of those incontestably real and absolute movements which we ourselves produce. This time we have mobility in its essence, and we feel that it mingles with an effort whose duration is an indivisable continuity. But as a certain space will have been crossed, our intelligence, which seeks fixity everywhere, assumes after the event that movement has been *exactly fitted on* to this space (as though it, movement, could coincide with immobility!) and that the mobile *exists* in turn in each of the points of the line it is moving along. At most we can say that it would have been at one of these particular points if it had stopped sooner—if, in view of a shorter movement we had made an entirely different effort. It is only a step from there to seeing in movement just a series of positions; the duration of movement will then break up into "moments" corresponding to each of the positions. But the moments of time and the positions of the mobile are only snapshots which our understanding has taken of the continuity of movement and duration. In these juxtaposed views one has a practical substitute for time and movement which conforms to the exigencies of language until such time as language lends itself to the exigencies of computation; but one has only an artificial means of recomposing: time and movement are something else.

We shall say as much for change; the understanding breaks it up into successive and distinct states, supposed to be invariable. If one looks a little more closely at each of these states, noticing that it varies, asking how it could endure if it did not change, the understanding hastens to replace it by a series of shorter states, which in their turn break up if necessary, and so forth ad infinitum. But how can we help seeing that the essence of duration is to flow, and that the fixed placed side by side with the fixed will never constitute anything which has duration. It is not the "states," simple snapshots we have taken once again along the course of change, that are real; on the contrary, it is flux, the continuity of transition, it is change itself that is real. This change is indivisible, it is even substantial. If our intelligence insists on judging it to be insubstantial, to give it some vague kind of support, it is because it has replaced this change by a series of adjacent states; but this multiplicity is artificial as is also the unity one endows it with. What we have here is merely an uninterrupted thrust of change —of a change always adhering to itself in a duration which extends indefinitely.

These reflections engendered many doubts as well as great hopes in my mind. I told myself that metaphysical problems had perhaps been badly propounded, but that precisely for that reason it was no longer advisable to believe them "eternal," that is, insoluble. Metaphysics dates from the day when Zeno of Elea pointed out the inherent contradictions of movement and change, as our intellect represents them. To surmount these difficulties raised by the intellectual representation of movement and change, to get around them by an increasingly subtle intellectual labor, required the principal effort of ancient and modern philosophers. It is thus that metaphysics was led to seek the reality of things above time, beyond what moves and what changes, and consequently outside what our senses and consciousness perceive. As a result it could be nothing but a more or less artificial arrangement of concepts, a hypothetical construction. It claimed to go beyond experience; what it did in reality was merely to take a full and mobile experience, lending itself to a probing ever-deepening and as a result pregnant with revelations—and to substitute for it a fixed extract, desiccated and empty, a system of abstract general ideas, drawn from that very experience or rather from its most superficial strata. One might as well discourse on the subject of the cocoon from which the butterfly is to emerge, and claim that fluttering, changing, living butterfly finds its *raison d'être* and fulfillment in the immutability of its shell. On the contrary, let us unfasten the cocoon, awaken the chrysalis; let us restore to movement its mobility, to change its fluidity, to time its duration. Who knows but what the "great insoluble problems" will remain attached to the outer shell? They were not concerned with either movement or change or time, but solely with the conceptual cocoon which we mistakenly took for them or for their equivalent. Metaphysics will then become experience itself; and duration will be revealed as it really is—unceasing creation, the uninterrupted up-surge of novelty.

For that is what our habitual representation of movement and change hinders us from seeing. If movement is a series of positions and change a series of states, time is made up of distinct parts immediately adjacent to one another. No doubt we still say that they follow one another, but in that case this succession is similar to that of the images on a cinematographic film: the film could be run off ten, a hundred, even a thousand times faster without the slightest modification in what was being shown; if its speed were increased to infinity, if the unrolling (this time, away from the apparatus) became instantaneous, the pictures would still be the same. Succession thus understood, therefore, adds nothing; on the contrary, it takes something away; it marks a deficit; it reveals a weakness in our perception, which is forced by this weakness to divide up the film image by image instead of grasping it in the aggregate. In short, time thus considered is no more than a space in idea where one imagines to be set out in line all past, present and future events, and in addition, something which prevents them from appearing in a single perception: the unrolling in duration would be this very incompletion, the addition of a negative quantity. Such, consciously or unconsciously, is the thought of most philosophers, in accordance with the demands of the understanding, the necessities of language and the symbolism of science. *Not one of them has sought positive attributes in time.* They treat succession as a co-existence which has failed to be achieved, and duration as a non-eternity. That is why, in spite of all their efforts, they cannot succeed in conceiving the radically new and unforeseeable. I speak not only of those philosophers who believe in so rigorous a concatenation of phenomena and events that effects must be deduced from causes: such philosophers imagine that the future is given in the present, that it is theoretically visible in it, that to the present it will add nothing new. But even those few who have believed in free will, have reduced it to a simple "choice" between two or more alternatives, as if these alternatives were "possibles" outlined beforehand, and as if the will was limited to "bringing about" ("realizer") one of them. They therefore still admit even if they do not realize it, that everything is given. They seem to have no idea whatever of an act which might be entirely new (at least inwardly) and which in no way would exist, not even in the form of the purely possible, prior to its realization. But this is the very nature of a free act. To perceive it thus, as indeed we must do with any creation, novelty or unpredictable occurrence whatsoever, we have to get back into pure duration.

Try, for instance, to call up today the act you will accomplish tomorrow, even if you know what you are going to do. Your imagination perhaps evokes the movement to be gone through; but what you will think and feel in doing it you can know nothing of today, because your state tomorrow will include all the life you will have lived up until that moment, with whatever that particular moment is to add to it. To fill this state in advance with what it should contain you will need exactly the time which separates today from tomorrow, for you cannot shorten psychological life by a single instant without modifying its content. Can you shorten the length of a melody without altering its nature? The inner life, is that very melody. In supposing therefore that you know what you will be doing tomorrow you foresee only the external shape of your action; any effort to imagine its interior beforehand will fill up a duration which, from one lengthening to another, will lead you to the moment when the action is accomplished and when there can no longer be any question of foreseeing it. What will it be, if action is truly free—that is to say, created whole—in its outer design as well as in its inner coloring, at the moment it is accomplished?

Radical indeed is the difference between an evolution whose continuous phases penetrate one another by a kind of internal growth, and an unfurling whose distinct parts are placed in juxtaposition to one another. The fan one spreads out might be opened with increasing rapidity, and even instantaneously; it would still display the same embroidery, prefigured on the silk. But a real evolution, if ever it is accelerated or retarded, is entirely modified within; its acceleration or retardation is precisely that internal modification. Its content and its duration are one and the same thing.

It is true that alongside the states of consciousness which live this unshrinkable and inextensible duration, there are material systems which time merely glides over. Of the phenomena which follow from them one can really say that they are the unfurling of a fan, or better still, the unrolling of a cinematographic film. Calculable ahead of time, they existed prior to their realization in the form of possibles.

Such are the systems studied by astronomy, physics and chemistry. Does the material universe in its entirety form a system of this kind? When our science assumes this, it simply means by so doing to discard everything in the universe which is not calculable. But the philosopher who does not want to discard anything is really obliged to ascertain that the states of our material world are contemporaneous with the history of our consciousness. As the latter endures the former must be bound in some way to real duration. In theory, the film upon which the successive states of a wholly calculable system are pictured could be run off at any speed at all without changing a thing on it. In fact, this speed is fixed, since the unrolling of the film corresponds to a certain duration of our inner life—to that one and to no other. The film which is unrolling is therefore in all probability attached to consciousness which has duration and which regulates its movement. As we have said, when one wishes to prepare a glass of sugared water one is obliged to wait until the sugar melts. This necessity for waiting is the significant fact. It shows that if one can cut out from the universe the systems for which time is only an abstraction, a relation, a number, the universe itself becomes something different. If we could grasp it in its entirety, inorganic but interwoven with organic beings, we should see it ceaselessly taking on forms as new, as original, as unforeseeable as our states of consciousness.

But we have so much trouble in distinguishing between an evolution and an unfurling, between the radically new and a rearrangement of the pre-existing, in fact, between creation and simple choice, that this distinction cannot be clarified in too many directions at once. Let us say then, that in duration, considered as a creative evolution, there is perpetual creation of possibility and not only of reality. Many will be loathe to admit it, because they will always believe that an event could not be accomplished if it had not been possible of accomplishment: so that before being real it must have been possible. But look at it closely: you will see that "possibility" signifies two entirely different things and that most of the time we waver between them, involuntarily playing upon the meaning of the word. When a musician composes a symphony was his work possible before being real? Yes, if by this we mean that there was no insurmountable barrier to its realization. But from this completely negative sense of the word we pass, inadvertently, to a positive sense: we imagine that everything which occurs could have been foreseen by any sufficiently informed mind, and that, in the form of an idea, it was thus pre-existent to its realization; an absurd conception in the case of a work of art, for from the moment that the musician has the precise and complete idea of the symphony he means to compose, his symphony is done. Neither in the artist's thought nor, what is more, in any other thought comparable to ours, whether impersonal or even simply virtual, did the symphony exist in its quality of being possible before being real. But can we not say as much of any state of the universe whatsoever, taken with all conscious and living beings?

Is it not richer in novelty, in the radical unforeseeable, than the symphony of even the greatest master?

Nevertheless the conviction still persists that even if it has not been conceived before being produced, *it could have been,* and in this sense from all eternity it has existed as possible, in some real or virtual intelligence. The examining of this illusion should tell us that it results from the very essence of our understanding. Things and events happen at certain moments; the judgment which determines the occurrence of the thing or the event can only come after them; it therefore has its date. But this date at once fades away, in virtue of the principle deep-rooted in our intellect, that all truth is eternal. If the judgment is true now, it seems to us it must always have been so. It matters not that it had never yet been formulated: it existed by right before existing in fact. To every true affirmation we attribute thus a retroactive effect; or rather, we impart to it a retrograde movement. As though a judgment could have pre-existed the terms which make it up! As though these terms did not date from the appearance of the objects they represent! As though the thing and the idea of the thing, its reality and its possibility, were not created at one stroke when a truly new form, invented by art or nature, is concerned!

The consequences of this illusion are innumerable. Our estimate of men and events is wholly impregnated with a belief in the retrospective value of true judgment, in a retrograde movement which truth, once posited, would automatically make in time. By the sole fact of being accomplished, reality casts its shadow behind it into the indefinitely distant past: it thus seems to have been pre-existent to its own realization, in the form of a possible. From this results an error which vitiates our conception of the past; from this arises our claim to anticipate the future on every occasion. We ask ourselves, for example, what the art, the literature, the civilization of tomorrow will be like; we picture approximately the graph of the evolution of societies; we go so far as to predict events in detail.

We can always, to be sure, link up the reality once it is accomplished, to the events which preceded it and to the circumstances in which it occurred; but taken from another angle, an entirely different reality (not just *any* reality, it is true) could just as well be linked up to the same circumstances and events. Are we to say then that by considering *all* sides of the present, extending it in every direction, we, now, should obtain all the possibles from which the future will choose, supposing it to have a choice? But in the first place these prolongations themselves might be additions of new qualities, created from nothing and, as such, absolutely unforeseeable and in the second place, a "side" of the present exists as a "side" only when our attention has isolated it, thus cutting a certain form out of the totality of present circumstances. How then could "all the sides" of the present exist before subsequent events have determined what forms the cuttings operated by our attention may have? These sides, it would seem, belong only in retrospect to a former present, that is to say to the past, and they possessed no more reality in that present, when it was a present, than the symphonies of future musicians have reality in our own actual present. To take a simple example, nothing prevents us today from associating the romanticism of the nineteenth century with what was already romantic in the classical writers. But the romantic aspect of classicism is only brought by the retroactive effect of romanticism once it has appeared. If there had not been a Rousseau, a Chateaubriand, a Vigny, a Victor Hugo, not only should we never have perceived, but also *there would never really have existed,* any romanticism in the earlier classical writers, for this romanticism of theirs only materializes by lifting out of their work a certain aspect, and this slice (découpure), with its particular form, no more existed in classical literature before romanticism appeared on the scene than there exists, in the cloud floating by, the amusing design that an artist perceives in shaping to his fancy the amorphous mass. Romanticism worked retroactively on classicism as the artist's design worked on the cloud. Retroactively it created its own prefiguration in the past and an explanation of itself by its predecessors.

This amounts to saying that it is only by a lucky accident, or exceptional good fortune that we can accurately note in the present reality what will be of most interest for the future historian. When that historian studies our present he will be seeking in particular the explanation of his present, and more especially of what is new in his present. We today can have no idea whatsoever of this novelty, if it is to be a creation; how then could we be guided by it in choosing from among the facts those we are to register, or rather in fabricating facts by arranging the present reality in the light of it? The essential fact of modern times is the advent of democracy. It is incontestably true that in the past, as described by its contemporaries, we find the shadows of coming events; but those indications which are perhaps most interesting would have been noted then only had they known that humanity was moving in that direction; now the trend of that movement was at that time no more marked than any other, or rather it did not yet exist, since it was created by the movement itself—that is, by the forward march of the men who have progressively conceived and realized democracy. The premonitory signs are therefore, in our eyes, signs only because we now know the course, because the course has been completed. Neither the course, nor its direction, nor in consequence, its end were given when these facts came into being: hence they were not yet signs. Let us go still further. We were saying that the most important facts in this connection could have been neglected by contemporaries. But the truth is that most of these facts did not yet exist as facts at that time; they would exist retrospectively for us if we could now resuscitate the period in its entirety, and play the particular form of searchlight we call the democratic idea over the solid block of reality as it was then: the portions thus illuminated, thus brought into relief from the whole, with contours as original and unforeseeable as the design of a great master, would be the preparatory facts of democracy. In short, in order to bequeath to our descendants the explanation, by its antecedents, of the essential event of their time, that event would already have to take shape before our eyes, and there would have to be no real duration. We transmit to future generations what interests us, what our attention centers upon and even sketches, in the light of our past evolution, but not what the future will have made interesting to them by the creation of a new interest, by a new direction communicated to their attention. In other words then, the historical origins of the present in its most important aspect, cannot be completely elucidated, for they would only be restored in their completeness if it had been possible for the past to be expressed by its contemporaries in terms of an indeterminate and therefore unforeseeable future.

Let us take a color such as orange. As we also know red and yellow, we can consider orange as yellow in one sense, red in another, and say that it is composed of yellow and red. But suppose that, orange being what it is, neither yellow nor red had yet appeared in the world: would orange still be composed of those two colors? Obviously not. The sensation of red and the sensation of yellow, involving as they do a whole nervous and cerebral mechanism at the same time as certain special dispositions of consciousness, are creations of life which have happened, but which could have not happened; and if there had never been, either on our planet or any other, beings undergoing these two sensations, the sensation of orange would have been a simple sensation; never would the sensations of yellow and red have figured in it either as components or as aspects. I realize that our habitual logic protests. It says: "If the sensations of yellow and red enter into the composition of the sensation of orange today, they entered into it always, even though there was a time when neither one of them existed effectively: they were there virtually." But that is because our ordinary logic is a logic of retrospection. It cannot help throwing present realities, reduced to possibilities or virtualities, back into the past, so that what is compounded now must, in its eyes, always have been so. It does not admit that a simple state can, in remaining what it is, become a compound state solely because evolution will have created new viewpoints from which to consider it, and by so doing, created multiple elements in which to analyze it ideally. Our logic will not believe that if these elements had sprung forth as realities they would not have existed before that as possibilities, the possibility of a thing never being (except where that thing is a purely mechanical arrangement of pre-existing elements) more than the mirage, in the indefinite past, of reality that has come into being. If this logic we are accustomed to pushes the reality that springs forth in the present back into the past in the form of a possible, it is precisely because it will not admit that anything does spring up, that something is created and that time is efficacious. It sees in a new form or quality only a rearrangement of the old—nothing absolutely new. For it, all multiplicity resolves itself into a definite number of unities. It does not accept the idea of an indistinct and even undivided multiplicity, purely intensive or qualitative, which, while remaining what it is, will comprise an indefinitely increasing number of elements, as the new points of view for considering it appear in the world. To be sure, it is not a question of giving up that logic or of revolting against it. But we must extend it, make it more supple, adapt it to a duration in which novelty is constantly springing forth and evolution is creative.

Such was the chosen course upon which I embarked. Many others opened up before me and around me from the center in which I had put myself in order to recapture pure duration. But I kept to that one because I had

chosen first of all to try out my method on the problem of liberty. In so doing I should be getting back into
the flow of the inner life, of which philosophy seemed to
me too often to retain only the hardened outer shell. Had
not the novelist and moralist advanced farther in that
direction than the philosopher? Perhaps; but it was only
here and there, under the pressure of necessity, that they
had broken through the barrier; no one had as yet be-
thought himself of setting out methodically "in search
of time gone by" ("à la recherche du temps perdu").
Be that as it may, I give only some bits of information
on this subject in my first book and still restricted myself to certain allusions in the second, when I compared
the plane of action—wherein the past is contracted into
the present—with the dream plane, where, indivisible
and indestructible, the whole of the past is deployed. But
if it is the province of literature to undertake in this way
the study of the soul in the concrete, upon individual
examples, the duty of philosophy it seemed to me was to
lay down the general conditions of the direct, immediate
observation of oneself by oneself. This inner observation
is warped by habits we have developed; the chief example of this warping is doubtless the one which created
the problem of liberty—a pseudo-problem born of a
confusion of duration with extension. But there are
other pseudo-problems which seemed to have the same
origin: our moods appear to us as though they could be
separated, counted so to speak; certain of them, thus dis-
sociated, have as it were an intensity which is measurable; for each and every one of these states we think we
can substitute the words which designate them and which
ever after will cover them up; we then attribute to them
the fixity, the discontinuity, the generality of the words
themselves.

It is this covering that we must grasp in order to tear it
off. But we shall grasp it only if we consider first its
aspect and its structure, if in addition, we understand its
intended purpose. It is spatial by nature and has a social utility. Spatiality therefore, and in this quite spe-

cial sense, sociability, are in this case the real causes of
the relativity of our knowledge. Brushing aside this veil,
we get back to the immediate and reach an absolute.

From these early reflections came conclusions which
fortunately have become almost commonplace, but which,
at the time, appeared daring. They required that psychology break with associationism, which was universally accepted, if not as a doctrine, at least as a method.
They demanded still another break which at that time I
only half saw. Beside associationism there was Kantianism, whose influence, often combined with that of the
former, was no less powerful and wide-spread. Those
who repudiated the positivism of a Comte, or the agnos-
ticism of a Spencer dared not go so far as to question
the Kantian conception of the relativity of knowledge.
Kant had proved, so it was said, that our thought exerts
itself upon a matter previously scattered in Space and
Time, and thus prepared especially for man: the "thing
in itself" escapes us; to comprehend it, we would need
an intuitive faculty which we do not possess. On the contrary, from my analysis the result was that at least a part
of reality, our person, can be grasped in its natural
purity. Here, at any rate, the materials of our knowledge
have not been created, or ground out of shape and reduced to powder, by some malicious genius who has
afterwards thrown into some artificial receptacle such as
our consciousness, a psychological dust. Our person appears to us just as it is "in itself," as soon as we free
ourselves of the habits contracted for our greater convenience. But might it not be the same for other realities,
perhaps even for all of them? Was the "relativity of consciousness," which arrested the soaring of metaphysics,
original and essential? Or rather, might it not be acci-
dental and acquired? Would it not simply be due to
the fact that the intelligence has contracted habits necessary for every-day living; these habits, transferred to the
domain of speculation, bring us face to face with a
reality, distorted or made over, or at any rate, arranged;
but the arrangement does not force itself upon us irresist-

ibly; it comes from ourselves; what we have done we can undo; and we enter then into direct contact with reality. It was therefore not only a psychological theory, associationism, which I brushed aside; it was also and for a similar reason, a general philosophy such as Kantianism, and everything connected with it. Both of them, almost universally accepted at that time in their main outlines, appeared to me as *impedimenta* hindering philosophy and psychology from going ahead.

The only thing to do, then, was to go ahead. It was not enough to brush aside the obstacle. As a matter of fact, I undertook the study of psychological functions, then of psycho-physiological relation, then of life in general, always seeking direct vision, and in this way suppressing problems which did not concern the things themselves, but their translation into artificial concepts. I shall not stop here to go into something which would only show the extreme complication of a method to all appearance so simple; I shall speak of it again very briefly, in the next chapter. But since I began by saying that my primary concern was precision, let me end by pointing out that precision could not have been obtained, as I see it, by any other method. For lack of precision is commonly the including of a thing in too wide a genus, things and genera corresponding moreover to pre-existing words. But if one begins by casting off ready-made concepts, if one professes to have a direct vision of reality, if one sub-divides this reality taking into account its articulations, the new concepts one must form in order to express oneself will now be cut to the exact measure of the object; lack of precision will arise only from the extension of these concepts to other objects which they would include equally in their generality, but which will have to be studied in themselves, outside of these concepts, when one wishes to know them in their turn.

II *Introduction*

THE STATING OF PROBLEMS

Duration and intuition.—Nature of intuitive knowledge.—In what sense it is clear.—Two kinds of clarity.
—The Intelligence.—Value of intellectual knowledge.—
Abstractions and metaphors.—Metaphysics and science.
—Under what condition they can be mutually helpful.—
On mysticism.—On the independence of the mind.—
Must we accept the "terms" of the problems?—The philosophy of the body politic.—General ideas.—True and
false problems.—Kantian criticism and the theories of
knowledge.—The "intellectualist" illusion.—Methods of
teaching.—*Homo loquax.*—The philosopher, the scholar
and the "intelligent man."

These conclusions on the subject of duration were, as
it seemed to me, decisive. Step by step they led me to
raise intuition to the level of a philosophical method.
"Intuition," however, is a word whose use caused me
some degree of hesitation. Of all the terms which designate a mode of knowing, it is still the most appropriate; and yet it leads to a certain confusion. Because a
Schelling, a Schopenhauer and others have already called
upon intuition, because they have more or less set up intuition in opposition to intelligence, one might think
that I was using the same method. But of course, their
intuition was an immediate search for the eternal!
Whereas, on the contrary, for me it was a question,
above all, of finding true duration. Numerous are the
philosophers who have felt how powerless conceptual
thought is to reach the core of the mind. Numerous,
consequently, are those who have spoken of a supra-in-
tellectual faculty of intuition. But as they believed that

the intelligence worked within time, they have concluded that to go beyond the intelligence consisted in getting outside of time. They did not see that intellectualized time is space, that the intelligence works upon the phantom of duration, not on duration itself, that the elimination of time is the habitual, normal, commonplace act of our understanding, that the relativity of our knowledge of the mind is a direct result of this fact, and that hence, to pass from intellection to vision, from the relative to the absolute, is not a question of getting outside of time (we are already there) ; on the contrary, one must get back into duration and recapture reality in the very mobility which is its essence. An intuition, which claims to project itself with one bound into the eternal, limits itself to the intellectual. For the concepts which the intelligence furnishes, the intuition simply substitutes one single concept which includes them all and which consequently is always the same, by whatever name it is called: Substance, Ego, Idea, Will. Philosophy, thus understood, necessarily pantheistic, will have no difficulty in explaining everything deductively, since it will have been given beforehand, in a principle which is the concept of concepts, all the real and all the possible. But this explanation will be vague and hypothetical, this unity will be artificial, and this philosophy would apply equally well to a very different world from our own. How much more instructive would be a truly intuitive metaphysics, which would follow the undulations of the real! True, it would not embrace in a single sweep the totality of things; but for each thing it would give an explanation which would fit it exactly, and it alone. It would not begin by defining or describing the systematic unity of the world: who knows if the world is actually one? Experience alone can say, and unity, if it exists, will appear at the end of the search as a result; it is impossible to posit it at the start as a principle. Furthermore, it will be a rich, full unity, the unity of a continuity, the unity of our reality, and not that abstract and empty unity, which has come from one supreme generalization, and which could just as well be that of any possible world whatsoever. It is true that philosophy then will demand a new effort for each new problem. No solution will be geometrically deduced from another. No important truth will be achieved by the prolongation of an already acquired truth. We shall have to give up crowding universal science potentially into one principle.

The intuition we refer to then bears above all upon internal duration. It grasps a succession which is not juxtaposition, a growth from within, the uninterrupted prolongation of the past into a present which is already blending into the future. It is the direct vision of the mind by the mind—nothing intervening, no refraction through the prism, one of whose facets is space and another, language. Instead of states contiguous to states, which become words in juxtaposition to words, we have here the indivisible and therefore substantial continuity of the flow of the inner life. Intuition, then, signifies first of all consciousness, but immediate consciousness, a vision which is scarcely distinguishable from the object seen, a knowledge which is contact and even coincidence. —Next, it is consciousness extended, pressing upon the edge of an unconscious which gives way and which resists, which surrenders and which regains itself: through the rapid alternating of obscurity and light, it makes us see that the unconscious is there; contrary to strict logic, it affirms that the psychological can be consciousness as much as it likes, there is nevertheless a psychological unconsciousness.—Does it not go even further? Is it merely the intuition of ourselves? Between our consciousness and other consciousnesses the separation is less clear-cut than between our body and other bodies, for it is space which makes these divisions sharp. Unreflecting sympathy and antipathy, which so often have that power of divination, give evidence of a possible interpenetration of human consciousnesses. It would appear then that phenomena of psychological endosmosis exist. It may be that intuition opens the way for us into consciousness in general.—But is it only with consciousnesses that we are in sympathy? If every living being is born, develops and dies, if life is an evolution and if duration is in this case a reality, is there not also an intuition of the vital, and consequently a metaphysics of life, which might in a sense prolong the science of the living? Science will certainly throw more and more light on the physico-chemical nature of organized matter, but the underlying cause of this organization, which we can easily see does not come within the realm either of pure mechanism or of finality (in the proper sense) and is neither pure unity nor distinct multiplicity, and which in fact our understanding will characterize by simple negations, this cause, shall we not get down to it by recapturing through consciousness the vital impetus within us?—Let us go still further. Above and beyond the organizing process, unorganized matter appears as though decomposable into systems over which time slips without penetrating, systems which belong to the realm of science and to which the understanding can be applied. But the material universe in its entirety *keeps* our consciousness *waiting;* it waits itself. Either it endures, or it is bound up in our own duration. Whether it is connected with the mind by its origins or by its function, in either case it has to do with intuition through all the real change and movement that it contains. It is my belief, in fact, that the idea of differential, or rather of fluxion, was suggested to science by a vision of this kind. Metaphysical in its origins, it became scientific as it grew more rigorous, that is, expressible in static terms. In short, pure change, real duration, is a thing spiritual or impregnated with spirituality. Intuition is what attains the spirit, duration, pure change. Its real domain being the spirit, it would seek to grasp in things, even material things, their participation in spirituality—I should say in divinity were I not aware of all the human element still in our consciousness, however purified and spiritualized. This human element is precisely what makes it possible for the intuitional effort to be accomplished at different levels on different points, and to give in various philosophies results which do not coincide with one another even though they are in no way incompatible.

Let no one ask me for a simple and geometrical definition of intuition. It is only too easy to show that the word is taken in meanings which cannot be deduced mathematically from one another. An eminent Danish philosopher has pointed out four of them. I should be inclined to say that there are more! Of what is not abstract and conventional but real and concrete, and all the more so of what is not reconstitutable with known components, in other words, of that thing which has not been cut out of the whole of reality either by the understanding or by common sense or by language, one cannot give any idea unless one takes views of it that are multiple, complementary and not at all equivalent. God forbid that I should compare the small with the great, my effort with that of the masters! But the variety of the functions and aspects of intuition, as I describe it, is nothing beside the multiplicity of meanings the words "essence" and "existence" have in Spinoza, or the terms "form," "power," "act" . . . etc., in Aristotle. Glance over the list of meanings of the word eidos in the *Index Aristotelicus*: you will see how much they differ. If one considers two sufficiently divergent meanings, they will almost seem to be mutually exclusive. They are not exclusive because the chain of intermediary meanings links them up. By making the necessary effort to embrace the whole, one perceives that one is in the real and not in the presence of a mathematical essence which could be summed up in a simple formula.

There is, however, a fundamental meaning: to think intuitively is to think in duration. Intelligence starts ordinarily from the immobile, and reconstructs movement as best it can with immobilities in juxtaposition. Intuition starts from movement, posits it, or rather perceives it as reality itself, and sees in immobility only an abstract moment, a snapshot taken by our mind, of a mobility. Intelligence ordinarily concerns itself with things, meaning by that, with the static, and makes of change an accident which is supposedly superadded. For intuition the essential is change: as for the thing, as intelligence understands it, it is a cutting which has been made out of the becoming and set up by our mind as a substitute for the whole. Thought ordinarily pictures to itself the new as a new arrangement of pre-existing elements; nothing is ever lost for it, nothing is ever created. Intuition, bound up to a duration which is growth, perceives in it an uninterrupted continuity of unforeseeable novelty; it sees, it knows that the mind draws from itself more than it has, that spirituality consists in just that, and that reality, impregnated with spirit, is creation. The habitual labor of thought is easy and can be prolonged at will. Intuition is arduous and cannot last. Whether it be intellection or intuition, thought, of course, always utilizes language; and intuition, like all thought, finally becomes lodged in concepts such as duration, qualitative or heterogeneous multiplicity, unconsciousness—even differentiation, if one considers the notion such as it was to begin with. But the concept which is of intellectual origin is immediately clear at least for a mind which can put forth sufficient effort, while the idea which has sprung from an intuition ordinarily begins by being obscure, whatever our power of thought may be. The fact is that there are two kinds of clarity.

A new idea may be clear because it presents to us, simply arranged in a new order, elementary ideas which we already possessed. Our intelligence, finding only the old in the new, feels itself on familiar ground; it is at ease; it "understands." Such is the clarity we desire, are looking for, and for which we are always most grateful to whoever presents it to us. There is another kind that we submit to, and which, moreover, imposes itself only with time. It is the clarity of the radically new and absolutely simple idea, which catches as it were an intuition. As we cannot reconstruct it with pre-existing elements, since it has no elements, and as on the other hand, to understand without effort consists in recomposing the new from what is old, our first impulse is to say it is incomprehensible. But let us accept it provisionally, let us go with it through the various departments of our knowledge: we shall see that, itself obscure, it dissipates obscurities. By it the problems we considered insoluble will resolve themselves, or rather, be dissolved, either to disappear definitively, or to present themselves in some other way. From what it has done for these problems, it will in its turn, benefit. Each one of them, intellectual by nature, will communicate to it something of its intellectuality. Thus intellectualized, this idea can be aimed anew at problems which will have been of use to it after having made use of it; better still, it will clear up the obscurity which surrounded them, and will, as a result, become itself still clearer. One must therefore distinguish between the ideas which keep their light for themselves, making it penetrate immediately into their slightest recesses, and those whose radiation is exterior, illuminating a whole region of thought. These can begin by being inwardly obscure; but the light they project about them comes back in reflection, with deeper and deeper penetration; and they then have the double power of illuminating what they play upon and of being illuminated themselves.

Even then they must be given time. The philosopher has not always this patience. How much simpler it is to confine oneself to notions stored up in the language! These ideas were formed by the intelligence as its needs appeared. They correspond to a cutting out of reality according to the lines that must be followed in order to act conveniently upon it. Most frequently they distribute objects and facts according to the way they can be turned to account, throwing pell-mell into the same intellectual compartment everything which concerns the same need. When we react identically to different perceptions, we say that we are faced with objects "of the same kind." When we react in two directly opposed ways, we are dividing the objects into two "opposite kinds." What will be clear, then, by definition, is that which can be resolved into generalities thus obtained; obscure, that which can not be so reduced. Thus is explained the striking in-feriority of the intuitive point of view in philosophical controversy. Listen to the discussion between any two philosophers one of whom upholds determinism, and the other liberty: it is always the determinist who seems to be in the right. He may be a beginner and his ad-versary a seasoned philosopher. He can plead his cause nonchalantly, while the other sweats blood for his. It will always be said of him that he is simple, clear and right. He is easily and naturally so, having only to collect thought ready to hand and phrases ready-made: science, language, common sense, the whole of intelligence is at his disposal. Criticism of an intuitive philosophy is so easy and so certain to be well received that it will always tempt the beginner. Regret may come later—unless, of course, there is a native lack of comprehension and, out of spite, personal resentment toward everything that is not reducible to the letter, toward all that is properly spirit. That can happen, for philosophy too has its Scribes and its Pharisees.

To metaphysics, then, we assign a limited object, prin-cipally spirit, and a special method, mainly intuition. In doing this we make a clear distinction between meta-physics and science. But at the same time we attribute an equal value to both. I believe that they can both touch the bottom of reality. I reject the arguments ad-vanced by philosophers, and accepted by scholars, on the relativity of knowledge and the impossibility of at-taining the absolute.

Positive science, as a matter of fact, goes to sensible observation to obtain materials whose elaboration it en-trusts to the faculty of abstracting and generalizing, to judgment and reasoning, to the intelligence. Having started from pure mathematics, it continued through mechanics, then through physics and chemistry; it arrived somewhat late in the day at biology. Its original domain, which has continued to be its preferred domain, is that of inert matter. It is less at its ease in the organized world, where it treads its way with an assured step only if it relies upon physics and chemistry; it clings to the physico-chemical in vital phenomena rather than to what is really vital in the living. But great is its embarrassment when it reaches the mind. That does not mean that it cannot obtain some knowledge of it; but this knowledge becomes all the more vague the farther it gets away from the common border-line between mind and matter. One will never advance on this new terrain as on the old, relying solely on the power of logic. One must ceaselessly appeal from the "esprit géométrique" to the "esprit de finesse": still, there is always something metaphorical in the formulas, however abstract, at which one arrives; as though the intelligence was obliged to transpose the psychic into the physical in order to understand and explain it. On the contrary, as soon as it comes back to inert matter, the science which arises from pure intelligence finds itself at home. This is in no way surprising. Our intelligence is the prolongation of our senses. Before we speculate we must live, and life demands that we make use of matter, either with our organs, which are natural tools, or with tools, properly so-called, which are artificial organs. Long before there was a philosophy and a science, the role of the intelligence was already that of manufacturing instruments and guiding the action of our body on surrounding bodies. Science has pushed this labor of the intelligence much further, but has not changed its direction. It aims above all at making us masters of matter. Even when science is speculating, it is still devoting its attention to acting, the value of scientific theories being gauged constantly by the solidity of the grip they give us upon reality. But is that not precisely what should inspire us with complete confidence in positive science and also in the intelligence, its instrument? If the intellect has been made in order to utilize matter, its structure has no doubt been modeled upon that of matter. At least that is the simplest and most probable hypothesis. We should keep to it as long as it is not demonstrated to us that the intelligence deforms, transforms, constructs its object, or only brushes the surface, or grasps the mere semblance of it. Now nothing has ever been invoked by way of that demonstration, but the insoluble difficulties into which philosophy falls, the self-contradiction into which the intellect can fall when it speculates upon things as a whole—difficulties and contradictions we naturally come up against if the intellect is especially destined for the study of a part, and if we nevertheless mean to use it in knowing the whole. But it is not enough to say that. It is impossible to consider the mechanism of our intellect and the progress of our science without arriving at the conclusion that between intellect and matter there is, in fact, symmetry, concord and agreement. On one hand, matter resolves itself more and more, in the eyes of the scholar, into mathematical relations, and on the other hand, the essential faculties of our intellect function with an absolute precision only when they are applied to geometry.

Doubtless, it might have been possible for mathematical science not to take originally the form the Greeks gave it. No doubt it must also, whatever form it adopts, keep to a strict use of artificial signs. But prior to this formulated mathematics, which is in large measure made up of convention, there is another, virtual or implicit, which is natural to the human mind. If the necessity of working with certain symbols makes the approach to mathematics difficult for many of us, the mind, in compensation, as soon as it has surmounted the obstacle, moves in this domain with a facility it has nowhere else, evidence being in this case immediate and theoretically instantaneous, the effort to understand existing more often in fact but not in right. In any other order of study, on the contrary, there must be, for understanding, a maturation process of thought which in some way adheres to the result, essentially fills up duration, and cannot even theoretically be conceived as instantaneous. In short, we might believe in a divergence between matter and intellect if we were to consider in matter only the superficial impressions made upon our senses, and if we were to leave to our intellect the vague and hazy form it takes in its daily operations. But when we bring the intellect back to its precise contours and when we delve deeply enough into our sense-impressions so that matter begins to surrender to us its inner structure, we find that the articulations of the intellect apply exactly to those of matter. I therefore do not see why the science of matter should not reach an absolute. It instinctively assumes this scope, and all natural belief should be held as true, all appearance taken for reality, as long as its illusory character has not been established. Upon those who declare our science to be relative, upon those who claim that our knowledge deforms or constructs its object, now falls the burden of proof. And they cannot fulfill this obligation, for there is no room for the doctrine of the relativity of science when science and metaphysics are on their true ground, that to which we restore them.

We recognize, furthermore, that the limits within which the intellect works have a certain elasticity, its contours a certain haziness, and that its indecision is exactly what permits it to be applied in some degree to the things of the mind. Matter and mind have this in common, that certain superficial agitations of matter are expressed in our minds, superficially, in the form of sensations; and on the other hand, the mind, in order to act upon the body, must descend little by little toward matter and become spatialized. It follows that the intelligence, although turned toward external things, can still be exerted on things internal, provided that it does not claim to plunge too deeply.

But the temptation is great to carry to the very depth of the mind the application of those procedures which are successful as long as one remains near the surface. If one gives in to it, one will obtain purely and simply a physics of the mind traced upon that of bodies. Together these two physics will constitute a complete system of reality, what is sometimes called a metaphysics. How can one help but see that metaphysics thus understood fails to recognize the strictly spiritual in the mind, being only the extension to mind of what belongs to matter? And how can we help but see that in order to make this extension possible, we have had to take intellectual forms in a state of imprecision which still leaves them applicable to the superficial phenomena of the soul, and thereby condemns them to keeping less closely to the facts of the external world? Is it surprising that such a metaphysics, embracing both matter and mind at the same time, should give the effect of knowledge which is almost empty and in any case vague—almost empty on the side of mind, since it has been able effectively to retain only superficial aspects of the soul, systematically vague on the side of matter, because the intelligence of the metaphysician must have sufficiently loosened its mechanism, and given it sufficient play to enable it to work equally well at the surface of matter or the surface of mind?

Quite different is the metaphysics that we place side by side with science. Granting to science the power of explaining matter by the mere force of intelligence, it reserves mind for itself. In this realm, proper to itself, it seeks to develop new functions of thought. Everyone can have noticed that it is more difficult to make progress in the knowledge of oneself than in the knowledge of the external world. Outside onself, the effort to learn is natural; one makes it with increasing facility; one applies rules. Within, attention must remain tense and progress become more and more painful; it is as though one were going against the natural bent. Is there not something surprising in this? We are internal to ourselves, and our personality is what we should know best.

Yet such is not the case; our mind is as if it were in a strange land, whereas matter is familiar to it and in it the mind is at home. But that is because a certain ignorance of self is perhaps useful to a being which must exteriorize itself in order to act; it answers a necessity of life. Our action is exerted upon matter, and the farther the knowledge of matter has been pursued the more

efficacious is the action. It is doubtless to one's advantage, if one is to act effectively, to think of what one
will do, to understand what one has done, to have a clear
conception of what one might have done: nature invites
us to do so; it is one of the traits which distinguishes
man from the animal, completely intent as it is on the
impression of the moment. But nature asks of us only a
quick glance at our inner selves; we then perceive the
mind, but the mind preparing to shape matter, already
adapting itself to it, assuming something of the spatial,
the geometric, the intellectual. A knowledge of the mind,
in so far as it is properly spiritual, would rather keep us
from that end. We draw nearer to it, on the contrary,
when we study the structure of things. Thus nature
turns mind away from mind, turns mind toward matter. But in that way we see how we can, if we like, indefinitely widen, deepen, and intensify the vision of the
mind which has been granted us. Since the insufficiency
of this vision is due in the first place to the fact that it is
directed upon the mind already "spatialized" and divided into mental compartments where matter can be
inserted, let us separate the mind from the space in
which it is so at home, from the materiality which it
takes to itself in order to rest upon matter. In so doing
we shall restore it to itself and be able to comprehend it
immediately. This direct vision of the mind by the mind
is the chief function of intuition, as I understand it.

Intuition will be communicated only by the intelligence. It is more than idea; nevertheless in order to be
transmitted, it will have to use ideas as a conveyance. It
will prefer, however, to have recourse to the most concrete ideas, but those which still retain an outer fringe of
images. Comparisons and metaphors will here suggest
what cannot be expressed. That will not constitute a
detour; it will amount to going straight to the goal.
If one were constantly to speak an abstract, so-called
"scientific" language, one would be giving of mind
only its imitation by matter, for abstract ideas have been
drawn from the external world and always imply a spa-

tial representation: and yet one would think one had analyzed mind. Abstract ideas alone would, therefore, in such a case, be inviting us to imagine mind on the model of matter and to think it by transposition, that is, in the exact meaning of the word, by metaphor. Let us not be duped by appearances: there are cases in which it is imagery in language which knowingly expresses the literal meaning, and abstract language which unconsciously expresses itself figuratively. The moment we reach the spiritual world, the image, if it merely seeks to suggest, may give us the direct vision, while the abstract term, which is spatial in origin and which claims to express, most frequently leaves us in metaphor.

To sum it all up, what is wanted is a difference in method between metaphysics and science: I do not acknowledge a difference in value between the two. Less modest in my claims for science than most scholars have been, I consider that a science founded on experience as the moderns understand it, can attain the essence of the real. No doubt it embraces no more than a part of reality; but some day it will reach the bottom of that part; in any case, it will approach it indefinitely. It is, therefore, already fulfilling half of the program of the old metaphysics: it could be called metaphysics did it not prefer to keep the name of science. There remains the other half. This half seems to me to get back by right to a metaphysics which also starts from experience, and which, too, is itself capable of attaining the absolute: we should call it science, did not science prefer to limit itself to the other part of reality. Metaphysics, then, is not the superior of positive science; it does not come, after science, to consider the same object in order to obtain a higher knowledge of it. To suppose such a connection between them, as is the almost invariable custom among philosophers, is to wrong both of them: science, which one condemns to relativity; metaphysics, which will never be anything more than a hypothetical and vague knowledge, since science will necessarily have taken to itself in advance everything precise and certain that can be known of its object. Quite different is the relation I establish between metaphysics and science. It is my belief that they are, or that they can become, equally precise and certain. They both bear upon reality itself. But each one of them retains only half of it so that one might see in them, if one wished, two subdivisions of science or two departments of metaphysics, if they did not mark divergent directions of the activity of thought.

Precisely because they are on the same level, they have points in common and each one can, upon these points, be verified by the other. To establish between metaphysics and science a difference in dignity, to assign to them the same object, that is to say, the totality of things, stipulating that the one shall look at them from below and the other from above, is to exclude this mutual aid and reciprocal verification: in that case, metaphysics is, of necessity—unless it loses all contact with the real —a condensed extract or hypothetical extension of science. Instead of this, let us allot to them different objects; to science let us leave matter, and to metaphysics, mind: as mind and matter touch one another, metaphysics and science, all along their common surface, will be able to test one another, until contact becomes fecundation. The results obtained on either side will of necessity be linked, because matter links up with mind. If the insertion is not perfect, it will be because here is something to rectify in our science, or in our metaphysics, or in both. Metaphysics will thus, by its peripheral part, exert a salutary influence upon science. Conversely, science will communicate to metaphysics habits of precision which will spread through it from the periphery to the center. If only because its extremities will have to fit exactly upon those of positive science, our metaphysics will be that of the world in which we live, and not of all possible worlds. It will embrace realities.

That is to say that science and metaphysics will differ in object and method, but will commune in experience. Both of them will have put away the vague knowledge stored up in the usual concepts and transmitted by means of words. After all, what were we asking for metaphysics that had not already been obtained for science? For a long time the road had been barred to positive science by the claim made of reconstituting reality with the concepts set down in language. The "low" and the "high," the "heavy" and the "light," the "dry" and the "moist" were the elements one used in explaining the phenomena of nature; concepts were weighed, measured out and combined: it was an intellectual chemistry instead of physics. When it brushed concepts aside in order to look at things, even science seemed to revolt against intelligence; the "intellectualism" of that time recombined the material object, *a priori,* with elementary ideas. In reality, this science became more intellectualist than the inadequate physics which it replaced. It was obliged to become so, seeing that it was true, for matter and intellect are modeled upon one another, and in a science which reveals the exact configuration of matter our intellect necessarily finds its own image. The mathematical form which physics has taken is thus, at one and the same time, what best corresponds to reality and what is most satisfying to our understanding. Much less convenient will be the position of the true metaphysics. It also will begin by eliminating ready-made concepts; it also will rely upon experience. But that inner experience of which we speak will nowhere find a strictly appropriate language. It will of course be compelled to return to the concept, with at most the addition of the image; but then it will have to enlarge the concept, make it more flexible, and indicate, by the colored shading around the edges, that it does not contain the whole of experience. It is none the less true that metaphysics will have accomplished in its domain the reform that modern physics has brought about in its own.

Do not expect of this metaphysics simple conclusions or radical solutions. That would be tantamount to requiring that it be no more than a manipulation of concepts. That would also be leaving it in the region of the pure possible. In the realm of experience, on the contrary, with incomplete solutions and provisional conclusions, it will achieve an increasing probability which can ultimately become the equivalent of certitude. Suppose we take a problem which we shall state in the terms of traditional metaphysics: does the soul survive the body? It is easy to decide it once and for all by reasoning on pure concepts. We shall, then, define the soul and say with Plato that it is one and simple. We shall conclude that it cannot be dissolved. Therefore, it is immortal. Nothing could be clearer. But the conclusion holds good only if we accept the definition, that is, the construction. It is subordinated to this hypothesis; it is hypothetical. But suppose we give up constructing the idea of the soul as one constructs the idea of a triangle; let us look at the facts. If, as we believe, experience proves that only a minute part of conscious life is conditioned by the brain, it will follow that the suppression of the brain will probably leave conscious life subsisting. At least the burden of proof will rest now with him who denies the survival much more than with him who affirms it. It will only be a question of the degree of added life, I admit; we shall have to have other reasons, drawn this time from religion, to arrive at a higher form of precision and attribute to this life an endless duration. But, even from the philosophical point of view, there will no longer be any *if*: we shall affirm categorically— I mean without subordination to a metaphysical hypothesis—what we affirm, were we only to affirm it as being probable. The first thesis had the beauty of the definitive, but it was suspended in thin air, in the region of the simple possible. The other is unfinished, but it pushes strong roots down into the real.

A young science is always quick to dogmatize. Having only a limited experience at its disposal, it works less upon facts than upon a few simple ideas, suggested by the facts or not, that it then treats deductively. Metaphysics, more than any other science, was exposed to this danger. A whole labor of clearing away is necessary in order to open up the way to inner experience. True, the faculty of intuition exists in each one of us, but covered over by functions more useful to life. The metaphysician worked therefore *a priori* on concepts already fixed in language, as if, descended from heaven, they revealed a supra-sensible reality to the mind. Thus was born the Platonic theory of ideas. Carried on the wings of Aristotelianism and neo-Platonism it traversed the Middle Ages; it inspired, sometimes unwittingly, the philosophers of modern times. These were often mathematicians whose habits of mind led them to see in metaphysics only a broader mathematics, embracing quality at the same time as quantity. Geometrical unity and simplicity are thus explained by most philosophies, complete systems of definitively set problems, integrally resolved. But this is not the only kind of reason. We must remember that modern metaphysics gave itself an object analogous to that of religion. It started out from a conception of the divinity. Whether it confirmed or invalidated the dogma, it felt itself obliged to dogmatize. Although it was founded on reason alone, it had the security of judgment that the theologian gets from revelation. One may wonder, it is true, why it chose this point of departure. But the point is, it had no choice in the matter. As it was working outside of experience upon pure concepts, it had no alternative but to cling to a concept from which one might deduce everything and which contained everything. That was precisely the idea it had of God.

But why did it have this idea of God? That Aristotle had arrived at the point where he fused all concepts into a single one and posited as the principle of universal explanation a "Thought of Thought" closely related to the Platonic idea of the Good, and that modern philosophy, the continuator of Aristotle's, proceeded along a similar line, can, in an extremity, be understood. That God should have been called a principle which has nothing in common with the one humanity has always designated by the word *God,* is less easily comprehended.

The god of ancient mythology and the God of Christianity have very little resemblance, no doubt; but prayers are made to both, and both are interested in man: static or dynamic, religion considers this point fundamental. And yet philosophy still manages to call God a Being Whose essence would forbid Him to take any account of human invocations, as though, theoretically embracing all things, He was in fact blind to our sufferings and deaf to our prayers. In going more deeply into this point one would find the confusion, natural to the human mind, between an explanatory idea and an active principle. Things being brought back to their concepts, the concepts fitting into one another, one finally arrives at an idea of ideas, by which one imagines that everything is explained. Truth to tell, it does not explain very much, first because it accepts the subdivision and the distribution of the real into concepts which society has deposited in language and which it had most often brought about for the sake of convenience; and in the second place because the synthesis it makes of these concepts is empty of matter and purely verbal. One wonders how this essential point escaped profound philosophers and how they could believe that they were distinguishing in any way whatsoever the principle set up by them as an explanation of the world, while they were merely representing it conventionally by a sign. As I said above: no matter what name you give to the "thing itself," whether you make of it the Substance of Spinoza, the Ego of Fichte, the Absolute of Schelling, the Idea of Hegel, or the Will of Schopenhauer, it will be useless for the word to present itself with its well-defined signification: it will lose it; it will be emptied of all meaning from the moment it is applied to the totality of things. Speaking only of the last of these great "syntheses," isn't it evident that a Will is only will on condition that it is set off against what does not will? How then is mind to be set off against matter, if matter is itself will? To place will everywhere is the same as leaving it nowhere, for it is to identify the essence of what I feel within myself—

duration, outpouring, continuous creation—with the essence of what I perceive in things, where there is evidently repetition, previsibility, necessity. It makes little difference to me if one says "Everything is mechanism" or "Everything is will": in either case everything is identical. In both cases, "mechanism" and "will" become synonyms of "being" and consequently synonyms of each other. Therein lies the initial vice of philosophical systems. They think they are telling us something about the absolute by giving it a name. But once again the word can have a definite meaning when it designates a thing; it loses that meaning as soon as you apply it to all things. Yet once again, I know what will is if you mean by that my faculty of willing, or that faculty in creatures resembling me, or even the vital urge of organized beings, if it is to be analogous to my impulse of consciousness. But the more you increase the extension of the term, the more you diminish comprehension of it. If you include matter within its extension, you empty its comprehension of the positive characteristics by which spontaneity stands out against mechanism and liberty against necessity. When finally the word arrives at the point where it designates everything that exists, it means no more than existence. What advantage is there then in saying that the world is will, instead of simply stating that it is?

But the concept thus arrived at with its undetermined content, or rather lack of content, the concept which is no longer anything at all, we insist that it be everything. One therefore calls upon the God of religion Who is determination itself and, in addition, essentially active. He is at the summit of being: we make what we wrongly take to be the summit of knowledge coincide with Him. Something of the adoration and respect which humanity bestows upon Him passes, therefore, into the principle which has been embellished with His name. And that, to a large extent, is the source of the dogmatism of modern philosophy.

The truth is that an existence can be given only in

an experience. This experience will be called vision or contact, exterior perception in general, if it is a question of a material object; it will take the name of intuition when it has to do with the mind. How far does intuition go? It alone will be able to say. It catches hold of a thread: it is for it to see whether this thread goes as far up as heaven or stops at some distance from the earth. In the first case, metaphysical experience will be bound up with that of the great mystics: I think I can state for my part that the truth lies there. In the second case, these two metaphysical experiences will remain isolated from one another without being mutually repugnant on that account. However one looks at it, philosophy will have raised us above the human state.

It already frees us of certain speculative certitudes when it posits the problem of the mind in terms of mind and not of matter, when, in a general way, it makes it unnecessary for us to employ concepts to do work for which most of them are not meant. These concepts are included in words. They have most often been elaborated by the social organism in view of an object which has nothing to do with metaphysics. In order to form them society has cut out reality according to its needs. Why should philosophy accept a division which in all probability will not correspond to the articulations of the real? This division, however, it does usually accept. It accepts the problem as it is posited by language. It is therefore condemned in advance to receive a ready-made solution or, at best, simply to choose between the two or three only possible solutions, which are co-eternal to this positing of the problem. One might just as well say that all truth is already virtually known, that its model is patented in the administrative offices of the state, and that philosophy is a jig-saw puzzle where the problem is to construct with the pieces society gives us the design it is unwilling to show us. One might just as well assign to the philosopher the role and the attitude of the school-boy, who seeks the solution persuaded that if he had the boldness to risk a glance at the master's book, he would find it there, set down opposite the question. But the truth is that in philosophy and even elsewhere it is a question of *finding* the problem and consequently of *positing* it, even more than of solving it. For a speculative problem is solved as soon as it is properly stated. By that I mean that its solution exists then, although it may remain hidden and, so to speak, covered up: the only thing left to do is to *uncover* it. But stating the problem is not simply uncovering, it is inventing. Discovery, or uncovering, has to do with what already exists actually or virtually; it was therefore certain to happen sooner or later. Invention gives being to what did not exist; it might never have happened. Already in mathematics and still more in metaphysics, the effort of invention consists most often in raising the problem, in creating the terms in which it will be stated. The stating and solving of the problem are here very close to being equivalent; the truly great problems are set forth only when they are solved. But many little problems are in the same position. I open an elementary treatise on philosophy. One of the first chapters deals with pleasure and pain. There the student is asked a question such as this: "Is pleasure happiness, or not?" But first one must know if pleasure and happiness are genera corresponding to a natural division of things into sections. Strictly speaking the phrase could signify simply: "Given the ordinary meaning of the terms *pleasure* and *happiness* should one say that happiness consists in a succession of pleasures?" It is then a question of vocabulary that is being raised; it can be solved only by finding out how the words "pleasure" and "happiness" have been used by the writers who have best handled the language. One will moreover have done a useful piece of work; one will have more accurately defined two ordinary terms, that is, two social habitudes. But if one claims to be doing more, to be grasping realities and not to be re-examining conventions, why should one expect terms, which are perhaps artificial, (whether they are or not is not yet known since the object has not been studied) to state a problem which concerns the very nature of things? Suppose that in examining the states grouped under the name of pleasure they are found to have nothing in common except that they are states which man is seeking: humanity will have classified these very different things in one genus because it found them of the same practical interest and reacted toward all of them in the same way. Suppose on the other hand, that one arrives at an analogous result in analyzing the idea of happiness. Immediately the problem disappears or rather is dissolved in entirely new problems of which we can know nothing, and whose terms we do not even possess, before having studied in itself the human activity of which society had formed from the outside, in order to arrive at the general ideas of *pleasure* and *happiness,* views that were perhaps artificial. Even then one must be assured that the concept of "human activity" itself is in accordance with a natural division. In this disarticulation of the real according to its own tendencies lies the principal difficulty, as soon as one leaves the domain of matter for that of mind.

This amounts to saying that the question of the origin and value of general ideas arises on the occasion of any philosophical problem, and it calls for a particular solution in each case. The discussions which have been raised around it fill the history of philosophy. Perhaps it would be advisable to ask oneself, before any discussion, if these ideas do really constitute a genus and if it would not be precisely in dealing with general ideas that one would have to guard against generalities. Doubtless one can easily keep the general idea of general idea, if one insists. It is enough to say that we agree to call general idea a representation which groups an indefinite number of things under the same name: most words will thus correspond to a general idea. But the important question for the philosopher is to know by what operation, for what reason, and especially in virtue of what structure of the real, things can thus be grouped, and this question does not admit of a unique and simple solution.

Let me say at once that psychology seems to me to be wandering aimlessly in research of this kind when it has no guiding thread. Behind the working of the mind, which is the act, there is function. Behind general ideas there is the faculty of conceiving or perceiving generalities. The vital significance of this faculty must first of all be determined. In the labyrinth of acts, states and faculties of mind, the thread which one must never lose is the one furnished by biology. *Primum vivere.* Memory, imagination, conception and perception, generalization in short, are not there "for nothing, for pleasure." It really seems, to listen to certain theorists, that the mind fell from heaven with a subdivision into psychological functions whose existence simply needs to be recognized: because these functions are such, they will no doubt be used in such a manner. I believe on the contrary that it is because they are useful, because they are necessary to life, that they are what they are: one must refer to the fundamental exigencies of life to explain their presence and to justify it if need be, I mean in order to know if the ordinary subdivision into such or such faculties is artificial or natural, and if in consequence we should maintain it or modify it. All our observations on the mechanism of function will be warped if we have badly cut it out of the continuity of the psychological tissue. Shall we say that the exigencies of life are analogous in men, animals and even plants, that our method therefore runs the risk of neglecting what is characteristically human in man? Without the slightest doubt: once psychological life is cut out and distributed, all is not finished; the growth and even the transfiguration of each faculty in man remains to be followed. But one will have at any rate some chance of not having traced arbitrary divisions in the mind's activity and more than one would fail in untangling plants whose stems and foliage are entwined and interlaced if one dug down to the roots.

Let us apply this method to the problem of general ideas: we shall find that every living being, perhaps even every organ, every tissue of a living being generalizes, I mean classifies, since it knows how to gather, in the environment in which it lies, from the most widely differing substances or objects, the parts or elements which can satisfy this or that one of its needs; the rest it disregards. Therefore it isolates the characteristic which interests it, going straight to a common property; in other words, it classifies, and consequently abstracts and generalizes. Doubtless, in almost all cases and probably in all other animals except man, abstraction and generalization are actually experienced and not thought. Yet, in the animal itself, we find representations which lack only reflection and some disinterestedness to be general ideas in the full sense of the term: if not, how should a cow that is being led stop before a meadow, no matter which, simply because it enters into the category that we call grass or meadow? And how should a horse distinguish a stable from a granary, a road from a field, hay from oats? Moreover, to conceive, or rather to perceive generality in this way is also the characteristic of man in so far as he is animal, has instincts and needs. Without the intervention of his reflection or even his consciousness, a resemblance can be drawn from the most widely differing objects by one of his tendencies; it will classify these objects into a genus and create a general idea, acted rather than thought. These automatically extracted generalities are even much more numerous in man, who adds to instinct habits more or less capable of imitating the instinctive act. If we pass now to the complete general idea, I mean conscious, reflected, created with intention, we shall find most often at its base this automatic extraction of resemblances which is the essential of generalization. In one sense, nothing resembles anything, since all objects are different. In another sense everything resembles everything, since one will always find, by climbing high enough on the ladder of generalities, some artificial genus into which two different objects

taken at random can go. But between impossible generalization and useless generalization there is another
which is called forth in a prefiguration by the tendencies,
habits, gestures and attitudes, the complexes of movements automatically accomplished or sketched, which are
at the origin of most human general ideas. The resemblance between things or states, which we declare we
see, is above all the quality common to these states or
things, of obtaining from our body the same reaction,
of making it sketch the same attitude and begin the same
movements. The body extracts from the material or
moral environment whatever has been able to influence
it, whatever interests it: it is the identity of reaction to
different actions which, playing upon them, gives them
resemblance or brings it out. Thus a bell, under the
most varied form of impact—a blow with the knuckle,
a breath of wind, an electric current—will give out a
sound which is always the same, will in that way convert
these forms of impact into bell-ringers, and thus will
make them resemble one another, individuals constituting a genus simply because the bell remains the same:
bell, and nothing but bell, it cannot do otherwise, if it
reacts at all, than ring. It goes without saying that when
reflection has raised to the state of pure thought representations which were scarcely more than the insertion of
consciousness into a material frame, that is, attitudes and
movements, it will form voluntarily, directly, by imitation, general ideas which will be nothing more than ideas.
It will receive powerful assistance in this from the word,
which will again furnish representation with a frame
into which it can fit, but this time one that is more spiritual than corporeal. It is none the less true that in order
to realize the true nature of concepts, and attack with
some chance of success problems relating to general
ideas, one will always have to look to the impact of
thought upon the motor attitudes or habits, generalization being originally little else than habit, rising from
the field of action to that of thought.

But, once the origin and structure of the general idea

have thus been fixed, once the necessity of its appearance has been established, and furthermore, once the imitation of nature by the artificial construction of general ideas is noted, it still remains for us to find out how natural general ideas, which serve as a model to others, are possible, and why experience presents us with resemblances which we have only to translate into generalities. Among these resemblances there are some, naturally, which go to the fundamental root of things. Those will produce general ideas which will still be, to a certain extent, relative to the convenience of the individual and society, but which science and philosophy will have only to separate from this matrix to obtain a more or less approximate vision of some aspect of reality. They are few in number and the immense majority of general ideas are those which society has prepared for language with a view to conversation and action. Nevertheless, even among this majority we are especially referring to here, there are many which, by a series of intermediaries, after all sorts of manipulations, simplifications, and deformations, are linked with the small number of ideas which translate essential resemblances. It will often be instructive to go back with them, by a fairly long detour, to the resemblance to which they are linked. It might be useful, therefore, at this point to digress upon what one might call objective generalities, inherent in reality itself. Limited in number as they may be, they are important both for themselves and for the confidence they radiate, lending something of their firmness to genera that are wholly artificial, just as banknotes printed in excess owe what little value they possess to the gold remaining in the coffers.

Going more deeply into this point, one would perceive, I think, that resemblances divide into three groups, the second of which will probably have to be subdivided as positive science progresses. The resemblances of the first category are biological in essence: they would have it that life should work *as if* life itself had general ideas, those of genus and species, *as if* it followed a certain limited number of structural plans, *as if* it had instituted general properties of life, finally and above all as if, by the double effect of hereditary transmission (for what is *innate*) and more or less slow transformation, it had wished to arrange the living in a hierarchical series, along a scale where the resemblances between individuals are more numerous the higher one goes. Whether one expresses onself thus in terms of finality, or whether one attributes special properties to living matter, which imitate the intelligence, or indeed finally whether one adheres to some intermediate hypothesis, in principle it is always in reality itself (even if our classification is inexact in fact) that our subdivisions into species, genera, etc.—generalities which we translate into general ideas —will be based. And quite as well founded in right will be those resemblances which correspond to organs, tissues, cells, or even anything else which goes to make up living beings.

Now, if we pass from the organized to the unorganized, from living matter to matter inert and not yet informed by man, we find real genera but genera of quite a different character: qualities, such as colors, flavors, odors; elements or combinations, such as oxygen, hydrogen, water; finally, physical forces like gravity, heat, electricity. But what here brings the representations of individual groups under the general idea is an entirely different thing. Without going into detail, without complicating this explanation by taking into account shades of meaning, and further qualifying ahead of time anything exaggerated in our distinction, and finally agreeing to give the word "resemblance" its most precise and also its narrowest meaning, we say that in the first case the principle of classification is resemblance properly so-called, and in the second it is identity. A certain shade of red can be identical to itself in all objects in which it is found. One could say the same of two notes of the same pitch, the same intensity and the same tone. Furthermore, rightly or wrongly, we feel we are progressing toward identical elements or events as we further examine matter and resolve the chemical into physical, the physical into mathematical. Now, a simple logic can claim that resemblance is a partial identity and that identity is a complete resemblance; nevertheless, experience teaches us something entirely different. If one ceases to give the word "resemblance" the vague and somewhat popular meaning we gave it to begin with, if one seeks to give "resemblance" its exact meaning through a comparison with "identity," it will be found, I believe, that identity is something *geometrical* and resemblance something *vital*. The first has to do with measure, the other belongs rather to the domain of art: it is often a purely aesthetic feeling which prompts the evolutionary biologist to suppose related forms between which he is the first to see a resemblance: the very design he gives these forms reveals at times the hand and especially the eye of the artist. But if the identical thus contrasts so strongly with the resembling, there might be grounds for seeking to determine, for this new category of general ideas as for the other, what makes it possible.

Such an investigation could achieve its object only in a more advanced state of our knowledge of matter. Let us be content with a word on the hypothesis to which our deeper examination of life would lead us. If there is green which in thousands and thousands of different places is the same green (at least to our eye, or approximately), if it is the same for other colors, and if the differences of color depend upon the more or less great frequency of the elementary physical events we condense into color perception, the possibility of these frequencies presenting us at all times and in all circumstances with a few specific colors comes from the fact that all possible frequencies are (within certain limits, of course) everywhere and always realized. Then those which correspond to our various colors will necessarily be produced with all the others, at whatever time or place; the repetition of the identical, which in this case makes it possible to constitute genera, will have no other origin. With modern physics more and more clearly revealing to us differences in number behind our distinctions of quality, an explanation of this genus probably is valid for all the genera and all the elementary generalities (capable of being combined by us to form others) which we find in the world of inert matter. The explanation would be completely satisfactory, it is true, only if it also explained why our perception picks up, in the immense field of frequencies, those particular frequencies which will be the various colors—why, in the first place, it picks any up; why in the second place, it picks up those rather than others. I have answered this special question in an earlier work by defining living being as a certain power to act, determined in quantity and quality: it is this virtual action which extracts from matter our real perceptions, information it needs for its own guidance, condensations within an instant of our duration of thousands, millions, trillions of events taking place in the enormously less drawn-out duration of things. This difference of tension exactly measures the interval between physical determination and human liberty, at the same time that it explains their duality and coexistence. If, as I believe, the appearance of man or of some being of the same essence is the raison d'être of life on our planet, it must be said that all the categories of perception, not only of men but of animals and even of plants (which can behave *as though* they had perceptions), correspond, on the whole, to the choice of a certain *order of greatness* for condensation. That is a simple hypothesis, but it seems to me to issue quite naturally from the speculations of physics on the structure of matter. What would become of the table upon which I am at this moment writing if my perception, and consequently my action, was made for the order of greatness to which the elements, or rather the events, which go to make up its materiality, correspond? My action would be dissolved; my perception would embrace, at the place where I see my table and in the short moment I have to look at it, an immense universe and a no less interminable history. It would be impossible for me to understand how this moving immensity can become, so that I may act upon it, a simple rectangle, motionless and solid. It would be the same for all things and all events: the world in which we live, with the actions and reactions of its parts upon each other, is what it is by virtue of a certain choice in the scale of greatness, a choice which is itself determined by our power of acting. Nothing would prevent other worlds, corresponding to another choice, from existing with it, in the same place and the same time: in this way twenty different broadcasting stations throw out simultaneously twenty different concerts which coexist without any one of them mingling its sounds with the music of another, each one being heard, complete and alone, in the apparatus which has chosen for its reception the wave-length of that particular station. But let us not give too much of our attention to a question we found in our path. There is no need of a hypothesis on the intimate structure of matter to see that the conceptions which correspond to the properties and actions of matter, are possible or are what they are only by reason of the mathematics imminent in things. That is all I wished to recall in order to justify a classification of general ideas which places on one side the geometric, and on the other, the vital—the former bringing with it identity, and the latter, resemblance.

We must now go on to the third category we mentioned, to general ideas created whole by human speculation and action. Man is essentially a manufacturer. Nature, in denying him ready-made instruments like those the insects have, for example, has given him intelligence, that is to say, the power of inventing and constructing an indefinite number of tools. Now, no matter how simple the thing made, it is done after a model, perceived or imagined: the genus defined by either the model itself or the diagram of its construction is real. All our civilization thus rests upon a certain number of general ideas with whose contents we are sufficiently acquainted, since we made them, and which are invaluable, since we could not live without them. That, in part, explains the belief in the absolute reality of Ideas in general, perhaps even in their divinity. We know what role it plays in ancient philosophy, and even in our own. All general ideas benefit from the objectivity of certain among them. We might add that the productive activity of man is not exerted solely upon matter. Once in possession of the three kinds of general ideas we have enumerated, especially of the latter, our intelligence has what we called the general idea of general idea. It can then construct general ideas as it likes. It begins naturally with those which can be of greatest advantage to social life, or simply which are connected with social life; then will come those which concern pure speculation; and finally those one constructs for no particular reason, for the mere pleasure of doing so. But for almost all the concepts which do not belong in our first two categories, that is, for the immense majority of general ideas, it is the interest of society with that of individuals, it is the exigencies of conversation and action, which preside at their birth.

Let us finish this long digression upon which we embarked to show to what extent there is a need for recasting and sometimes completely setting aside conceptual thought in order to arrive at a more intuitive philosophy. This philosophy, we were saying, will often turn aside from the social vision of the object already made; it will ask us to participate, in spirit, in the act which makes it. It will therefore turn us back, on this particular point, in the direction of the divine. What is essentially human is, in fact, the labor of an individual thought which accepts, just as it is, its insertion into social thought and which utilizes pre-existing ideas as it utilizes any other tool furnished by the community. But there is already something quasi divine in the effort, however humble it may be, of a mind which re-inserts itself into the vital impetus, the generator of societies which in turn are the generators of ideas.

This effort will exorcise certain phantom problems

which obsess the metaphysician, that is to say, each one of us. I should like to talk about those distressing and insoluble problems which have no bearing on what is, but bear rather upon what is not. Such is the problem of the origin of being: "How can it be that something exists—matter, mind, or God? There must have been a cause, and a cause of the cause, and so on indefinitely." We go back then from cause to cause; and if we stop somewhere along the way, it is not because our intelligence seeks nothing beyond that, it is because our imagination finally shuts its eyes, as though over the abyss, to avoid dizziness. Such, again, is the problem of order in general: "Why an ordered reality, where our thought finds itself as in a mirror? Why is the world not incoherent?" I say that these problems relate to what is not rather than to what is. Never indeed would one be astonished at the existence of something —matter, mind, God—if one did not implicitly admit the possible existence of nothing. We imagine, or better still, we think we imagine, that being filled a void and that nothingness logically existed before being: primordial reality—whether we call it matter, mind or God— would then be superadded, and that is incomprehensible. In the same way one would not ask oneself why order exists if one did not think one conceived a disorder which presumably submitted to order and which consequently preceded it, at least ideally. Order would therefore need to be explained, while disorder, existing by right, would not demand explanation. Such is the point of view at which one is in danger of remaining as long as one merely seeks to comprehend. But let us go further and try to engender (we can do so obviously only in thought). To the extent that we distend our will, tend to reabsorb our thought in it and get into greater sympathy with the effort which engenders things, these formidable problems recede, diminish, disappear. For we feel that a divinely creative will or thought is too full of itself, in the immensity of its reality, to have the slightest idea of a lack of order or lack of being. To imagine the possibility of absolute disorder, all the more the possibility of nothingness, would be for it to say to itself that it might have not existed at all, and that would be a weakness incompatible with its nature which is force. The more we turn toward this creative will, the more the doubts which trouble the sane and normal man seem to us abnormal and morbid. Take for example the doubter who closes a window, then returns to verify its closing, then verifies his verification, and so forth. If we ask him what his motives are he will answer that he might have opened the window each time he tried to close it more securely. And if he is a philosopher he will transpose intellectually the hesitation of his conduct into this question: "How can one be sure, definitively sure, that one has done what one intended to do?" But the truth is that his power of action is defective, and therein lies the evil from which he suffers: he had only partial will to accomplish the act, and that is why the accomplished act leaves him only partial certitude. Now can we solve the problem this man sets himself? Obviously not, but neither do we set the problem; therein lies our superiority. At first glance I might think there is more in him than in me because we both shut the window and he, in addition, raises a philosophical question while I do not. But the question which in his case is superadded to the task accomplished represents in reality only something negative; it is not something more, but something less; it is a deficit of the will. Such is exactly the effect certain "great problems" produce in us when we set ourselves again in the direction of generating thought. They recede toward zero as fast as we approach this generating thought, as they fill only that space between it and us. Thus we discover the illusion of him who thinks he is doing more by raising these problems than by not raising them. One might just as well think that there is more in a half-consumed bottle than in a full one, because the latter contains only wine, while in the former there is wine and emptiness in addition.

But as soon as we have intuitively perceived the true, our intellect recovers itself, corrects itself, intellectually formulates its error. It has received the suggestion; it furnishes the verification. As the diver feels out the wreck on the sea floor that the aviator has pointed out from the air, so the intellect immersed in the conceptual environment verifies from point to point, by contact, analytically, what has been the object of a synthetic and super-intellectual vision. If it had not been for a warning from without, the thought of a possible illusion would never even have occurred to it, for its illusion was a part of its nature. Shaken from its slumber, it will analyze the ideas of disorder, of nothingness and their like. It will recognize—if only for an instant, even though the illusion were to reappear the moment it had been dispelled—that one cannot suppress one arrangement without another arrangement taking its place, or take away matter without some other matter replacing it. "Disorder" and "nothingness" in reality designate therefore a presence—the presence of a thing or an order which does not interest us, which blunts our effort or our attention; it is our disappointment being expressed when we call this presence absence. Consequently, to speak of the absence of all order and all things, that is, to speak of absolute disorder and absolute nothingness, is to pronounce words void of meaning, *flatus vocis*, since a suppression is simply a substitution envisaged by a single one of its two sides, and since the abolition of all order and all things would be a substitution with but a single side—an idea which has exactly as much existence as a round square. When the philosopher speaks of chaos and nothingness he is only carrying over into the order of speculation—raised to the absolute and consequently emptied of all meaning, of all effective content— two ideas made for practical use and which were related to a particular kind of matter or order, but not to all order or all matter. That being so, what becomes of the two problems of the origin of order and the origin of being? They fade away since they only arise if one repre-

sents being and order as "what turned up," and consequently nothingness and *dis*order as possibles or at least
as conceivables. But those are only words, mirages of
ideas.

Let human thought but become impregnated with
this conviction, let it be freed of this obsession: immediately it begins to breathe. It no longer worries over
questions which retarded its progress. The difficulties
raised for example by ancient skepticism and modern
criticism in turn are seen to disappear. It can equally
well ignore Kantian philosophy and the "theories of
knowledge" which derive from it; it will not pay any
attention to them. The whole object of the *Critique of
Pure Reason* is, in fact, to explain how a particular
order is superadded to supposedly incoherent materials.
And we know what price it makes us pay for this explanation according to which the human mind imposes
its form upon a "sensible diversity" of unexplained
origin; and the order we find in things is the order we
ourselves put in them. With the result that science would
be legitimate, but relative to our faculty of knowing, and
metaphysics impossible, since there would be no knowledge outside of science. The human mind is thus rele-
gated to a corner, like a schoolboy in disgrace: it cannot
turn its head around to see reality as it is.—Nothing is
more natural than this if one has not noticed that the
idea of absolute disorder is contradictory, or rather,
inexistent, a mere word by which one designates an oscillation of the mind between two different orders: in
which case it is absurd to suppose that disorder logically
or chronologically precedes order. The merit of Kantianism has been to develop a natural illusion in all its consequences, and to present it in its most systematic form.
But it has preserved this illusion; it even rests upon it.
Once we dispel the illusion we immediately restore to the
human mind, through science and through metaphysics,
the knowledge of the absolute.

We come back, then, once more to our point of departure. We were saying that philosophy must be brought

to a higher precision, put in a position to solve more special problems, be made an auxiliary to, and if need be, reformer of positive science. Let us have done with great systems embracing all the possible, and sometimes even the impossible! Let us be content with the real, mind and matter. But let us demand of our theory that it embrace the real so closely that between the two no other interpretation can find room. There will then be but one philosophy as there is only one science. Both will be accomplished by a collective and progressive effort. It is true that we shall have to bring about a perfecting of the philosophical method, symmetrical with and complementary to what positive science formerly received.

Such is the doctrine that certain people had judged to be directed against Science and the Intelligence. It was a two-fold error, but one from which it was possible to learn. An analysis of it will be useful.

Beginning with the first point, let us note that it was not the real scholars who in general accused me of attacking science. One of them might now and again have criticized this or that one of my views: and this precisely because he judged it to be scientific, because I had transported into the field of science, where he felt at home, a problem of pure philosophy. Let me repeat, what I wanted was a philosophy which would submit to the control of science and which in turn could enable science to progress. And I think it can be said that I found it, since psychology, neurology, pathology, biology have become more and more open to my views, at first judged to be paradoxical. But even had they remained paradoxical these views would never have been anti-scientific. They would always have borne witness to an effort to constitute a metaphysics having a common frontier with science and therefore being able to lend itself to verification on a great many points. Had one not trudged the length of that frontier, had it simply been noted that there was one and that metaphysics and science could therefore meet, one would already have understood the place I assign to positive science; no philosophy, I said, not even positivism, has placed it so high; to science, as to metaphysics, I have attributed the power of attaining an absolute. I have asked science simply to remain scientific, and not to take on an unconscious metaphysics which then presents itself to the ignorant or the half-educated under the mask of science. For more than half a century this "scientism" stood in the way of metaphysics. Every effort of intuition was discouraged in advance; it dashed itself against negations thought to be scientific. It is true that in more than one case these negations emanated from real scholars. They were dupes, actually, of the false metaphysics claimed to have been drawn from science and which, rebounding upon science, distorted it on many points. It went so far as to distort observation, interposing itself in certain cases between the observer and the facts. I thought I had given in an earlier work the demonstration of this fact based upon precise examples, in particular upon the subject of aphasia, to the greater good of science and, at the same time, philosophy. But suppose even that one does not care to be enough either of a metaphysician or a scholar to enter into these considerations, that one refuses to be interested in the contents of the doctrine, that one is ignorant of the method: a simple glance cast upon the applications shows what an amount of scientific circumvallation it demands before the slightest problem is attacked. Nothing more is necessary to see the place that I make for science. In reality, the chief difficulty of philosophical research as we understand it lies there. To reason on abstract ideas is easy; metaphysical construction is only a game, however slightly one is pre-disposed to it. To penetrate the mind intuitively is perhaps more painful, but no philosopher will work at it for long at a stretch; he will have quickly perceived each time what he is capable of perceiving. On the other hand, if one accepts such a method one will never have made enough preparatory studies, never have learned enough. Here is a philosophical problem. We have chosen it, we have met it. It blocks our way, hence we must brush aside the obstacle or give up philosophizing. No subterfuge is possible; farewell to the dialectical artifice which lulls the attention to sleep and which, in dreams, gives the illusion of progress. The difficulty must be resolved and the problem analyzed in its elements. Where will it lead us? No one knows. No one will even be able to say what that science is to which the new problems will appertain. It might be a science which is completely foreign. What is more, it will not be enough to become familiar with it or even to go deeply into it: sometimes there will be no alternative but to re-form certain procedures, certain habits, certain theories, governing oneself exactly by the facts and the reasons which have brought up new questions. Very well then, we shall do so; we shall initiate ourselves into the science we do not know, we shall study it, and if need be, make it over. And what if it takes months or even years? We shall devote to the task the time required. But supposing one lifetime is not sufficient? Several lifetimes will achieve success; no philosopher henceforth is obliged to construct the whole of philosophy. This is the language that we would speak to the philosopher. Such is the method we propose to him. It demands that he be always ready, no matter what his age, to become a student once more.

As a matter of fact, philosophy is not far from that stage. The change has already been realized on certain points. If my views were generally judged to be paradoxical when they made their appearance, some of them are commonplace today; others bid fair to become so. Let us admit that they could not at first be accepted. It would have meant tearing oneself away from deeply-rooted habits, veritable extensions of nature. All our ways of speaking, thinking, perceiving imply in effect that immobility and immutability are there by right, that movement and change are superadded, like accidents, to things which, by themselves, do not move and, in themselves, do not change. The representation of change is that of qualities or states, which supposedly

follow one another in a substance. Each of these qualities, each of these states would be something stable,
change being made of their succession: as for substance,
whose role is to support the states and qualities which
succeed one another, it would be stability itself. Such is
the logic immanent in our languages and formulated
once and for all by Aristotle: the intelligence has as its
essence to judge, and judgment operates by the attribu-
tion of a predicate to a subject. The subject, by the sole
fact of being named, is defined as invariable; the variation will reside in the diversity of the states that one will
affirm concerning it, one after another. In proceeding
thus, by apposition of a predicate to a subject, from the
stable to the stable, we follow the bent of our intelligence, we conform to the demands of our language and,
in a word, obey nature. For nature has predestined man
to social life; she has demanded work in common; and
this work will be possible if we put on one side the absolutely definitive stability of the subject and on the
other side the stabilities of the qualities and states,
which will turn out to be attributes. In enunciating the
subject we lean our communication up against a knowledge that our interlocutors already possess, since substance is supposed to be invariable; they now know upon
which point to direct their attention; then will come the
information we wish to give them, in the expectation of
which we placed them in introducing the substance, and
which brings them the attribute. But it is not only in shaping us for social life, in leaving us complete latitude for the
organization of society, in thus rendering language
necessary that nature has predestined us to see in change
and movement only accidents, to set immutability and
immobility up as essences or substances, as supports.
It must be added that our perception itself proceeds
according to this philosophy. From the continuity of
extension, it cuts out chosen elements precisely in such
a way that they can be treated as invariable while they
are being contemplated. When the variation is too strong
to pass unnoticed we say that the state with which we

were concerned has given place to another which will not vary any more than the first. Here again it is nature preparing individual and social action which has traced the main lines of our language and our thought without, however, making them coincide exactly, and also leaving enough place for contingency and variability. To convince oneself of this, it will be enough to compare to our duration what one might call the duration of things: two rhythms vastly different, calculated in such a way that in the shortest perceptible interval of our time are contained trillions of oscillations or more generally of external events which repeat; this immense history that would take us hundreds of centuries to unfold, we apprehend in an indivisible synthesis. Thus perception, thought, language, all the individual or social activities of the mind, conspire to bring us face to face with objects that we can take to be invariable and immobile while we consider them, as it also brings us face to face with persons, including our own, which will become in our eyes objects and, at the same time, invariable substances. How can we uproot so profound an inclination? How can we bring the human mind to reverse the direction of its customary way of operating, beginning with change and movement, envisaged as reality itself, and no longer to see in halts or states mere snapshots taken of what is moving reality? The human mind would have to be shown that if the habitual movement of thought is practically useful, handy for conversation, coöperation, action, it leads to philosophical problems which are and which will remain insoluble, because they are presented backwards. It is precisely because they were seen to be insoluble and because they did not appear to be badly presented that one arrived at the conclusion that all knowledge was relative and the absolute, impossible of attainment. This explains in the main the success of positivism and of Kantianism, the almost general attitudes of mind prevailing when I first went in for philosophy. This attitude of humiliation was gradually to be renounced as the true cause of the irreducible antinomies came to be perceived. These antinomies were of man's making. They did not come from things themselves but from an automatic transfer to speculation of habits contracted in action. What a careless attitude of the intellect had done, an effort on the part of the intellect could undo. And for the human mind that would be a liberation.

Let us hasten to add that a method that is being proposed is understood only if it is applied to an example. In this case the example was ready to hand. It was a matter of getting once more to the point where we could grasp the inner life beneath the juxtaposition of our states that we effect in a spatialized time. The experiment was within reach of everyone, and those who were willing to make it had no difficulty in getting an idea of the substantiality of the ego, as of its duration. It is, we were saying, indivisible and indestructible continuity of a melody where the past enters into the present and forms with it an undivided whole which remains undivided and even indivisible in spite of what is added at every instant, or rather, thanks to what is added. We have the intuition of it; but as soon as we seek an intellectual representation of it we line up, one after another, states which have become distinct like the beads of a necklace and therefore require, in order to hold them together, a thread which is neither this nor that, nothing that resembles beads, nothing that resembles anything whatsoever—an empty entity, a simple word. Intuition gives us the thing whose spatial transposition, whose metaphorical translation alone, is seized by the intellect.

That is clear enough for our own substance. What are we to think of the substances of things? When I began to write, physics had not yet made the decisive advances which were to bring a change in its ideas on the structure of matter. But convinced, even then, that immobility and invariability were only views taken of moving and changing reality, I could not believe that matter, whose solid image had been obtained through the immobilization of changes and hence perceived as qualities, was composed of solid elements like it. No matter how much one refrained from any imaged representation of the atom, corpuscle, ultimate element, whatever it might be, it was nevertheless a *thing* serving as support to movements and changes, and consequently in itself was not changing, in itself not moving. Sooner or later, I thought, the idea of support would have to be abandoned. I said something on the subject in my first book, but I got no further than "movements of movements," without being able to find a more exact expression for what I wanted to say. I tried to get nearer to the idea in my second work. I went still further in my lectures on "the perception of change." The same reason which was later to lead me to write that "evolution cannot be reconstituted with fragments of the product of evolution" made me think that the solid must be resolved into something entirely different from solid. The inevitable propensity of our mind to imagine the element as fixed was legitimate in other domains since it is something action requires; but precisely for that reason, speculation in this case had to guard against it. But I could only draw attention to this point. Sooner or later, I thought, physics will be brought around to the point of seeing in the fixity of the element a form of mobility. When that time came, it is true, science would probably give up looking for an imaged representation of it, the image of a movement being that of a moving point (that is to say, always of a minute solid). In actual fact, the great theoretical discoveries of recent years have led physicists to suppose a kind of fusion between the wave and the corpuscle—between substance and movement, as I should express it. One very profound philosopher who began as a mathematician came to envisage a piece of iron as "a melodic continuity."

Long indeed would be the list of "paradoxes" more or less related to my fundamental "paradox," which have little by little bridged the interval between improbability and probability, and have reached the point of being common-place. Once again it was not enough that I started from a direct experiment; the results of this experiment could not be adopted unless the progress of the outward experiment and of all the processes of reasoning related to it imposed its adoption. I myself was in that position: certain consequences of my first reflection were not clearly perceived and definitively accepted by me until I had reached them again along a completely different road.

I shall cite as example my conception of the psychophysiological relation. When I set myself the problem of the reciprocal action of mind and body upon one another, it was solely because I had met it in my study of "the immediate data of consciousness" (*Essais sur les données immédiates de la conscience*). At that time freedom appeared to me to be a fact; but on the other hand the affirmation of universal determinism, established by savants as a rule of method, was generally accepted by philosophers as a scientific dogma. Was human freedom compatible with the determinism of nature? As freedom had become for me an undoubted fact, I had dealt with it to the exclusion of almost everything else in my first book: determinism could come to terms with it the best it could; it would have to do so, as no theory can resist a fact for long. But the problem I had avoided throughout my first work now presented itself as inescapable. Faithful to my method, I tried to get the problem stated in less general terms and even, if possible, to give it a concrete form, to shape it to certain facts upon which direct observation could be based. It is not necessary to relate here how the traditional problem of "the relation of mind and body" contracted before me to the point where it became no more than that of the cerebral localization of the memory, and how this last question, much too vast itself, came little by little to concern nothing but the memory of words, still more especially, the maladies of this particular memory, the aphasias. The study of the different forms of aphasia which I pursued with the sole desire of getting at the pure facts, showed me that between the consciousness and the organism there was a relation that no reasoning could have constructed *a priori,* a correspondence which was neither parallelism nor epiphenomenalism, nor anything resembling them. The role of the brain was to choose at any moment, among memories, those which could illuminate the action begun, and to exclude the others. Those memories capable of being inserted into the motor framework forever changing, but always prepared, emerged once more to consciousness; the rest remained in the unconscious. The role of the body was thus to reproduce in action the life of the mind, to emphasize its motor articulations as the orchestra conductor does for a musical score; the brain did not have thinking as its function but that of hindering the thought from becoming lost in dream; it was the organ of *attention to life.* Such was the conclusion to which I was led by the specially detailed study of normal and pathological facts, more generally through external observation. But only then did I become aware of the fact that inward experience in the pure state, in giving us a "substance" whose very essence is to endure and consequently continually to prolong into the present an indestructible past, would have relieved me from seeking, and would even have forbidden me to seek, where memories are preserved. They preserve themselves, as we admit, for example, when we pronounce a word. In order to pronounce it we have to remember the first half of it while we are articulating the second. But no one will think that the first has been immediately deposited in a drawer, cerebral or otherwise, so that consciousness may come for it a moment later. But if that is the case for the first half of the word, it will be the same for the preceding word, which is an integral part of it as far as sound and meaning are concerned; it will be the same from the beginning of the sentence, and the preceding sentence, and the whole discourse that we could have made very long, indefinitely long had we wished. Now, our whole life, from the time of our first

awakening to consciousness, is something like this indefinitely prolonged discourse. Its duration is substantial,
indivisible insofar as it is pure duration. Thus I could,
if necessary, have saved several years of research. But
as my intellect did not differ from that of other men, the
strength of conviction which accompanied my intuition
of duration, when I kept to the inner life, did not
extend very much further. Above all, with what I had
noted of this inner life in my first book, I could not
have gone as deeply as I was later led to do into the
diverse intellectual functions, memory, association of
ideas, abstraction, generalization, interpretation, attention. Psycho-physiology on the one hand, psycho-pathology on the other, directed the scrutiny of my consciousness to more than one problem which, had it not been
for them, I should have neglected to study, and the
study of these problems made me state them otherwise.
The results thus obtained were not without their effect
upon psycho-physiology and psycho-pathology themselves. To confine myself to the latter science, I shall
mention simply the growing importance that considerations of psychological tension, of attention to life and all
that had to do with "schizophrenia" gradually assumed
in it. Even my idea of integral conservation of the
past has more and more found its empirical verification
in the vast collection of experiments instituted by the
disciples of Freud.

Slower still in being accepted are views situated at the
point of convergence of three different speculations, and
not simply of two. These are metaphysical. They concern
the apprehension of matter by mind and should put an
end to the old conflict between realism and idealism by
shifting the line of demarcation between subject and object, between mind and matter. Here again the problem
resolves itself by being stated differently. Psychological
analysis alone had shown me successive planes of consciousness in the memory, from the "dream plane," the
most extensive of all, upon which is spread out as on the
base of a pyramid the whole past of the person, up to the

point comparable to the peak, where memory is no more than the perception of the actual with nascent actions which prolong it. Is this perception of all surrounding bodies seated in the organized body? Such is the general belief. The action of the surrounding bodies is exerted upon the brain by the intermediary of the sense organs; in the brain inextensive sensation and perceptions are elaborated: these perceptions are presumably projected outward by the consciousness and cover, as it were, external objects. But the comparison of the data of psychology with that of physiology showed me something quite different. The hypothesis of an eccentric projection of the sensations appeared to me as being false when considered superficially, less and less intelligible the deeper one went into it, but natural enough when one took into account the direction to which psychology and philosophy had been committed and the inevitable illusion into which one fell when one cut up reality in a certain way in order to state problems in certain terms. One was obliged to imagine in the brain some representation of reduced size, some miniature of the outer world, which became still more reduced and even non-extensive in order to pass from the brain into consciousness: the latter, furnished with space as with a "form," restored extent to the non-extended and regained, through a reconstruction, the external world. All these theories fell to the ground with the illusion which had given them birth. It is not in us, it is in them that we perceive objects; it is at least in them that we should perceive them if our perception was "pure." After all, I simply came back to the idea of common sense. "One would," I wrote, "greatly astonish a man unaccustomed to philosophical speculations by telling him that the object he had before him, which he sees and touches, exists only in his mind and for his mind, or even more generally, exists only for a mind, as Berkeley would have it. . . . But on the other hand, we should astonish that interlocutor just as much by telling him that the object is quite different from what one perceives in. . . . Therefore, for common

sense, the object is in itself picturesque as we perceive
it: it is a picture, but a picture which exists in itself."
How could a doctrine which took its stand from the
point of view of common sense appear so strange? One
can easily understand it when one follows the development of modern philosophy and when one sees how
from the outset it is orientated toward idealism, yielding
to an urge which was the same as that of modern science
in its inception. Realism was stated in the same way; it
was formulated by opposition to idealism, utilizing the
same terms; so that it built up among philosophers
certain habits of mind, in virtue of which the distinction
between the "objective" and "subjective" was decided
in approximately the same way by everyone, whatever
the relation established between the two terms and to
whatever school one belonged. It was extremely difficult
to give up these habits; I was conscious of the almost
painful and endless effort I had to make, myself, in
order to get back to a point of view so strongly resembling that of common sense. The first chapter of
"Matter and Memory," in which I gave the results
of my reflections on "images," was judged obscure by all
who had some habit of philosophical speculation, and
even because of that habit. I do not know whether the
obscurity has disappeared: what is certain is that the
theories of knowledge which have recently come into
being, especially abroad, seem to leave aside the terms
in which Kantians and anti-Kantians agreed to state
the problem. Philosophers return to the immediately
given, or are tending toward it.

So much for Science, and for the reproach I incurred
for combatting it. As for the Intelligence, there was
no need to become so agitated on its account. Why
was it not consulted in the first place? Being intelligence, and consequently understanding everything, it
would have understood and said that I wished it nothing
but well. In reality, what people were defending against
me was, in the first place, a dry rationalism made up for

the most part of negations, and whose negative side I eliminated merely by proposing certain solutions; and in the second place, perhaps principally, a verbalism which still vitiates a large part of knowledge and which I wanted definitely to cast aside.

What, really, is intelligence? It is the human way of thinking. It has been given to us, as instinct has been given to the bee, in order to direct our conduct. Since nature destined us to master and utilize matter, the intelligence evolves with ease only in space, and feels at its ease only in the unorganized. By its origin it tends toward fabrication; it manifests itself in an activity which serves as prelude to mechanical art and by a language which announces science—all the rest of primitive mentality being belief and tradition. The normal development of the intellect then takes place, therefore in the direction of science and technique (technicité). A mechanics still in the crude stage brings forth a mathematics still imprecise: this latter having become scientific and causing the other sciences to spring up around it, indefinitely perfects mechanical art. So science and art introduce us into the intimacy of a matter which the one thinks and the other manipulates. From this standpoint the intellect would, in principle, finally reach an absolute. It would then be completely itself. Vague at the outset because it was only a presentiment of matter, it takes shape more clearly the more precisely it knows matter. But precise or vague, it is the attention that mind gives to matter. How then could mind still be intellect when it turns upon itself? We can give things whatever names we choose and I see no great objection, I repeat, to knowledge of the mind by the mind still being called intelligence, if one insists. But then it will be necessary to specify that there are two intellectual functions, the one the inverse of the other, for mind thinks mind only in climbing back up the slope of habits acquired in contact with matter, and these habits are what one currently calls intellectual tendencies. Is it not better to designate by another name a function which certainly is not what one ordinarily calls intelligence? I call it intuition. It represents the attention that the mind gives to itself, over and above, while it is fixed upon matter, its object. This supplementary attention can be methodically cultivated and developed. Thus will be constituted a science of the mind, a veritable metaphysics which will define the mind positively instead of simply denying, concerning it, all that we know about matter. In understanding metaphysics in that way, in assigning to intuition the knowledge of the mind, we withdraw nothing from the intellect, for we claim that the metaphysics which was the product of pure intelligence eliminated time, that hence it repudiated the mind or defined it by negations: this purely negative knowledge of the mind we shall be glad to leave to the intelligence, if the intelligence insists upon keeping it; we claim simply that there is another. On no point whatever, then, do we diminish the intelligence; we do not drive it away from any of the territory it has occupied up to the present; and, where it is completely at home, we attribute to it a power which modern philosophy has generally contested. Only, beside it, we note the existence of another faculty capable of another kind of knowledge. Thus we have on one hand science and mechanical art, which have to do with pure intellect; on the other hand, metaphysics, which calls upon intuition. Between these two extremities, then, will be placed the sciences of moral life, social life and even organic life— the former more intuitive, the latter more intellectual. But intuitive or intellectual, knowledge will be stamped with the seal of precision.

There is nothing precise, on the contrary, in conversation, which is the usual source of "criticism." Whence come the ideas therein exchanged? What is the significance of words? One must not think that social life is a habit acquired and transmitted. Man is organized for the life of the state as the ant is for the ant-hill, but with this difference, that the ant possesses ready-made means of attaining its end, while we bring what is necessary to reinvent them and to vary their form. Even though each word of our speech is conventional, language is not therefore a convention, and it is as natural for man to speak as to walk. Now, what is the original function of language? It is to establish a communication with a view to coöperation. Language transmits orders or warnings. It prescribes or describes. In the first case, it is the call to immediate action; in the second, it is the description of the thing or some one of its properties, with a view to action. But in either case the function is industrial, commercial, military, always social. The things that language describes have been cut out of reality by human perception in view of human work to be done. The properties which it indicates are the calls made by the thing to a human activity. The word will therefore be the same, as I was saying, when the suggested step to be taken is the same, and our mind will attribute to various things the same property, will imagine them in the same way, will in fact group them under the same idea wherever the suggestion of the same advantage to be gained, the same action to be done, calls forth the same word. Such are the origins of the word and the idea. Both of them have doubtless evolved. They are no longer as blatantly utilitarian. Nevertheless they do remain utilitarian. Social thought is unable not to keep its original structure. Is it intellect or intuition? I am quite content to have intuition let its light filter in to it: there is no thought without "esprit de finesse," and the "esprit de finesse" is the reflection of the intuition in the intellect. I am quite willing to admit that this very modest share of intuition has become enlarged, that it has given birth to poetry, then to prose, and converted into instruments of art, words which, at first, were only signals: by the Greeks especially was this miracle wrought. It is no less true that thought and language, originally destined to organize the work of men in space, are intellectual in essence. But it is, necessarily,

vague intellectuality—a very general adaptation of
mind to matter which society is to use. There is nothing
more natural than that philosophy should at first have
been content with it and that it began by being pure
dialectic. It had nothing else at its disposal. A Plato,
an Aristotle adopt the cutting out of reality that they
find already made in language: "dialectic," which is
related to dialegein, dialegisthai, means at the same time
"dialogue" and "distribution"; a dialectic like Plato's
was both a conversation where one sought to agree upon
the meaning of the word and a distribution of things
according to the indications of language. But sooner or
later this system of ideas modeled upon words had to
give place to an exact knowledge represented by more
precise signs; science would then be constituted by
taking matter explicitly as object, experimentation as
means, mathematics as ideal; the intelligence would thus
arrive at a complete understanding of materiality, and
consequently of itself as well. Sooner or later a philosophy would also be developed which would in its turn
shake itself free from the word, but this time to go in
the opposite direction to mathematics and to accentuate,
in primitive and social knowledge, the intuitive instead
of the intellectual. Between intuition and intelligence
thus intensified, language had, however, to remain. It
remains in fact what it has always been. However
much it has become burdened with more science and
more philosophy it nevertheless continues to fulfill its
function. The intelligence which at first was identified
with it and which shared in its imprecision, has been
made more precise in science; it has taken hold of
matter. Intuition, which made its influence felt on
language, would like to broaden out into philosophy and
become co-extensive with the mind. Between them
meanwhile, between these two forms of thought in the
solitary state, subsists thought in common, which was
at first the whole of human thought. It is this thought
which language continues to express. It acquired ballast
from science, I admit; but the scientific mind demands

that everything be continually called into question and language has need of stability. It is open to philosophy; but the philosophical mind is sympathetic to the endless renovation and re-invention which are at the bottom of things, and words have a definite meaning, a conventional value relatively fixed; they can express the new only as a rearrangement of the old. One currently and perhaps imprudently calls "reason" this conservative logic which governs thought in common; conversation greatly resembles conservation. It is there that it is at home. And there it exercises a legitimate authority. Theoretically, in fact, conversation should bear only upon things of the social life. And the essential object of society is to insert a certain fixity into universal mobility. Societies are just so many islands consolidated here and there in the ocean of becoming. This consolidation is more perfect in proportion as the social activity is more intelligent. The general intelligence which is the faculty of arranging concepts "reasonably" and handling words suitably, must therefore aid in the social life just as intelligence in the narrower sense of the word, which is the mathematical function of the mind, presides over the knowledge of matter. It is the first of these we have in mind when we say of a man that he is intelligent. By that we mean that he has the ability and the facility for combining the ordinary concepts and for drawing probable conclusions from them. One can hardly take issue with him on that account, as long as he confines himself to things of every-day life, for which the concepts were made. But one would hardly admit of a man who was merely intelligent undertaking to speak with authority on scientific questions seeing that the intellect, made precise in science, becomes a mathematical, physical and biological attitude of mind, and substitutes for words more appropriate signs. All the more should one forbid him to meddle in philosophy when the questions raised are no longer in the domain of the intelligence alone. But no, it is agreed that the intelligent man is on this point a competent man.

Against this I protest most vigorously. I hold the intelligence in high esteem, but I have a very mediocre opinion of the "intelligent man," whose cleverness consists in talking about all things with a show of truth.

Clever in speaking, prompt to criticize. Whoever has freed himself from words in order to turn to things, to find once more their natural articulations and to probe a problem experimentally, is perfectly well aware of what surprises await the mind. Beyond the strictly human, that is, social, domain, the probable is almost never true. Nature takes very little pains to facilitate our conversation. It is a far cry from concrete reality to the reality we should have reconstructed *a priori!* This reconstruction, however, is perfectly satisfactory to a mind which is merely critical, since its role is not to work on the thing, but to appraise what some one has said about it. How will it go about its appraisal except by comparing the solution which is given it, extracted from the thing, with the solution it would have arrived at with the current ideas, that is, with the words which are the repository of social thought? And what will its judgment signify, except that there is no further need for searching, that searching disturbs society, that we should draw a line below the vague forms of knowledge stored up in the language, total them up, and be satisfied? "We know everything," is the postulate of this method. No one would any longer dare to apply it to the criticism of physical or astronomical theories. But this is a current procedure in philosophy. Against him who has worked, struggled, toiled to cast aside ready-made ideas and to make contact with the thing, they oppose a solution which they claim is "reasonable." He who really seeks the truth should raise his voice in protest. It would rest with him to show that the faculty of criticizing, thus understood, amounts to a fixed determination to shut one's eyes to the truth, and that the only acceptable criticism would be a new study, more deeply pursued but equally direct, of the thing itself. Unfortunately he himself is only too inclined to criticize on every occasion, when, in effect, he has been able to examine only two or three questions. In denying to pure "intelligence" the power of appreciating what he is doing, he would be depriving himself of the right to judge in cases where he is neither philoso pher nor savant, but simply "intelligent." He therefore prefers to adopt the common illusion. Everything encourages him, moreover, in this illusion. It is a common practice to consult incompetent men on a difficult point simply because they have acquired notoriety through their competence in quite different matters. One encourages in them, and more especially fortifies in the public mind the idea that there exists a general faculty of knowing things without having studied them, an "intelligence" which is neither simply the habit of handling in conversation the concepts useful in social life, nor the mathematical function of the mind, but a certain power of obtaining from social concepts the knowledge of the real by combining them more or less skilfully. This superior skill is what supposedly constitutes the superiority of the mind. As if true superiority could be anything but a greater force of attention! As if this attention was not necessarily specialized, that is to say, inclined by nature or habit toward certain objects rather than toward others! As if it was not direct vision, a vision which penetrates the veil of words, and as if it was not the very ignorance of things which gives so much facility in speaking of them! As far as I am concerned, I value scientific knowledge and technical competence as much as intuitive vision. I believe that it is of man's essence to create materially and morally, to fabricate things and to fabricate himself. *Homo faber* is the definition I propose. *Homo sapiens,* born of the reflection *Homo faber* makes on the subject of his fabrication, seems to me to be just as worthy of esteem as long as he resolves by pure intelligence those problems which depend upon it alone. One philosopher may be mistaken in the choice of these problems, but another philosopher will correct him; both will have worked to the best of their ability; both can merit our gratitude and admiration. *Homo faber, Homo sapiens,* I pay my respects to both, for they tend to merge. The only one to which I am antipathetic is *Homo loquax* whose thought, when he does think, is only a reflection upon his talk.

Old-time methods of teaching tended to form him and perfect him. Do they not still tend that way to a certain extent? Most certainly the defect is less marked here than in other countries. Nowhere more than in France does the master stir up the initiative of the student, even of the schoolboy. Nevertheless, much remains for us to do. I need not speak here of manual labor, of the role it could play in the school. We are too prone to regard it simply as a relaxation. We forget that the intellect is essentially the faculty of manipulating matter, that it at least began by being so, that such was nature's intention. Why then should the intellect not profit by manual training? We can go further and say that it is quite natural for the child to try its hand at constructing. By helping it, by furnishing it at least with opportunities, one would later obtain from the grown man a superior yield; one would greatly increase what inventiveness there is in the world.

A learning which is bookish from the outset compresses and suppresses activities which were only waiting to surge forth. Let us give the child exercise in manual training, but without allowing that teaching to sink to the level of a drill. Let us apply to a real master, that he may perfect the touch to the point of making it a sense of touch: the intelligence will go from the hand to the head. But I must not dwell too long on this point. In all subjects, letters or sciences, our teaching has remained too verbal. The time has gone by when it was enough to be a man of the world and to know how to converse on various subjects. If it is a question of science we set forth results above all. Would it not be better to initiate the students in methods? They would be put at once to practice; they would be invited to observe, to experiment, to work things out for themselves. How they would listen to us! How we should be understood! For the child is a seeker and an inventor, always on the watch for novelty, impatient of rule, in short, closer to nature than is the grown man. But the latter is essentially a sociable being, and it is he who does the teaching: he necessarily places in primary importance the whole collection of acquired results of which the social patrimony is composed, and of which he is legitimately proud. However, encylopaedic as the programme may be, what the pupil can assimilate from ready-made knowledge will amount to very little, will often be studied without relish, and always be quickly forgotten. There is no doubt that each of these results acquired by humanity is precious; but that is adult knowledge and the adult will find it when he needs it, if he has simply learned where to look for it. Rather let us cultivate a child's knowledge in the child, and avoid smothering under an accumulation of dry leaves and branches, products of former vegetations, the new plant which asks nothing better than to grow.

Could one not find similar defects in our teaching of literature (in spite of its superiority to that given in other countries)? It is true, lectures on the work of a great writer may be of use in making it better understood and better appreciated. Even then it is necessary for the pupil to have begun to like it and consequently to understand it. That is equivalent to saying that the child will first have to reinvent it, or in other words, appropriate to a certain extent the inspiration of the author. To do so he must fall into step with him by adopting his gestures, his attitudes, his gait, by which I mean learning to read the text aloud with the proper intonation and inflection. The intelligence will later add shades of meaning. But shade and color are nothing without design. Before intellection properly so-called, there is the perception of structure and movement; there is, on the page one reads, punctuation and rhythm.

Now it is in indicating this structure and rhythm, in taking into consideration the temporal relations between the various sentences of the paragraph and the various parts of each sentence, in following uninterruptedly the *crescendo* of thought and feeling to the point musically indicated as the culminating point that the art of diction consists.

It is wrong to treat it as an artistic accomplishment. Instead of coming at the end of one's studies, like an ornament, it should be at the beginning and throughout, as a support. Upon it we should place all the rest, if we did not yield here again to the illusion that the main thing is to discourse on things and that one knows them sufficiently when one knows how to talk about them. But one knows, one understands only what one can in some measure reinvent. There is a certain analogy, be it said in passing, between the art of reading as I have just described it and the intuition I recommend to the philosopher. On the page it has chosen from the great book of the world, intuition seeks to recapture, to get back the movement and rhythm of the composition, to live again creative evolution by being one with it in sympathy. But I have embarked upon too long a digression; it is time to end it. It is not for me to elaborate a program of education. I wanted simply to indicate certain habits of mind which I consider unfortunate and which the school too often encourages in fact, even though it repudiates them in principle. I wanted especially to protest once more against the substitution of concepts for things, and against what I have been calling the socialization of the truth. It was essential in primitive societies. It is natural to the human mind because the human mind is not intended for pure science, still less for philosophy. But this socialization must be reserved for practical truths for which it is made. It has no business in the domain of pure knowledge, science or philosophy.

Thus I repudiate facility. I recommend a certain manner of thinking which courts difficulty; I value effort above everything. How could certain people have mistaken my meaning? To say nothing of the kind of person who would insist that my "intuition" was instinct or feeling. Not one line of what I have written could lend itself to such an interpretation. And in everything I have written there is assurance to the contrary: my intuition is reflection. But because I called attention to the mobility at the base of things, it has been claimed that I encouraged a sort of relaxing of the mind. And because the permanence of substance was, in my eyes, a continuity of change, it has been said that my doctrine was a justification of instability. One might just as well imagine that the bacteriologist recommends microbic diseases to us when he shows us microbes everywhere, or that the physicist prescribes the exercise of swinging when he reduces natural phenomena to oscillations. A principle of explanation is one thing, a maxim of conduct is another. One could almost say that the philosopher who finds mobility everywhere is the only one who cannot recommend it, since he sees it as inevitable, since he discovers it in what people have agreed to call immobility. But the truth is that in spite of the fact that he views stability as a complexity of change or as a particular aspect of change, in spite of the fact that in some way he resolves stability into change he will none the less, like everybody else, distinguish stability and change. And for him, as for everyone, will arise the question of knowing to what extent it is the special appearance called stability, to what extent it is change pure and simple that he must recommend to human societies. His analysis of change leaves this question intact. If he has any common sense at all, he, like everyone else, will consider necessary a permanence of what is. He will say that institutions should furnish a relatively invariable framework for the diversity and mobility of individual designs. And he will understand perhaps better than other people the role of these institutions. Do they not continue in the domain of action, in laying down imperatives, the work of stabilization that the senses and

the understanding accomplish in the realm of knowledge
when they condense into perception the oscillations of
matter, and into concepts, the constant flow of things?
No doubt, in the rigid framework of institutions, sustained by that very rigidity, society evolves. In fact,
the duty of the statesman is to follow those variations
and to modify the institution while there is still time:
out of ten political errors, nine consist simply in believing that what has ceased to be true is still true. But
the tenth, which might be the most serious, will be no
longer to believe true what nevertheless, is still true.
In a general way action demands a firm basis (point
d'appui), and the living being tends essentially toward
efficacious action. That is why I saw in a certain stabilization of things the primordial function of consciousness.
Installed in universal mobility, I said, consciousness
contracts in a quasi-instantaneous vision an immensely
long history which unfolds outside it. The higher the
consciousness, the stronger is this tension of its own
duration in relation to that of things.

Tension, concentration, these are the words by which
I characterized a method which required of the mind,
for each new problem, a completely new effort. I should
never have been able to extract from my book *Matter
and Memory*, which preceded *Creative Evolution*, a true
doctrine of evolution (it would have been one in only
appearance) ; nor could I have extracted from my
Essay *on the immediate Data of Consciousness** a
theory of the relations of the soul and the body like the
one I set forth later in *Matter and Memory* (I should
have had only a hypothetical construction); nor from the
pseudo-philosophy to which I was devoted before the *Immediate Data*—that is to say from the general notions
stored up in language could I have extracted the conclusions on duration and the inner life which I presented in
this first work. My initiation into the true philosophical
method began the moment I threw overboard verbal

* Editor's note: English Title—*Time and Free Will.*

solutions, having found in the inner life an important field of experiment. After that, all progress was an enlarging of this field. It is an inclination natural to the human mind to extend a conclusion logically, to apply it to other objects without actually having enlarged the circle of its investigations, but it is one to which we must never yield. But that is what philosophy does quite ingenuously when it is pure dialectic, that is, when it attempts to construct a metaphysics with the rudimentary knowledge one finds stored up in language. It continues to do so when it sets up certain facts as "general principles" applicable to all things outside those facts. All my philosophical activity was a protestation against this way of philosophizing. I thus had to put aside important questions, which I could easily have made a show of answering by extending to them the results of my preceding works. I shall answer certain of these questions only if I am granted time and strength to solve them in themselves, for themselves. If not, grateful to my method for having given me what I believe to be the precise solution of a certain number of problems, finding that as far as I am concerned, I cannot get more out of it, I shall be content to stop where I am. One is never compelled to write a book.

III

THE POSSIBLE AND THE REAL

I should like to come back to a subject on which I have often spoken, the continuous creation of unforeseeable novelty which seems to be going on in the universe. As far as I am concerned, I feel I am experiencing it constantly. No matter how I try to imagine in detail what is going to happen to me, still how inadequate, how abstract and stilted is the thing I have imagined in comparison to what actually happens! The realization brings along with it an unforeseeable nothing which changes everything. For example, I am to be present at a gathering; I know what people I shall find there, around what table, in what order, to discuss what problem. But let them come, be seated and chat as I expected, let them say what I was sure they would say: the whole gives me an impression at once novel and unique, as if it were but now designed at one original stroke by the hand of an artist. Gone is the image I had conceived of it, a mere prearrangeable juxtaposition of things already known! I agree that the picture has not the artistic value of a Rembrandt or a Velasquez: yet it is just as unexpected and, in this sense, quite as original. It will be alleged that I did not know the circumstances in detail, that I could not control the persons in question, their gestures, their attitudes, and that if the thing as a whole provided me with something new it was because they produced additional factors. But I have the same impression of novelty before the unrolling of my inner life. I feel it more vividly than ever, before the action I willed and of which I was sole master. If I deliberate before acting, the moments of deliberation present themselves to my consciousness like the successive sketches a painter makes of his picture, each one unique of its kind; and no matter whether the act itself in its accomplishment realizes something willed and consequently foreseen, it has none the less its own particular form in all its originality.—Granted, someone will say; there is perhaps something original and unique in a state of soul; but matter is repetition; the external world yields to mathematical laws; a superhuman intelligence which would know the position, the direction, and the speed of all the atoms and electrons of the material universe at a given moment could calculate any future state of this universe as we do in the case of an eclipse of the sun or the moon.—I admit all this for the sake of argument, if it concerns only the inert world and at least with regard to elementary phenomena, although this is beginning to be a much debated question. But this "inert" world is only an abstraction. Concrete reality comprises those living, conscious beings enframed in inorganic matter. I say living and conscious, for I believe that the living is conscious by right; it becomes unconscious in fact where consciousness falls asleep, but even in the regions where consciousness is in a state of somnolence, in the vegetable kingdom for example, there is regulated evolution, definite progress, aging; in fact, all the external signs of the duration which characterizes consciousness. And why must we speak of an inert matter into which life and consciousness would be inserted as in a frame? By what right do we put the inert first? The ancients had imagined a World Soul supposed to assure the continuity of existence of the material universe. Stripping this conception of its mythical element, I should say that the inorganic world is a series of infinitely rapid repetitions or quasi-repetitions which, when totaled, constitute visible and previsible changes. I should compare them to the swinging of the pendulum of a clock: the swingings of the pendulum are coupled to the continuous unwinding of a spring linking them together and whose unwinding they mark; the repetitions of the inorganic world constitute rhythm in the life of conscious beings and measure their duration. Thus the living being essentially has duration; it has duration precisely because it is continuously elaborating what is new and because there is no elaboration without searching, no searching without groping. Time is this very hesitation, or it is nothing. Suppress the conscious and the living (and you can do this only through an artificial effort of abstraction, for the material world once again implies perhaps the necessary presence of consciousness and of life), you obtain in fact a universe whose successive states are in theory calculable in advance, like the images placed side by side along the cinematographic film, prior to its unrolling. Why, then, the unrolling? Why does reality unfurl? Why is it not spread out? What good is time? (I refer to real, concrete time, and not to that abstract time which is only a fourth dimension of space.) This, in days gone by, was the starting-point of my reflections. Some fifty years ago I was very much attached to the philosophy of Spencer. I perceived one fine day that, in it, time served no purpose, did nothing. Nevertheless, I said to myself, time is something. Therefore it acts. What can it be doing? Plain common sense answered: time is what hinders everything from being given at once. It retards, or rather it is retardation. It must, therefore, be elaboration. Would it not then be a vehicle of creation and of choice? Would not the existence of time prove that there is indetermination in things? Would not time be that indetermination itself?

If such is not the opinion of most philosophers, it is because human intelligence is made precisely to take things by the other end. I say intelligence, I do not say thought, I do not say mind. Along side of intelligence there is in effect the immediate perception by each of us of his own activity and of the conditions in which it is exercised. Call it what you will; it is the feeling we have of being creators of our intentions, of our decisions, of our acts, and by that, of our habits, our characters, ourselves. Artisans of our life, even artists when we so desire, we work continually, with the material furnished us by the past and present, by heredity and opportunity, to mold a figure unique, new, original, as unforeseeable, as the form given by the sculptor to the clay. Of this work and what there is unique about it we are warned, no doubt, even while it is being done, but the essential thing is that we do it. It is up to us to go deeply into it; it is not even necessary that we be fully conscious of it, any more than the artist needs to analyze his creative ability; he leaves that to the philosopher to worry about, being content, himself, simply to create. On the other hand, the sculptor must be familiar with the technique of his art and know everything that can be learned about it: this technique deals especially with what his work has in common with other works; it is governed by the demands of the material upon which he operates and which is imposed upon him as upon all artists; it concerns in art what is repetition or fabrication, and has nothing to do with creation itself. On it is concentrated the attention of the artist, what I should call his intellectuality. In the same way, in the creation of our character we know very little about our creative ability: in order to learn about it we should have to turn back upon ourselves, to philosophize, and to climb back up the slope of nature; for nature desired action, it hardly thought about speculation. The moment it is no longer simply a question of feeling an impulse within oneself and of being assured that one can act, but of turning thought upon itself in order that it may seize this ability and catch this impulse, the difficulty becomes great, as if the whole normal direction of consciousness had to be reversed. On the contrary we have a supreme interest in familiarizing ourselves with the technique of our action, that is to say in extracting from the conditions in which it is exercised, all that can furnish us with recipes and general rules upon which to base our conduct. There will be novelty in our acts thanks only to the repetition we have found in things. Our normal faculty of knowing is then essentially a power of extracting what stability and regularity there is in the flow of reality. Is it a question of perceiving? Perception seizes upon the infinitely repeated shocks which are light or heat, for example, and contracts them into relatively invariable sensations: trillions of external vibrations are what the vision of a color condenses in our eyes in the fraction of a second. Is it a question of conceiving? To form a general idea is to abstract from varied and changing things a common aspect which does not change or at least offers an invariable hold to our action. The invariability of our attitude, the identity of our eventual or virtual reaction to the multiplicity and variability of the objects represented is what first marks and delineates the generality of the idea. Finally, is it a question of understanding? It is simply finding connections, establishing stable relations between transitory facts, evolving laws; an operation which is much more perfect as the relation becomes more definite and the law more mathematical. All these functions are constitutives of the intellect. And the intellect is in the line of truth so long as it attaches itself, in its penchant for regularity and stability, to what is stable and regular in the real, that is to say to materiality. In so doing it touches one of the sides of the absolute, as our consciousness touches another when it grasps within us a perpetual efflorescence of novelty or when, broadening out, it comes into sympathy with that effort of nature which is constantly renewing. Error begins when the intellect claims to think one of the aspects as it thought the other, directing its powers on something for which it was not intended.

I believe that the great metaphysical problems are in general badly stated, that they frequently resolve themselves of their own accord when correctly stated, or else are problems formulated in terms of illusion which disappear as soon as the terms of the formula are more closely examined. They arise in fact from our habit of transposing into fabrication what is creation. Reality is global and undivided growth, progressive invention, duration: it resembles a gradually expanding rubber balloon assuming at each moment unexpected forms. But our intelligence imagines its origin and evolution as an arrangement and rearrangement of parts which supposedly merely shift from one place to another; in theory therefore, it should be able to foresee any one state of the whole: by positing a definite number of stable elements one has, predetermined, all their possible combinations. That is not all. Reality, as immediately perceived, is fullness constantly swelling out, to which emptiness is unknown. It has extension just as it has duration; but this concrete extent is not the infinite and infinitely divisible space the intellect takes as a place in which to build. Concrete space has been extracted from things. They are not in it; it is space which is in them. Only, as soon as our thought reasons about reality, it makes space a receptacle. As it has the habit of assembling parts in a relative vacuum, it imagines that reality fills up some absolute kind of vacuum. Now, if the failure to recognize radical novelty is the original cause of those badly stated metaphysical questions, the habit of proceeding from emptiness to fullness is the source of problems which are non-existent. Moreover, it is easy to see that the second mistake is already implied in the first. But I should like first of all to define it more precisely.

I say that there are pseudo-problems, and that they are the agonizing problems of metaphysics. I reduce them to two. One gave rise to theories of being, the other to theories of knowledge. The first false problem consists in asking oneself why there is being, why something or someone exists. The nature of what is is of little importance; say that it is matter, or mind, or both, or that matter and mind are not self-sufficient and manifest a transcendent Cause: in any case, when existences and causes are brought into consideration and the causes of these causes, one feels as if pressed into a race—if one calls a halt, it is to avoid dizziness. But just the same one sees, or thinks one sees, that the difficulty still exists, that the problem is still there and will never be solved. It will never, in fact, be solved, but it should never have been raised. It arises only if one posits a nothingness which supposedly precedes being. One says: "There could be nothing," and then is astonished that there should be something—or someone. But analyze that sentence: "There could be nothing." You will see you are dealing with words, not at all with ideas, and that "nothing" here has no meaning. "Nothing" is a term in ordinary language which can only have meaning in the sphere, proper to man, of action and fabrication. "Nothing" designates the absence of what we are seeking, we desire, expect. Let us suppose that absolute emptiness was known to our experience: it would be limited, have contours, and would therefore be something. But in reality there is no vacuum. We perceive and can conceive only occupied space. One thing disappears only because another replaces it. Suppression thus means substitution. We say "suppression," however, when, we envisage, in the case of substitution, only one of its two halves, or rather the one of its two sides which interests us; in this way we indicate a desire to turn our attention to the object which is gone, and away from the one replacing it.

We say then that there is nothing more, meaning by that, that what exists does not interest us, that we are interested in what is no longer there or in what might have been there. The idea of absence, or of nothingness, or of nothing, is therefore inseparably bound to that of suppression, real or eventual, and the idea of suppression is itself only an aspect of the idea of substitution. Those are the ways of thinking we use in practical life; it is particularly essential to our industry that our thought should be able to lag behind reality and remain attached, when need be, to what was or to what might be, instead of being absorbed by what is. But when we go from the domain of fabrication to that of creation, when we ask ourselves why there is being, why something or someone, why the world or God, exists and why not nothingness, when, in short, we set ourselves the most agonizing of metaphysical problems, we virtually accept an absurdity; for if all suppression is a substitution, if the idea of a suppression is only the truncated idea of a substitution, then to speak of a suppression of everything is to posit a substitution which would not be one, that is, to be self-contradictory. Either the idea of a suppression of everything has just about as much existence as that of a round square—the existence of a sound, *flatus vocis*—or else, if it does represent something, it translates a movement of the intellect from one object to another, preferring the one it has just left to the object it finds before it, and designates by "absence of the first" the presence of the second. We have posited the whole, then made each of its parts disappear one by one, without consenting to see what replaced it; it is therefore the totality of presences, simply arranged in a new order, that one has in mind in attempting to total up the absences. In other words, this so-called representation of absolute emptiness is, in reality, that of universal fullness in a mind which leaps indefinitely from part to part, with the fixed resolution never to consider anything but the emptiness of its dissatisfaction instead of the fullness of things. All of which amounts to saying that the idea of Nothing, when it is not that of a simple word, implies as much matter as the idea of All, with, in addition, an operation of thought.

I should say as much of the idea of disorder. Why is the universe well-ordered? How is rule imposed upon what is without rule, and form upon matter? How is it that our thought recognizes itself in things? This problem, which among the moderns has become the problem of knowledge after having been, among the ancients, the problem of being, was born of an illusion of the same order. It disappears if one considers that the idea of disorder has a definite meaning in the domain of human industry or, as we say, of fabrication, but not in that of creation. Disorder is simply the order we are not looking for. You cannot suppress one order even by thought, without causing another to spring up. If there is not finality or will, it is because there is mechanism; if the mechanism gives way, so much the gain for will, caprice, finality. But when you expect one of these two orders and you find the other, you say there is disorder, formulating what is in terms of what might or should be, and objectifying your regret. All disorder thus includes two things: outside us, one order; within us, the representation of a different order which alone interests us. Suppression therefore again signifies substitution. And the idea of a suppression of all order, that is to say, the idea of an absolute disorder, then contains a veritable contradiction, because it consists in leaving only a single aspect to the operation which, by hypothesis, embraced two. Either the idea of an absolute disorder represents no more than a combination of sounds, *flatus vocis,* or else, if it corresponds to something, it translates a movement of the mind which leaps from mechanism to finality, from finality to mechanism, and which, in order to mark the spot where it is, prefers each time to indicate the point where it is not. Therefore, in wishing to suppress order, you find yourself with two or more "orders." This is tantamount to saying that the conception of an order which is superadded to an "absence of order" implies an absurdity, and that the problem disappears.

The two illusions I have just mentioned are in reality only one. They consist in believing that there is *less* in the idea of the empty than in the idea of the full, *less* in the concept of disorder than in that of order. In reality, there is more intellectual content in the ideas of disorder and nothingness when they represent something than in those of order and existence, because they imply several orders, several existences and, in addition, a play of wit which unconsciously juggles with them.

Very well then, I find the same illusion in the case in point. Underlying the doctrines which disregard the radical novelty of each moment of evolution there are many misunderstandings, many errors. But there is especially the idea that the possible is *less* than the real, and that, for this reason, the possibility of things precedes their existence. They would thus be capable of representation beforehand; they could be thought of before being realized. But it is the reverse that is true. If we leave aside the closed systems, subjected to purely mathematical laws, isolable because duration does not act upon them, if we consider the totality of concrete reality or simply the world of life, and still more that of consciousness, we find there is more and not less in the possibility of each of the successive states than in their reality. For the possible is only the real with the addition of an act of mind which throws its image back into the past, once it has been enacted. But that is what our intellectual habits prevent us from seeing.

During the great war certain newspapers and periodicals sometimes turned aside from the terrible worries of the day to think of what would happen later once peace was restored. They were particularly preoccupied with the future of literature. Someone came one day to ask me my ideas on the subject. A little embarrassed, I declared I had none. "Do you not at least perceive," I was asked, "certain possible directions? Let us grant that one cannot foresee things in detail; you as a philosopher have at least an idea of the whole. How do you conceive, for example, the great dramatic work of tomorrow?" I shall always remember my interlocutor's surprise when I answered, "If I knew what was to be the great dramatic work of the future, I should be writing it." I saw distinctly that he conceived the future work as being already stored up in some cupboard reserved for possibles; because of my long-standing relations with philosophy, I should have been able to obtain from it the key to the storehouse. "But," I said, "the work of which you speak is not yet possible."—"But it must be, since it is to take place."—"No, it is not. I grant you, at most, that it *will have been possible.*" "What do you mean by that?"— "It's quite simple. Let a man of talent or genius come forth, let him create a work: it will then be real, and by that very fact it becomes retrospectively or retroactively possible. It would not be possible, it would not have been so, if this man had not come upon the scene. That is why I tell you that it will have been possible today, but that it is not yet so." "You're not serious! You are surely not going to maintain that the future has an effect upon the present, that the present brings something into the past, that action works back over the course of time and imprints its mark afterwards?"—"That depends. That one can put reality into the past and thus work backwards in time is something I have never claimed. But that one can put the possible there, or rather that the possible may put itself there at any moment, is not to be doubted. As reality is created as something unforeseeable and new, its image is reflected behind it into the indefinite past; thus it finds that it has from all time been possible, but it is at this precise moment that it begins to have been always possible, and that is why I said that its possibility, which does not precede its reality, will have preceded it once the reality has appeared. The possible is therefore the mirage of the present in the past; and as we know the future will finally constitute a present and the mirage effect is continually being produced, we are convinced that the image of tomorrow is already contained in our actual present, which will be the past of tomorrow, although we did not manage to grasp it. That is precisely the illusion. It is as though one were to fancy, in seeing his reflection in the mirror in front of him, that he could have touched it had he stayed behind it. Thus in judging that the possible does not presuppose the real, one admits that the realization adds something to the simple possibility: the possible would have been there from all time, a phantom awaiting its hour; it would therefore have become reality by the addition of something, by some transfusion of blood or life. One does not see that the contrary is the case, that the possible implies the corresponding reality with, moreover, something added, since the possible is the combined effect of reality once it has appeared and of a condition which throws it back in time. The idea immanent in most philosophies and natural to the human mind, of possibles which would be realized by an acquisition of existence, is therefore pure illusion. One might as well claim that the man in flesh and blood comes from the materialization of his image seen in the mirror, because in that real man is everything found in this virtual image with, in addition, the solidity which makes it possible to touch it. But the truth is that more is needed here to obtain the virtual than is necessary for the real, more for the image of the man than for the man himself, for the image of the.man will not be portrayed if the man is not first produced, and in addition one has to have the mirror."

That is what my interlocutor was forgetting as he questioned me on the theater of tomorrow. Perhaps too he was unconsciously playing on the meaning of the word "possible." *Hamlet* was doubtless possible before being realized, if that means that there was no insurmountable obstacle to its realization. In the particular sense one calls possible what is not impossible; and it stands to reason that this non-impossibility of a thing is the condition of its realization. But the possible thus understood is in no degree virtual, something ideally pre-existent. If you close the gate you know no one will cross the road; it does not follow that you can predict who will cross when you open it. Nevertheless, from the quite negative sense of the term "impossible" you pass surreptitiously, unconsciously to the positive sense. Possibility signified "absence of hindrance" a few minutes ago: now you make of it a "pre-existence under the form of an idea," which is quite another thing. In the first meaning of the word it was a truism to say that the possibility of a thing precedes its reality: by that you meant simply that obstacles, having been surmounted, were surmountable. But in the second meaning it is an absurdity, for it is clear that a mind in which the *Hamlet* of Shakespeare had taken shape in the form of possible would by that fact have created its reality: it would thus have been, by definition, Shakespeare himself. In vain do you imagine at first that this mind could have appeared before Shakespeare; it is because you are not thinking then of all the details in the play. As you complete them the predecessor of Shakespeare finds himself thinking all that Shakespeare will think, feeling all he will feel, knowing all he will know, perceiving therefore all he will perceive, and consequently occupying the same point in space and time, having the same body and the same soul: it is Shakespeare himself.

But I am putting too much stress on what is self-evident. We are forced to these considerations in discussing a work of art. I believe in the end we shall consider it evident that the artist in executing his work is creating the possible as well as the real. Whence comes it then that one might hesitate to say the same thing for nature? Is not the world a work of art incomparably richer than that of the greatest artist? And is there not as much absurdity, if not more, in supposing, in the work of nature, that the future is outlined in advance, that possibility existed before reality? Once more let me say I am perfectly willing to admit that the future states of a closed system of material points are calculable and hence visible in its present state. But, and I repeat, this system is extracted, or abstracted, from a whole which, in addition to inert and unorganized matter, comprises organization. Take the concrete and complete world, with the life and consciousness it encloses; consider nature in its entirety, nature the generator of new species as novel and original in form as the design of any artist: in these species concentrate upon individuals, plants or animals, each of which has its own character—I was going to say its personality (for one blade of grass does not resemble another blade of grass any more than a Raphael resembles a Rembrandt) ; lift your attention above and beyond individual man to societies which disclose actions and situations comparable to those of any drama: how can one still speak of possibles which would precede their own realization? How can we fail to see that if the event can always be explained afterwards by an arbitrary choice of antecedent events, a completely different event could have been equally well explained in the same circumstances by another choice of antecedent—nay, by the same antecedents otherwise cut out, otherwise distributed, otherwise perceived—in short, by our retrospective attention? Backwards over the course of time a constant remodeling of the past by the present, of the cause by the effect, is being carried out.

We do not see it, always for the same reason, always a prey to the same illusion, always because we treat as the more what is the less, as the less what is the more. If we put the possible back into its proper place, evolution becomes something quite different from the realization of a program: the gates of the future open wide; freedom is offered an unlimited field. The fault of those doctrines—rare indeed in the history of philosophy—which have succeeded in leaving room for indetermination and freedom in the world, is to have failed to see what their affirmation implied. When they spoke of indetermination, of freedom, they meant by indetermination a competition between possibles, by freedom a choice between possibles—as if possibility was not created by freedom itself! As if any other hypothesis, by affirming an ideal pre-existence of the possible to the real, did not reduce the new to a mere rearrangement of former elements! As if it were not thus to be led sooner or later to regard that rearrangement as calculable and foreseeable! By accepting the premiss of the contrary theory one was letting the enemy in. We must resign ourselves to the inevitable: it is the real which makes itself possible, and not the possible which becomes real.

But the truth is that philosophy has never frankly admitted this continuous creation of unforeseeable novelty. The ancients already revolted against it because, Platonists to a greater or less degree, they imagined that Being was given once and for all, complete and perfect, in the immutable system of Ideas: the world which unfolds before our eyes could therefore add nothing to it; it was, on the contrary, only diminution or degradation;

THE POSSIBLE AND THE REAL 105

its successive states measured as it were the increasing
or decreasing distance between what is, a shadow projected in time, and what ought to be, Idea set in eternity;
they would outline the variations of a deficiency, the
changing form of a void. It was Time which, according
to them, spoiled everything. The moderns, it is true, take
a quite different point of view. They no longer treat
Time as an intruder, a disturber of eternity; but they
would very much like to reduce it to a simple appearance. The temporal is, then, only the confused form
of the rational. What we perceive as being a succession
of states is conceived by our intellect, once the fog
has settled, as a system of relations. The real becomes
once more the eternal, with this single difference, that
it is the eternity of the Laws in which the phenomena
are resolved instead of being the eternity of the Ideas
which serve them as models. But in each case, we are
dealing with theories. Let us stick to the facts. Time is
immediately given. That is sufficient for us, and until
its inexistence or perversity is proved to us we shall
merely register that there is effectively a flow of unforeseeable novelty.

Philosophy stands to gain in finding some absolute
in the moving world of phenomena. But we shall gain
also in our feeling of greater joy and strength. Greater
joy because the reality invented before our eyes will give
each one of us, unceasingly, certain of the satisfactions
which art at rare intervals procures for the privileged; it
will reveal to us, beyond the fixity and monotony which
our senses, hypnotized by our constant needs, at first
perceived in it, ever-recurring novelty, the moving originality of things. But above all we shall have greater
strength, for we shall feel we are participating, creators
of ourselves, in the great work of creation which is the
origin of all things and which goes on before our eyes.
By getting hold of itself, our faculty for acting will become intensified. Humbled heretofore in an attitude of
obedience, slaves of certain vaguely-felt natural necessities, we shall once more stand erect, masters associated

with a greater Master. To such a conclusion will our study bring us. In this speculation on the relation between the possible and the real, let us guard against seeing a simple game. It can be a preparation for the art of living.

IV

PHILOSOPHICAL INTUITION

Lecture given at the Philosophical Congress in Bologna,
April 10th, 1911

I should like to submit to you some reflections on the philosophical mind. It seems to me—and more than one report presented at this Congress bears witness to the fact—that metaphysics at present is tending to become more simplified, to draw closer to life. I think this tendency is a correct one, and that it is along this line we should work. But in so doing we shall be doing nothing revolutionary; we shall merely be giving the most appropriate form to what is the foundation of all philosophy—I mean of any philosophy which is fully conscious of its function and destination. For the complication of the letter must not allow the simplicity of the spirit to be lost to view. If we confine ourselves entirely to doctrines already formulated, to the synthesis in which they then appear to embrace the conclusions of earlier philosophies and all the forms of acquired knowledge, we run the risk of underestimating the essentially spontaneous aspect of philosophical thought.

There is a remark that those of us who teach the history of philosophy might make, those who frequently have occasion to come back to the study of the same doctrines and to go ever more deeply into them. A philosophical system seems at first to appear as a complete edifice, expertly designed, where arrangements have been made for the commodious lodging of all problems. In contemplating it in that form we experience an aesthetic joy intensified by a professional satisfaction. Not only, in fact, do we find here order in complexity (an order to which we sometimes like to add our little word as we describe it) but we also have the satisfaction of telling ourselves that we know from whence come the materials and how the building is done. In the problems the philosopher has stated we recognize the questions that were being discussed around him. In the solutions he gives to them we think we recognize, arranged or disarranged, but only slightly modified, the elements of previous or contemporary philosophies. Such a view must have been given to him by this one, another has been suggested by someone else. With what we read, heard and learned we could doubtless reproduce most of what he did. We therefore set to work, we go back to the sources, we weigh the influences, we extract the similitudes, and in the end we distinctly see in the doctrine what we were looking for: a more or less original synthesis of the ideas among which the philosopher lived.

But if we go on constantly renewing contact with the philosopher's thought, we can, by a gradual impregnation, be brought to an entirely different view. I do not say that the work of comparison undertaken at the outset was time lost: without this preliminary effort to recompose a philosophy out of what is other than itself, and to link it up to the conditions which surrounded it, we should perhaps never succeed in grasping what it actually is; for the human mind is so constructed that it cannot begin to understand the new until it has done everything in its power to relate it to the old. But, as we seek to penetrate more fully the philosopher's thought instead of circling around its exterior, his doctrine is transformed for us. In the first place its complication diminishes. Then the various parts fit into one another. Finally the whole is brought together into a single point, which we feel could be ever more closely approached even though there is no hope of reaching it completely.

In this point is something simple, infinitely simple, so extraordinarily simple that the philosopher has never

succeeded in saying it. And that is why he went on talking all his life. He could not formulate what he had in
mind without feeling himself obliged to correct his formula, then to correct his correction: thus, from theory
to theory, correcting when he thought he was completing, what he has accomplished, by a complication which
provoked more complication, by developments heaped
upon developments, has been to convey with an increasing
approximation the simplicity of his original intuition.
All the complexity of his doctrine, which would go on
ad infinitum, is therefore only the incommensurability
between his simple intuition and the means at his
disposal for expressing it.

What is this intuition? If the philosopher has not
been able to give the formula for it, we certainly are
not able to do so. But what we shall manage to recapture and to hold is a certain intermediary image between
the simplicity of the concrete intuition and the complexity of the abstractions which translate it, a reced-
ing and vanishing image, which haunts, unperceived perhaps, the mind of the philosopher, which follows him
like his shadow through the ins and outs of his thought
and which, if it is not the intuition itself, approaches it
much more closely than the conceptual expression, of necessity symbolical, to which the intuition must have recourse in order to furnish "explanation." Let us look
closely at this shadow: by doing so we shall divine the
attitude of the body which projects it. And if we try to
imitate this attitude, or better still to assume it ourselves,
we shall see as far as it is possible what the philosopher
saw.

What first of all characterizes this image is the power
of *negation* it possesses. You recall how the demon of
Socrates proceeded: it checked the philosopher's will at
a given moment and prevented him from acting rather
than prescribing what he should do. It seems to me that
intuition often behaves in speculative matters like the
demon of Socrates in practical life; it is at least in this
form that it begins, in this form also that it continues to

give the most clear-cut manifestations: it forbids. Faced with currently-accepted ideas, theses which seemed evident, affirmations which had up to that time passed as scientific, it whispers into the philosopher's ear the word: *Impossible!* Impossible, even though the facts and the reasons appeared to invite you to think it possible and real and certain. Impossible, because a certain experience, confused perhaps but decisive, speaks to you through my voice, because it is incompatible with the facts cited and the reasons given, and because hence these facts must have been badly observed, these reasonings false. What a strange force this intuitive power of negation is! How is it that the historians of philosophy have not been more greatly struck by it? Is it not obvious that the first step the philosopher takes, when his thought is still faltering and there is nothing definite in his doctrine, is to reject certain things definitively? Later he will be able to make changes in what he affirms; he will vary only slightly what he denies. And if he varies in his affirmations, it will still be in virtue of the power of negation immanent in intuition or in its image. He will have allowed himself lazily to deduce consequences according to the rules of a rectilinear logic; and then suddenly, in the face of his own affirmation he has the same feeling of impossibility that he had in the first place in considering the affirmations of others. Having in fact left the curve of his thought, to follow straight along a tangent, he has become exterior to himself. He returns to himself when he gets back to intuition. Of these departures toward an affirmation and these returns to the primary intuition are constituted the zigzaggings of a doctrine which "develops," that is to say which loses itself, finds itself again, and endlessly corrects itself.

Let us get rid of this complication and get back to the simple intuition, or at least to the image which translates it: in so doing we see the doctrine freed of those conditions of time and place upon which it seemed to depend. Doubtless the problems which the philosopher

worked upon were the problems which presented themselves in his day; the science he used or criticized was the
science of his time; in the theories he expounds one
might even find, by looking for them, the ideas of his
contemporaries and his predecessors. How could it be
otherwise? In order to have the new understood, it
must be expressed in terms of the old; and the problems
already stated, the solutions provided, the philosophy
and science of the times in which he lived, all these
have been for each great thinker the material he was
obliged to use to give a concrete form to his thought.
Not to mention that it has been traditional, from
ancient times, to present all philosophy as a complete
system, which includes everything one knows. But it
would be a strange mistake to take for a constitutive
element of doctrine what was only the means of expressing it. Such is the first error to which we are
exposed, as I was just saying, when we undertake the
study of a system. So many partial resemblances strike
us, so many parallels seem to be indicated, so many
pressing appeals to our ingenuity and erudition are
sent out from all directions, that we are tempted to
recompose the philosopher's thought with fragments
of ideas gathered here and there, praising him afterwards, of course, for having been able—as we have just
shown ourselves to be—to execute a pretty piece of
mosaic. But the illusion does not last long, for we soon
perceive that in the very places where the philosopher
seems to be repeating things already said, he is thinking
them in his own way. We then abandon the idea of
recomposing; but in so doing we tumble more often
than not into another illusion, less serious perhaps but
more tenacious than the first. We are inclined to imagine
the doctrine—even though it be that of a master—as
growing out of earlier philosophies and representing
"a moment of an evolution." This time, to be sure, we
are not completely wrong, for a philosophy resembles an
organism rather than an assemblage, and it is still better
to speak of evolution in this case than of composition.

But this new comparison, in addition to the fact that it attributes more continuity to the history of thought than is really in it, has the disadvantage of keeping our attention fixed upon the external complication of the system and upon what its superficial form allows us to foresee, instead of inviting us to put our finger on the novelty and simplicity of the inner content. A philosopher worthy of the name has never said more than a single thing: and even then it is something he has tried to say, rather than actually said. And he has said only one thing because he has seen only one point: and at that it was not so much a vision as a contact: this contact has furnished an impulse, this impulse a movement, and if this movement, which is as it were a kind of swirling of dust taking a particular form, becomes visible to our eyes only through what it has collected along its way, it is no less true that other bits of dust might as well have been raised and that it would still have been the same whirlwind. Thus a thought which brings something new into the world is of course obliged to manifest itself through the ready-made ideas it comes across and draws into its movement; it seems thus, as it were, relative to the epoch in which the philosopher lived; but that is frequently merely an appearance. The philosopher might have come several centuries earlier; he would have had to deal with another philosophy and another science; he would have given himself other problems; he would have expressed himself by other formulas; not one chapter perhaps of the books he wrote would have been what it is; and nevertheless he would have said the same thing.

Let me take an example. I have appealed to your professional memories: with your permission I am going to recall some of my own. As professor in the Collège de France I devote one of my courses each year to the history of philosophy. In that way I have been able, during several consecutive years, to practice at length upon Berkeley and Spinoza the experiment I have just decribed. I shall not discuss Spinoza; he would take us too far afield. Nevertheless I know of nothing more instructive than the contrast between the form and the matter of a book like the *Ethics:* on the one hand those tremendous things called Substance, Attribute and Mode, and the formidable array of theorems with the close network of definitions, corollaries and scholia, and that complication of machinery, that power to crush which causes the beginner, in the presence of the *Ethics,* to be struck with admiration and terror as though he were before a battleship of the Dreadnought class; on the other hand, something subtle, very light and almost airy, which flees at one's approach, but which one cannot look at, even from afar, without becoming incapable of attaching oneself to any part whatever of the remainder, even to what is considered essential, even to the distinction between Substance and Attribute, even to the duality of Thought and Extension. What we have behind the heavy mass of concepts of Cartesian and Aristotelian parentage, is that intuition which was Spinoza's, an intuition which no formula, no matter how simple, can be simple enough to express. Let us say, to be content with an approximation, that it is the feeling of a coincidence between the act by which our mind knows truth perfectly, and the operation by which God engenders it; the idea that the "conversion" of the Alexandrians, when it becomes complete, is indistinguishable from their "procession," that when man, sprung from divinity, succeeds in returning to it, he perceives that what he had at first taken to be two opposed movements of coming and going are in fact a single movement—moral experience in this case undertaking to resolve a logical contradiction and to fuse, by an abrupt suppression of Time, the movement of coming with that of going. The closer we get to this original intuition the better we understand that if Spinoza had lived before Descartes he would doubtless have written something other than what he wrote, but that given Spinoza living and writing, we were certain to have Spinozism in any case.

I come to Berkeley, and since it is he whom I take as

example you will not think it amiss that I analyze him in detail: brevity here could only be at the expense of a strict examination of the subject. A mere glance over the work of Berkeley is enough to see that, as if of itself, it resolves into four fundamental theses. The first, which defines a certain idealism and to which is linked up the new theory of vision (although the philosopher had judged it wise to present the latter as independent) the first, I say, would be formulated thus: "Matter is a cluster of ideas." The second consists in the claim that abstract and general ideas are merely words: that is nominalism. The third thesis affirms the reality of minds and characterizes them by the will: let us say that it is spiritualism and voluntarism. The last, which we might call theism, posits the existence of God, basing itself principally on the consideration of matter. Now, nothing would be easier than to find these four theses, formulated in practically the same terms, among the contemporaries or predecessors of Berkeley. The fourth is found among the theologians. The third was in Duns Scotus; Descartes said somewhat the same thing. The second fed the controversies of the Middle Ages before becoming an integral part of the philosophy of Hobbes. As to the first, it greatly resembles the "occasionalism" of Malebranche, the idea and even the formula of which we should already discover in certain texts of Descartes; nor, for that matter had Descartes been the first to point out that dreams have every appearance of reality and that there is nothing in any of our perceptions taken separately which guarantees us the existence of a thing outside us. Thus, with the philosophers of already distant times or even, if we do not care to go back too far, with Descartes and Hobbes to whom Locke might be added, we shall have the elements necessary for the external reconstitution of Berkeley's philosophy: we shall at most leave him his theory of vision, which would then constitute his own individual work and whose originality, reflected through the rest, would give to the doctrine as a whole its original aspect. Let us then take these slices of ancient and modern philosophy, put them in the same bowl, add by way of vinegar and oil a certain aggressive impatience with regard to mathematical dogmatism and the desire, natural in a philosopher bishop, to reconcile reason with faith, mix well and turn it over and over conscientiously, and sprinkle over the whole, like so many savoury herbs, a certain number of aphorisms culled from among the Neo-Platonists: we shall have—if I may be pardoned the expression—a salad which, at a distance, will have certain resemblance to what Berkeley accomplished.

Well, anyone who went about it in this way would be incapable of penetrating Berkeley's thought. I am not speaking of the difficulties and impossibilities which he would come up against in explaining the details: a strange sort of "nominalism" that was, which ended by raising a number of general ideas to the dignity of eternal essences, immanent in the divine Intelligence! a strange negation of the reality of bodies that which is expressed by a positive theory of the nature of matter, a fertile theory, as far removed as possible from the sterile idealism which tries to assimilate perception to dreaming! What I mean to say is that it is impossible for us to examine Berkeley's philosophy carefully without seeing the four theses we have discovered in it first approach, then penetrate one another, in such a way that each of them seems to become pregnant with the other three, to take on breadth and depth, and become radically distinguished from the earlier or contemporary theories with which one could superficially identify it. Perhaps this second point of view from which the doctrine appears as an organism and not as a mere assemblage, is still not the definitive point of view. It is at least closer to the truth. I cannot go into all the details; but nevertheless I must indicate for at least one or two of the four theses, how any of the others could be extracted from them.

Let us take idealism. It does not consist merely in saying that bodies are ideas. What good would that do? We should indeed be obliged to continue to affirm everything about these ideas that experience has led us to affirm about bodies, and we should simply have substituted one word for another; for Berkeley surely does not think that matter will cease to exist when he has stopped living. What Berkeley's idealism signifies is that matter is co-extensive with our representation of it; that it has no interior, no underneath; that it hides nothing, contains nothing; that it possesses neither power nor virtuality of any kind; that it is spread out as mere surface and that it is no more than what it presents to us at any given moment. The word "idea" ordinarily indicates an existence of this kind, I mean to say a completely realized existence, whose being is indistinguishable from its seeming, while the word "thing" makes us think of a reality which would be at the same time a reservoir of possibilities; that is why Berkeley prefers to call bodies ideas rather than things. But if we look upon his "idealism" in the light, we see that it coincides with his "nominalism"; for the more clearly this second thesis takes shape in the philosopher's mind, the more evidently it is restricted to the negation of general abstract ideas— *abstracted,* that is, *extracted* from matter: it is clear in fact that one cannot extract something from what contains nothing, nor consequently make a perception yield something other than the perception itself. Color being but color, resistance being only resistance, you will never find anything in common between resistance and color, you will never discover in visual data any element shared by the data of touch. If you claim to abstract from the data of either something which will be common to all, you will perceive in examining that something that you are dealing with a word: therein lies the nominalism of Berkeley; but there also, at the same time, is the "new theory of vision." If an extension which would be at once visual and tactile is only a word, it is all the more so with an extension which would involve all the senses at once: there again is nominalism, but there too is the refutation of the Cartesian theory of matter. Let us not even talk any more about extension; let us simply note that in view of the structure of language the two expressions "I have this perception" and "this perception exists" are synonymous, but that the second, introducing the same word "existence" into the description of totally different perceptions, invites us to believe that they have something in common between them and to imagine that their diversity conceals a fundamental unity, the unity of a "substance" which is, in reality, only the word *existence* hypostasized: there you have the whole idealism of Berkeley; and this idealism, as I was saying, is identical with his nominalism.—Let us go on now, with your permission, to the theory of God and the theory of minds. If a body is made of "ideas" or, in other words, if it is entirely passive and determinate, having neither power nor virtuality, it cannot act on other bodies; and consequently the movements of bodies must be the effect of an active power, which has produced these bodies themselves and which, because of the order which the universe reveals, can only be an intelligent cause. If we are mistaken when under the name of general ideas we set up as realities the names that we have given to groups of objects or perceptions more or less artificially constituted by us on the plane of matter, such is not the case when we think we discover, behind this plane, the divine intentions: the general idea which exists only on the surface and which links body to body is no doubt only a word, but the general idea which exists in depth, relating bodies to God or rather descending from God to bodies, is a reality; and thus the nominalism of Berkeley quite naturally calls for this development of the doctrine as found in the *Siris,* and which has wrongly been considered a Neo-Platonic fantasy; in other words, the idealism of Berkeley is only one aspect of the theory which places God behind all the manifestations of matter. Finally, if God imprints in each one of us perceptions, or as Berkeley says, "ideas," the being which gathers up these perceptions, or rather which goes to meet them, is quite the reverse of an idea:

it is a will, though one which is constantly limited by divine will. The meeting-place of these two wills is precisely what we call matter. If the *percipi* is pure passivity the *percipere* is pure activity. Human mind, matter, divine mind therefore become terms which we can express only in terms of one another. And the spiritualism of Berkeley is itself found to be only an aspect of any one of the other three theses.

Thus the various parts of the system interpenetrate, as in a living being. But, as I was saying at the beginning, the spectacle of this reciprocal penetration doubtless gives us a more precise idea of the body of the doctrine; it still does not enable us to reach the soul.

We shall get closer to it, if we can reach the mediating *image* referred to above—an image which is almost matter in that it still allows itself to be seen, and almost mind in that it no longer allows itself to be touched—a phantom which haunts us while we turn about the doctrine and to which we must go in order to obtain the decisive signal, the indication of the attitude to take and of the point from which to look. Did the mediating image which takes shape in the mind of the interpreter, as he progresses in his study of the work, exist originally in the same form in the master's thought? If it was not that particular one, it was another, which could belong to a different order of perceptions and have no material resemblance whatsoever to it, but which nevertheless would equal it in value as two translations of the same work in different languages equal one another. Perhaps these two images, perhaps even other images, still equivalent, were present all at once, following the philosopher step by step in procession through the evolutions of his thought. Or perhaps he did not perceive any one of them clearly, being content only at rare intervals to make contact directly with that still more subtle thing, intuition itself; but then we are indeed forced, as interpreters, to re-establish the intermediary image, unless we are prepared to speak of the "original intuition" as a vague thought and of the "spirit of the doctrine" as an abstraction, whereas this spirit is as concrete and this intuition as precise as anything in the system.

In Berkeley's case, I think I see two different images and the one which strikes me most is not the one whose complete indication we find in Berkeley himself. It seems to me that Berkeley perceives matter as a *thin transparent film* situated between man and God. It remains transparent as long as the philosophers leave it alone, and in that case God reveals Himself through it. But let the metaphysicians meddle with it, or even common sense in so far as it deals in metaphysics: immediately the film becomes dull, thick and opaque, and forms a screen because such words as Substance, Force, abstract Extension, etc. slip behind it, settle there like a layer of dust, and hinder us from seeing God through the transparency. The image is scarcely indicated by Berkeley himself though he has said in so many words "that we first raise a dust and then complain we cannot see." But there is another comparison, often evoked by the philosopher, which is only the auditory transposition of the visual image I have just described: according to this, matter is a language which God speaks to us. That being so, the metaphysics of matter thickening each one of the syllables, marking it off, setting it up as an independent entity, turns our attention away from the meaning to the sound and hinders us from following the divine word. But, whether we attach ourselves to the one or to the other, in either case we are dealing with a simple image that we must keep in view, because if it is not the intuition generating the doctrine, it is immediately derived from it, and approximates it more than any of the theses taken individually, more even than the combination of all of them.

Is it possible for us to recapture this intuition itself? We have just two means of expression, concept and image. It is in concepts that the system develops; it is into an image that it contracts when it is driven back to the intuition from which it comes: so that, if one wishes to go beyond the image by rising above it, one necessarily falls back on concepts, and on concepts more vague, even more general than those from which one started in search of the image and the intuition. Reduced to this form, bottled as it were the moment it comes from the spring, the original intuition will then become superlatively insipid and uninteresting: it will be banal in the extreme. If we were to say for example that Berkeley considers the human soul as partially united with God and partly independent, that it is conscious of itself at every moment as of an imperfect activity which would join a higher activity if there were not, interposed between the two, something which is absolutely passive, we should be expressing all of the original intuition of Berkeley that can be directly translated into concepts, and still we should have something so abstract as to be almost empty. Let us stick to these formulas since we cannot find better ones, but let us try to put a little life into them. Let us take all that the philosopher has written, let us bring back these scattered ideas to the image from which they had descended; and let us raise them enclosed now in the image, up to the abstract formula enlarged by its absorption of the image and ideas, let us now attach ourselves to this formula and watch it, simple as it is, grow simpler still, all the more simple for our having pushed into it a greater number of things; finally let us rise with it, go up to the point where everything that was given extended in the doctrine contracts in tension: we shall picture to ourselves this time how from this center of force, which is moreover inaccessible, there springs the impulse which gives the impetus, that is to say the intuition itself. It is from this that the four theses of Berkeley came, because this movement met on its way the ideas and problems the contemporaries of Berkeley were raising. In other times Berkeley would doubtless have formulated other theses; but, the movement being the same, these theses would have been situated in the same way with regard to one another; they would have had the same relationship to one another, like new words of a new sentence through which runs the thread of an old meaning: and it would have been the same philosophy.

The relation of a philosophy to earlier and contemporary philosophies is not, then, what a certain conception of the history of systems would lead us to assume. The philosopher does not take pre-existing ideas in order to recast them into a superior synthesis or combine them with a new idea. One might as well believe that in order to speak we go hunting for words that we string together afterwards by means of a thought. The truth is that above the word and above the sentence there is something much more simple than a sentence or even a word: the meaning, which is less a thing thought than a movement of thought, less a movement than a direction. And just as the impulsion given to the embryonic life determines the division of an original cell into cells which in turn divide until the complete organism is formed, so the characteristic movement of each act of thought leads this thought, by an increasing sub-division of itself, to spread out more and more over the successive planes of the mind until it reaches that of speech. Once there it expresses itself by means of a sentence, that is, by a group of pre-existing elements; but it can almost arbitrarily choose the first elements of the group provided that the others are complementary to them; the same thought is translated just as well into diverse sentences composed of entirely different words, provided these words have the same connection between them. Such is the process of speech. And such also is the operation by which a philosophy is constituted. The philosopher does not start with pre-existing ideas; at most one can say that he arrives at them. And when he gets there the idea thus caught up into the movement of his mind, being animated with a new life like the word which receives its meaning from the sentence, is no longer what it was outside the vortex.

One would find the same kind of relationship between a philosophical system and the whole body of scientific knowledge of the epoch in which the philosopher lived.

There is a certain conception of philosophy which requires that all the effort of the philosopher should be to
embrace in one large synthesis the results of the particular sciences. Indeed, the philosopher, for a long time,
was he who possessed universal knowledge; and today
even, when the multiplicity of particular sciences, the diversity and complexity of methods, the enormous mass
of facts collected make the accumulation of all human
knowledge in a single mind impossible, the philosopher
remains the man of universal knowledge, in this sense,
that if he can no longer know everything, there is nothing that he should not have put himself in a position to
learn. But does it necessarily follow, that his task is to
take possession of existing science to bring it to increasing degrees of generality, and to proceed, from condensation to condensation, to what has been called the
unification of knowledge? May I be pardoned if I consider it strange that this conception of philosophy is
proposed to us in the name of science, out of respect for
science: I know of no conception more offensive to
science or more injurious to the scientist. Here, if you
like, is a man who, over a long period of time, has
followed a certain scientific method and laboriously
gained his results, who says to us: "Experience, with
the help of reasoning, leads to this point; scientific
knowledge begins here, it ends there; such are my conclusions"; and the philosopher would have the right to
answer: "Very well, leave it to me, and I'll show you
what I can do with it! The knowledge you bring me
unfinished, I shall complete. What you put before me in
bits I shall put together. With the same materials, since
it is understood that I shall keep to the facts which you
have observed, with the same kind of work, since I must
restrict myself as you did to induction and deduction, I
shall do more and better than you have done." Truly a
very strange pretension! How could the profession of
philosopher confer upon him who exercises it the power
of advancing farther than science in the same direction

as science? That certain scientists are more inclined
than others to forge ahead and to generalize their results,
more inclined also to turn back and to criticize their
methods, that in this particular meaning of the word
they should be dubbed philosophers, moreover that
each science can and should have its own philosophy
thus understood, I am the first to admit. But that
particular philosophy is still science, and he who
practices it is still a scientist. It is no longer a question,
as it was a moment ago, of setting up philosophy as a
synthesis of the positive sciences and of claiming, in
virtue of the philosopher's mind alone, to raise oneself
above science in the generalization of the same facts.

Such a conception of the role of the philosopher would
be unfair to science. But how much more unfair to philosophy! Is it not evident that if the scientist stops at
a certain point along the road of generalization and synthesis it is because beyond that point objective experience and sure reasoning do not permit us to advance?
And hence in claiming to go further in the same direction, should we not be placing ourselves systematically
in the arbitrary or at least the hypothetical? To make
of philosophy an ensemble of generalities which goes beyond scientific generalization, is to insist that the philosopher be content with the plausible and that probability be sufficient for him. I am perfectly well aware
that for most of those who follow our discussions from a
distance, our domain is in fact that of the simple possible, at most that of the probable; they would be very
much inclined to say that philosophy begins where certitude leaves off. But who among us would like philosophy to be in such a situation? Doubtless everything is
not equally verified or verifiable in what a philosophy
brings us, and it is the essence of the philosophical
method to demand that at many moments, on many
points, the mind should take risks. But the philosopher
runs these risks only because he has insured himself and
because there are things of which he feels himself un-

shakeably certain. He will make us certain in our turn to the extent that he is able to communicate to us the intuition from whence he draws his strength.

The truth is that philosophy is not a synthesis of particular sciences, and that if it often places itself on the terrain of science, if it sometimes embraces in a simpler vision the objects of science, it is not by intensifying science, it is not by carrying the results of science to a higher degree of generality. There would not be place for two ways of knowing, philosophy and science, if experience did not present itself to us under two different aspects; on the one hand in the form of facts side by side with other facts, which repeat themselves more or less, which can to a certain extent be measured, and which in fact open out in the direction of distinct multiplicity and spatiality; on the other hand in the form of a reciprocal penetration which is pure duration, refractory to law and measurement. In both cases, experience signifies consciousness; but in the first case, consciousness unfolds outward and externalizes itself in relation to itself in the exact measure to which it perceives things as external to one another; in the second, it turns back within itself, it takes possession of itself and develops in depth. In thus probing its own depth does it penetrate more deeply into the interior of matter, of life, or reality in general? One could dispute this if consciousness had been superadded to matter as an accident; but I believe I have shown that such a hypothesis, according to the way in which it is generally taken, is absurd or false, self-contradictory or contradicted by the facts. One might still dispute it, if human consciousness, although related to a higher and vaster consciousness, had been put aside, as if man had to stand in a corner of nature like a child being punished. But no! the matter and life which fill the world are equally within us; the forces which work in all things we feel within ourselves; whatever may be the inner essence of what is and what is done, we are of that essence. Let us then go down into our own inner selves: the deeper the point we touch, the stronger will be the thrust which sends us back to the surface. Philosophical intuition is this contact, philosophy is this impetus. Brought back to the surface by an impulsion from the depth, we shall regain contact with science as our thought opens out and disperses. Philosophy then must be able to model itself upon science, and an idea of so-called intuitive origin which could not manage, by dividing itself and subdividing its divisions, to cover the facts observed outwardly and the laws by which science joins them to each other, which would not be capable even of correcting certain generalizations and of rectifying certain observations, would be pure fantasy; it would have nothing in common with intuition. But on the other hand the idea which succeeds in fitting perfectly this dispersion of itself upon the facts and laws, was not obtained by a unification of external experience; for the philosopher did not arrive at unity, he started from it. I am speaking, naturally, of a unity which is at once restricted and relative, like the unity which marks off a living being from the rest of the universe. The process by which philosophy seems to assimilate the results of positive science, like the operation in the course of which a philosophy appears to re-assemble in itself the fragments of earlier philosophies, is not a synthesis but an analysis.

Science is the auxiliary of action. And action aims at a result. The scientific intelligence asks itself therefore what will have to be done in order that a certain desired result be attained, or more generally, what conditions should obtain in order that a certain phenomenon take place. It goes from an arrangement of things to a re-arrangement, from a simultaneity to a simultaneity. Of necessity it neglects what happens in the interval; or if it does concern itself with it, it is in order to consider other arrangements in it, still more simultaneities. With methods meant to seize the ready-made, it cannot in general enter into what is being done, it cannot follow the moving reality, adopt the becoming which is the life of things. This last task belongs to philosophy. While the scientist, obliged to take immobile views of movement and to gather repetitions along a path where nothing is repeated, intent also dividing reality conveniently on successive planes where it is deployed in order to submit it to the action of man, is obliged to use craft with nature, to adopt toward it the wary attitude of an adversary, the philosopher treats nature as a comrade. The rule of science is the one posited by Bacon: obey in order to command. The philosopher neither obeys nor commands; he seeks to be at one with nature. From this point of view, moreover, the essence of philosophy is the spirit of simplicity. Whether we contemplate the philosophical spirit in itself or in its works, whether we compare philosophy to science or one philosophy with other philosophies, we always find that any complication is superficial, that the construction is a mere accessory, synthesis a semblance: the act of philosophizing is a simple one.

The more we become imbued with this truth, the more we shall be inclined to take philosophy out of the school and bring it into closer contact with life. No doubt the attitude of common-sense, as it results from the structure of the senses, of intelligence and of language, is nearer to the attitude of science than to that of philosophy. By that I do not mean only that the general categories of our thoughts are the very categories of science, that the highways traced by our senses across the continuity of the real are those along which science will travel, that perception is a science in the process of being born, science an adult perception, and that ordinary knowledge and scientific knowledge, both destined to prepare our action upon things, are necessarily two visions of a kind, although of unequal precision and range; what I wish particularly to say, is that ordinary knowledge is forced, like scientific knowledge and for the same reasons, to take things in a time broken up into an infinity of particles, pulverized so to speak, where an instant which does not endure follows another equally without duration. Movement is for it a series of positions, change a series of qualities, and becoming, generally, a series of states. It starts from immobility (as though immobility could be anything but an appearance, comparable to the special effect that one moving body produces upon another when both move at the same rate in the same direction), and by an ingenious arrangement of immobilities it recomposes an imitation of movement which it substitutes for movement itself: an operation which is convenient from a practical standpoint but is theoretically absurd, pregnant with all the contradictions, all the pseudo-problems that Metaphysics and Criticism find before them.

But precisely because it is right there that common sense turns its back upon philosophy, all we shall have to do is to have it make a volte-face on that point in order to head it again in the direction of philosophical thought. Intuition doubtless admits of many degrees of intensity, and philosophy many degrees of depth; but the mind once brought back to real duration will already be alive with intuitive life and its knowledge of things will already be philosophy. Instead of a discontinuity of moments replacing one another in an infinitely divided time, it will perceive the continuous fluidity of real time which flows along, indivisible. Instead of surface states covering successively some neutral stuff and maintaining with it a mysterious relationship of phenomenon to substance, it will seize upon one identical change which keeps ever lengthening as in a melody where everything is becoming but where the becoming, being itself substantial, has no need of support. No more inert states, no more dead things; nothing but the mobility of which the stability of life is made. A vision of this kind, where reality appears as continuous and indivisible, is on the road which leads to philosophical intuition.

For, in order to reach intuition it is not necessary to transport ourselves outside the domain of the senses and of consciousness. Kant's error was to believe that it was. After having proved by decisive arguments that no dialectical effort will ever introduce us into the beyond and that an effective metaphysics would necessarily be an intuitive metaphysics, he added that we lack this intuition and that this metaphysics is impossible. It would in fact be so if there were no other time or change than those which Kant perceived and which, moreover, we too must reckon with; for our usual perception cannot get out of time nor grasp anything else than change. But the time in which we are naturally placed, the change we habitually have before us, are a time and change that our senses and our consciousness have reduced to dust in order to facilitate our action upon things. Undo what they have done, bring our perception back to its origins, and we shall have a new kind of knowledge without having been obliged to have recourse to new faculties.

If this knowledge is generalized, speculation will not be the only thing to profit by it. Everyday life can be nourished and illuminated by it. For the world into which our senses and consciousness habitually introduce us is no more than the shadow of itself: and it is as cold as death. Everything in it is arranged for our maximum convenience, but in it, everything is in a present which seems constantly to be starting afresh; and we ourselves, fashioned artificially in the image of a no less artificial universe, see ourselves in the instantaneous, speak of the past as of something done away with, and see in memory a fact strange or in any case foreign to us, an aid given to mind by matter. Let us on the contrary grasp ourselves afresh as we are, in a present which is thick, and furthermore, elastic, which we can stretch indefinitely backward by pushing the screen which masks us from ourselves farther and farther away; let us grasp afresh the external world as it really is, not superficially, in the present, but in depth, with the immediate past crowding upon it and imprinting upon it its impetus; let us in a word become accustomed to see all things *sub specie durationis:* immediately in our galvanized perception what is taut becomes relaxed, what is dormant awakens, what is dead comes to life again. Satisfactions which art will never give save to those favored by nature and fortune, and only then upon rare occasions, philosophy thus understood will offer to all of us, at all times, by breathing life once again into the phantoms which surround us and by revivifying us. In so doing philosophy will become complementary to science in practice as well as in speculation. With its applications which aim only at the convenience of existence, science gives us the promise of well-being, or at most, of pleasure. But philosophy could already give us joy.

V

THE PERCEPTION OF CHANGE

My first words are words of thanks to the University
of Oxford for the great honor she has done me in inviting me to address her. I have always thought of Oxford
as one of the few sanctuaries where, reverently main-
tained, passed on by each generation to the next, the
warmth and radiance of ancient thought are preserved.
But I also know that this attachment to antiquity does
not prevent your University from being very modern and
very much alive. More especially in what concerns
philosophy, am I struck to see with what profundity and
what originality the ancient philosophers are studied
here (did not one of your most eminent masters only
recently touch up the interpretation of the Platonic
theory of Ideas on its essential points?) ; and I am also
struck, on the other hand, by the fact that Oxford is in
the vanguard of the philosophical movement with the
two extreme conceptions of the nature of truth: integral
rationalism and pragmatism. This alliance of past and
present is fruitful in all fields, nowhere more so than in
philosophy. To be sure, we have something new to do,
and perhaps the moment has come to be fully alive to
it; but the fact that it is new does not mean that it
must be revolutionary. Let us rather study the ancients,
become imbued with their spirit and try to do, as far
as possible, what they themselves would be doing were
they living among us. Endowed with our knowledge (I
do not refer so much to our mathematics and physics,
which would perhaps not radically alter their way of
thinking, but especially our biology and psychology), they
would arrive at very different results from those they
obtained. That is what particularly strikes me in the

problem I have undertaken to deal with here, that of change.

I chose it, because I consider it fundamental, and because I believe that if one were convinced of the reality of change and if one made an effort to grasp it, everything would become simplified, philosophical difficulties, considered insurmountable, would fall away. Not only would philosophy gain by it, but our everyday life—I mean the impression things make upon us and the reaction of our intelligence, our sensibility and our will upon things—would perhaps be transformed and, as it were, transfigured. The point is that usually we look at change but we do not see it. We speak of change, but we do not think about it. We say that change exists, that everything changes, that change is the very law of things: yes, we say it and we repeat it; but those are only words, and we reason and philosophize as though change did not exist. In order to think change and see it, there is a whole veil of prejudices to brush aside, some of them artificial, created by philosophical speculation, the others natural to common sense. I believe we shall end by coming to an agreement about them, and shall thus form a philosophy in which everyone will collaborate, upon which everyone will be able to agree. That is why I should like to fix two or three points upon which it seems to me agreement has already been reached; it will gradually be extended to the rest of them. The first lecture therefore will deal less with change itself than with the general characteristics of a philosophy attached to the intuition of change.

Here, first of all, is a point upon which every one will agree. If the senses and the consciousness had an unlimited scope, if in the double direction of matter and mind the faculty of perceiving was indefinite, one would not need to conceive any more than to reason. Conceiving is a make-shift when perception is not granted us, and reasoning is done in order to fill up the gaps of perception or to extend its scope. I do not deny the utility of abstract and general ideas—any more than I question the value of bank-notes. But just as the note is only a promise of gold, so a conception has value only through the eventual perceptions it represents. It is not, of course, merely a question of the perception of a thing, or a quality, or a state. One can conceive an order, a harmony, and more generally a *truth,* which then becomes a *reality.* I say that we agree on this point. Everyone could see for himself, in fact, that the most ingeniously assembled conceptions and the most learnedly constructed reasonings collapse like a house of cards the moment the fact—a single fact really seen—collides with these conceptions and these reasonings. There is not a single metaphysician, moreover, not one theologian, who is not ready to affirm that a perfect being is one who knows all things intuitively without having to go through reasoning, abstraction and generalization. There is no difficulty therefore about the first point.

And there will not be any more about the second, which we come to now. The insufficiency of our faculties of perception—an insufficiency verified by our faculties of conception and reasoning—is what has given birth to philosophy. The history of doctrines attests it. The conceptions of the earliest Greek thinkers were certainly very close to perception, since it was by the transformations of a sensible element like water, air or fire, that they completed the immediate sensation. But from the time the philosophers of the school of Elea, criticizing the idea of transformation, had shown or thought they had shown the impossibility of keeping so close to the sense-data, philosophy started off along the road it has since traveled, the road leading to a "supra-sensible" world: one was to explain things henceforth with pure "ideas." It is true that for the ancient philosophers the intelligible world was situated outside and above the one our senses and consciousness perceive: our faculties of perception showed us only shadows projected in time and space by immutable and eternal Ideas. For the moderns, on the contrary, these essences are constitutive of sensible things themselves; they are veritable substances, of which phenomena are only the surface covering. But all of them, ancient and modern, are agreed in seeing in philosophy a substitution of the concept for the percept. They all appeal from the insufficiency of our senses and consciousness to the faculties of the mind no longer perceptive, I mean to the functions of abstraction, generalization and reasoning.

On the second point we can therefore be agreed. I come then to the third, which, I imagine, will not occasion any discussion either.

If such is really the philosophical method, there is not, there cannot be *a* philosophy as there is *a* science; on the contrary there will always be as many different philosophies as there are original thinkers. How could it be otherwise? No matter how abstract a conception may be it always has its starting point in a perception. The intellect combines and separates; it arranges, disarranges and co-ordinates; it does not create. It must have a matter, and this matter can only reach it through the senses or the consciousness. A philosophy which constructs or completes reality with pure ideas will therefore only be substituting for or adding to our concrete perceptions as a whole, some particular one of them it has elaborated, thinned down, refined and thereby converted into abstract and general idea. But there will always be something arbitrary in its choice of that privileged perception, for positive science has taken for itself all that is incontestably common to different things; or in other words *quantity,* and all that remains for philosophy therefore is the domain of *quality,* where everything is heterogeneous to everything else, and where a part will never represent the whole except in virtue of a contestable if not arbitrary decree. One can always oppose other decrees to this one. And many different philosophies will spring up, armed with different concepts. They will struggle indefinitely with one another.

Here, then, is the question which arises, and which I consider essential. Since any attempt at purely conceptual philosophy calls forth antagonistic efforts, and since, in the field of pure dialectics there is no system to which one cannot oppose another, should we remain in that field or, (without, of course, ceasing to exercise our faculties of conception and reasoning), ought we not rather return to perception, getting it to expand and extend? I was saying that it is the insufficiency of natural perception which has driven philosophers to complete perception by conception—the latter having as its function to fill in the spaces between the data of the senses or of consciousness and in that way to unify and systematize our knowledge of things. But the examination of doctrines shows us that the faculty of conceiving, as it advances in this work of integration, is forced to eliminate from the real a great number of qualitative differences, to extinguish in part our perceptions, and to weaken our concrete vision of the universe. For the very reason that each philosophy is led, willy-nilly, to proceed in this way, it gives rise to opposing philosophies, each of which picks up something of what the other has dropped. The method, therefore, goes contrary to the purpose: it should in theory extend and complete perception; it is obliged in fact to require that many perceptions stand aside so that some one of them may become representative of the others. —But suppose that instead of trying to rise above our perception of things we were to plunge into it for the purpose of deepening and widening it. Suppose that we were to insert our will into it, and that this will, expanding, were to expand our vision of things. We should obtain this time a philosophy where nothing in the data of the senses or the consciousness would be sacrificed: no quality, no aspect of the real would be substituted for the rest ostensibly to explain it. But above all we should have a philosophy to which one could not oppose others, for it would have left nothing outside of itself that other doctrines could pick up; it would have taken everything. It would have taken every thing that is given, and even more, for the senses and consciousness, urged on by this philosophy to an exceptional effort, would have given it more than they furnish naturally. To the multiplicity of systems contending with one another, armed with different concepts, would succeed the unity of a doctrine capable of reconciling all thinkers in the same perception—a perception which moreover would grow ever larger, thanks to the combined effort of philosophers in a common direction.

It will be said that this enlarging is impossible. How can one ask the eyes of the body, or those of the mind, to see more than they see? Our attention can increase precision, clarify and intensify; it cannot bring forth in the field of perception what was not there in the first place. That's the objection.—It is refuted in my opinion by experience. For hundreds of years, in fact, there have been men whose function has been precisely to see and to make us see what we do not naturally perceive. They are the artists.

What is the aim of art if not to show us, in nature and in the mind, outside of us and within us, things which did not explicitly strike our senses and our consciousness? The poet and the novelist who express a mood certainly do not create it out of nothing; they would not be understood by us if we did not observe within ourselves, up to a certain point, what they say about others. As they speak, shades of emotion and thought appear to us which might long since have been brought out in us but which remained invisible; just like the photographic image which has not yet been plunged into the bath where it will be revealed. The poet is this revealing agent. But nowhere is the function of the artist shown as clearly as in that art which gives the most important place to imitation, I mean painting. The great painters are men who possess a certain vision of things which has or will become the vision of all men. A Corot, a Turner—not to mention others —have seen in nature many an aspect that we did not notice. Shall it be said that they have not seen but created, that they have given us products of their imagination, that we adopt their inventions because we like them and that we get pleasure from looking at nature through the image the great painters have traced for us? It is true to a certain extent; but, if it were only that, why should we say of certain works—those of the masters—that they are true? Where would the difference be between great art and pure fancy? If we reflect deeply upon what we feel as we look at a Turner or a Corot, we shall find that, if we accept them and admire them, it is because we had already perceived something of what they show us. But we had perceived without seeing. It was, for us, a brilliant and vanishing vision, lost in the crowd of those visions, equally brilliant and equally vanishing, which become overcast in our ordinary experience like "dissolving views" and which constitute, by their reciprocal interference, the pale and colorless vision of things that is habitually ours. The painter has isolated it; he has fixed it so well on the canvas that henceforth we shall not be able to help seeing in reality what he himself saw.

Art would suffice then to show us that an extension of the faculties of perceiving is possible. But how does this extension work?—Let us notice that the artist has always been considered an "idealist." We mean by that that he is less preoccupied than ourselves with the positive and material side of life. He is, in the real sense of the word, "absent-minded." Why then, being detached from reality to a greater degree, does he manage to see in it more things? We should not understand why if the vision we ordinarily have of external objects and of ourselves were not a vision which we had been obliged to narrow and drain by our attachment to reality, our need for living and acting. As a matter of fact, it would be easy to show that the more we are preoccupied with living, the less we are inclined to contemplate, and that the necessities of action tend to limit the field of vision. I cannot go into a demonstration of this point; I am of the opinion that an entirely new light would illuminate many psychological and psycho-physiological questions if we recognized that distinct perception is merely cut, for the purposes of practical existence, out of a wider canvas. In psychology and elsewhere, we like to go from the part to the whole, and our customary system of explanation consists in reconstructing ideally our mental life with simple elements, then in supposing that the combination of these elements has really produced our mental life. If things happened this way, our perception would as a matter of fact be inextensible; it would consist of the assembling of certain specific materials, in a given quantity, and we should never find anything more in it than what had been put there in the first place.

But the facts, taken as they are, without any mental reservation about providing a mechanical explanation of the mind, suggest an entirely different interpretation. They show us, in normal psychological life, a constant effort of the mind to limit its horizon, to turn away from what it has a material interest in not seeing. Before philosophizing one must live; and life demands that we put on blinders, that we look neither to the right, nor to the left nor behind us, but straight ahead in the direction we have to go. Our knowledge, far from being made up of a gradual association of simple elements, is the effect of a sudden dissociation: from the immensely vast field of our virtual knowledge, we have selected, in order to make it into actual knowledge, everything which concerns our action upon things; we have neglected the rest. The brain seems to have been constructed with a view to this work of selection. That could easily be shown by the way in which the memory works. Our past, as we shall see in our next lecture, is necessarily automatically preserved. It survives complete. But our practical interest is to thrust it aside, or at least to accept of it only what can more or less usefully illuminate and complete the situation in the present. The brain serves to bring about this choice: it actualizes the useful memories, it keeps in the lower strata of the consciousness those which are of no use. One could say as much for perception. The auxiliary of action, it isolates that part of reality as a whole that interests us; it shows us less the things themselves than the use we can make of them. It classifies, it labels them beforehand; we scarcely lock at the object, it is enough for us to know to which category it belongs. But now and then, by a lucky accident, men arise whose senses or whose consciousness are less adherent to life. Nature has forgotten to attach their faculty of perceiving to their faculty of acting. When they look at a thing, they see it for itself, and not for themselves. They do not perceive simply with a view to action; they perceive in order to perceive —for nothing, for the pleasure of doing so. In regard to a certain aspect of their nature, whether it be their consciousness or one of their senses, they are born *detached;* and according to whether this detachment is that of a certain particular sense, or of consciousness, they are painters or sculptors, musicians or poets. It is therefore a much more direct vision of reality that we find in the different arts; and it is because the artist is less intent on utilizing his perception that he perceives a greater number of things.

Well, what nature does from time to time, by distraction, for certain privileged individuals, could not philosophy of such a matter attempt, in another sense and another way, for everyone? Would not the role of philosophy under such circumstances be to lead us to a completer perception of reality by means of a certain displacement of our attention? It would be a question of *turning* this attention *aside* from the part of the universe which interests us from a practical viewpoint and *turning it back* toward what serves no practical purpose. This conversion of the attention would be philosophy itself.

At first glance it would seem that this has long since been done. More than one philosopher has in fact said that in order to philosophize he had to be detached, and that speculation was the reverse of action. We were speaking a few moments ago of the Greek philosophers: not one of them expressed the idea more forcefully than

Plotinus. "All action," he said (and he even added "all fabrication") "weakens contemplation."

And, faithful to the spirit of Plato, he thought that the discovery of truth demanded a conversion of the mind, which breaks away from the appearances here below and attaches itself to the realities above: "Let us flee to our beloved homeland!"—But as you see, it was a question of "fleeing." More precisely, for Plato and for all those who understand metaphysics in that way, breaking away from life and converting one's attention consisted in transporting oneself immediately into a world different from the one we inhabit, in developing other faculties of perception than the senses and consciousness. They did not believe that this education of the attention might most frequently consist in removing its blinders, in freeing it from the contraction that it is accustomed to by the demands of life. They were not of the opinion that the metaphysician, for at least half of his speculations, should continue to look at what every one looks at: no, he had always to turn toward something else. That is why they invariably call upon faculties of vision other than those we constantly exercise in the knowledge of the external world and of ourselves.

And precisely because he disputed the existence of these transcendent faculties, Kant believed metaphysics to be impossible. One of the most profound and important ideas in the *Critique of Pure Reason* is this: if metaphysics is possible, it is through a vision and not through a dialectic. Dialectics leads to contrary philosophies; it demonstrates the thesis as well as the antithesis of antinomies. Only a superior intuition (which Kant calls an "intellectual" intuition), that is, a *perception* of metaphysical reality, would enable metaphysics to be constituted. The most obvious result of the Kantian *Critique* is thus to show that one could only penetrate into the beyond by a vision, and that a doctrine has value in this domain only to the extent that it contains perception: take this perception, analyze it, recompose it, turn it round and round in all directions, cause it to undergo the most subtle operations of the highest intellectual chemistry, you will never get from your crucible anything more than you have put into it; as much vision as you have put into it, just so much will you find; and reasoning will not have made you go one step *beyond* what you had perceived in the first place. That is what Kant brought out so clearly and that, it seems to me, is the greatest service he rendered to speculative philosophy. He definitively established that, if metaphysics is possible, it can be so only through an effort of intuition. —Only, having proved that intuition alone would be capable of giving us a metaphysics, he added: this intuition is impossible.

Why did he consider it impossible? Precisely because he pictured a vision of the kind—I mean a vision of reality "in itself"—that Plotinus had imagined, as those who have appealed to metaphysical intuition have imagined it. By that they all understood a faculty of knowing which would differ radically from consciousness as well as from the senses, which would even be orientated in the opposite direction. They have all believed that to break away from practical life was to turn one's back upon it.

Why did they believe that? Why did Kant, their adversary, share their mistake? How is it they one and all had this conception even if they drew opposite conclusions from it—they constructing a metaphysics, and he declaring metaphysics impossible?

They believed it because they imagined that our senses and consciousness, as they function in everyday life, make us grasp movement directly. They believed that by our senses and consciousness, working as they usually work, we actually perceive the change which takes place in things and in ourselves. Then, as it is incontestable that in following the usual data of our senses and consciousness we arrive in the speculative order at insoluble contradictions, they concluded that contradiction was inherent in change itself and that in order to avoid this contradiction one had to get out of the sphere of change and lift oneself above Time. Such is the position taken by the metaphysician as well as by those who, along with Kant, deny the possibility of metaphysics.

Metaphysics, as a matter of fact, was born of the arguments of Zeno of Elea on the subject of change and movement. It was Zeno who, by drawing attention to the absurdity of what he called movement and change, led the philosophers—Plato first and foremost—to seek the true and coherent reality in what does not change. And it is because Kant believed that our senses and consciousness are in fact exerted in a real Time, that is, in a Time which changes continuously, in a duration which endures; it is because, on the other hand, he took into account the relativity of the usual data of our senses and consciousness (a relativity which he laid down, furthermore, long before the transcendent conclusion of his endeavor that he considered metaphysics impossible without an entirely different kind of vision from that of the senses and the consciousness—a vision, moreover, no trace of which he found in man).

But if we could prove that what was considered as movement and change by Zeno first, and then by metaphysicians in general, is neither change nor movement, that of change they retained what does not change, and of movement what does not move, that they took for an immediate and complete perception of movement and change a crystallization of this perception, a solidification with an eye to practice—and if we could show on the other hand, that what Kant took for time itself was a time which neither flows nor changes nor endures; then, in order to avoid such contradictions as those which Zeno pointed out and to separate our everyday knowledge from the relativity to which Kant considered it condemned, we should not have to get outside of time (we are already outside of it!), we should not have to free ourselves or change (we are already only too free of

it!); on the contrary, what we should have to do is to
grasp change and duration in their original mobility.
Then we should not only see many difficulties drop away
one by one, and more than one problem disappear; but
through the extension and revivification of our faculty of
perceiving, perhaps also (though for the moment it is
not a question of rising to such heights) through a
prolongation which privileged souls will give to intuition, we should re-establish continuity in our knowledge
as a whole—a continuity which would no longer be
hypothetical and constructed, but experienced and lived.
Is a work of this kind possible? That is what we shall
seek to determine, at least as far as the knowledge of
our surroundings is concerned, in our second lecture.

Second Lecture

You gave me such sustained attention yesterday that
you must not be surprised if I am tempted to take advantage of it today. I am going to ask you to make a
strenuous effort to put aside some of the artificial schema
we interpose unknowingly between reality and us. What
is required is that we should break with certain habits of
thinking and perceiving that have become natural to us.
We must return to the direct perception of change and
mobility. Here is an immediate result of this effort. *We
shall think of all change, all movement, as being absolutely indivisible.*

Let us begin with movement. I have my hand at point
A. I move it over to point *B,* traversing the interval
AB. I say that this movement from *A* to *B* is by nature
simple.

But of this each one of us has the immediate sensation. No doubt while we are moving our hand from *A*
to *B* we say to ourselves that we could stop it at an intermediary point, but in that case we should not have to
do with the same movement. There would no longer be
a single movement from *A* to *B;* there would be, by hypothesis, two movements, with an interval. Neither from
within, through the muscular sense, nor from without

through sight, should we still have the same perception. If I leave my movement from *A* to *B* as it is, I feel it undivided and must declare it to be indivisible.

It is true that, when I watch my hand going from *A* to *B* and describing the interval *AB,* I say: "The interval *AB* can be divided into as many parts as I wish, therefore the movement from *A* to *B* can be divided into as many parts as I like, since this movement is applied exactly upon this interval." Or again: "At each instant of its trajectory, the mobile passes through a certain point, therefore one can distinguish in the movement as many stages as one likes, therefore the movement is infinitely divisible." But let us reflect for a moment. How could the movement *be applied upon* the space it traverses? How can something moving coincide with something immobile? How could the moving object *be* in a point of its trajectory passage? It *passes through,* or in other terms, it *could be there.* It would be there if it stopped; but if it should stop there, it would no longer be the same movement we were dealing with. It is always by a single bound that a passing is completed, when there is no break in the passage. The bound may last a few seconds, or days, months, years: it matters little. The moment it is one single bound, it is indecomposable. Only, once the passage is effected, as the trajectory is space and space is indefinitely divisible, we imagine that movement itself is indefinitely divisible. We like to imagine it because, in a movement, it is not the change of position which interests us, it is the positions themselves, the one the movement has left, the one it will take, the one it would take if it stopped on the way. We need immobility, and the more we succeed in imagining movement as coinciding with the immobilities of the points of space through which it passes, the better we think we understand it. To tell the truth, there never is real immobility, if we understand by that an absence of movement. Movement is reality itself, and what we call immobility is a certain state of things analogous to that produced when two trains move at the same speed, in the same direction, on parallel tracks: each of the two trains is then immovable to the travelers seated in the other. But a situation of this kind which, after all, is exceptional, seems to us to be the regular and normal situation, because it is what permits us to act upon things and also permits things to act upon us: the travelers in the two trains can hold out their hands to one another through the door and talk to one another only if they are "immobile," that is to say, if they are going in the same direction at the same speed. "Immobility" being the prerequisite for our action, we set it up as a reality, we make of it an absolute, and we see in movement something which is superimposed. Nothing is more legitimate in practice. But when we transport this habit of mind into the domain of speculation, we fail to recognize the true reality, we deliberately create insoluble problems, we close our eyes to what is most living in the real.

I need not recall the arguments of Zeno of Elea. They all involve the confusion of movement with the space covered, or at least the conviction that one can treat movement as one treats space, divide it without taking account of its articulations. Achilles, they say, will never overtake the tortoise he is pursuing, for when he arrives at the point where the tortoise was the latter will have had time to go further, and so on indefinitely. Philosophers have refuted this argument in numerous ways, and ways so difficult that each of these refutations deprives the others of the right to be considered definitive. There would have been, nevertheless, a very simple means of making short work of the difficulty: that would have been to question Achilles. For since Achilles finally catches up to the tortoise and even passes it, he must know better than anyone else how he goes about it. The ancient philosopher who demonstrated the possibility of movement by walking was right: his only mistake was to make the gesture without adding a commentary. Suppose then we ask Achilles to comment on his race: here, doubtless, is what he will answer: "Zeno insists that I go from the point where I am to the point the tortoise has left, from that point to the next point it has left, etc., etc.; that is his procedure for making me run. But I go about it otherwise. I take a first step, then a second, and so on: finally, after a certain number of steps, I take a last one by which I skip ahead of the tortoise. I thus accomplish a series of indivisible acts. My course is the series of these acts. You can distinguish its parts by the number of steps it involves. But you have not the right to disarticulate it according to another law, or to suppose it articulated in another way. To proceed as Zeno does is to admit that the race can be arbitrarily broken up like the space which has been covered; it is to believe that the passage is in reality applied to the trajectory; it is making movement and immobility coincide and consequently confusing one with the other."

But that is precisely what our usual method consists in. We argue about movement as though it were made of immobilities and, when we look at it, it is with immobilities that we reconstitute it. Movement for us is a position, then another position, and so on indefinitely. We say, it is true, that there must be something else, and that from one position to another there is the *passage* by which the interval is cleared. But as soon as we fix our attention on this passage, we immediately make of it a series of positions, even though we still admit that between two successive positions one must indeed assume a passage. We put this passage off indefinitely the moment we have to consider it. We admit that it exists, we give it a name; that is enough for us: once that point has been satisfactorily settled we turn to the positions preferring to deal with them alone. We have an instinctive fear of those difficulties which the vision of movement as movement would arouse in our thought; and quite rightly, once we have loaded movement down with immobilities. If movement is not everything, it is nothing; and if to begin with we have supposed that immobility can be a reality, movement will slip through our fingers when we think we have it.

I have spoken of movement; but I could say the same for any change whatever. All real change is an indivisible change. We like to treat it as a series of distinct states which form, as it were, a line in time. That is perfectly natural. If change is continuous in us and also in things, on the other hand, in order that the uninterrupted change which each of us calls "me" may act upon the uninterrupted change that we call a "thing," these two changes must find themselves, with regard to one another, in a situation like that of the two trains referred to above. We say, for example, that an object changes color, and that change here consists in a series of shades which would be the constitutive elements of change and which, themselves, would not change. But in the first place, if each shade has any objective existence at all, it is an infinitely rapid oscillation, it is change. And in the second place, the perception we have of it, to the extent that it is subjective, is only an isolated, abstract aspect of the general state of our person, and this state as a whole is constantly changing and causing this so-called invariable perception to participate in its change; in fact, there is no perception which is not constantly being modified. So that color, outside of us, is mobility itself, and our own person is also mobility. But the whole mechanism of our perception of things, like the mechanism of our action upon things has been regulated in such a way as to bring about, between the external and the internal mobility, a situation comparable to that of our two trains—more complicated, perhaps, but of the same kind: when the two changes, that of the object and that of the subject, take place under particular conditions, they produce the particular appearance that we call a "state." And once in possession of "states," our mind recomposes change with them. I repeat, there is nothing more natural: the breaking up of change into states enables us to act upon things, and it is useful in a practical sense to be interested in the states rather than in the change itself. But what is favorable to action in this case would be fatal to speculation. If you imagine a change as being really composed of states, you at once cause insoluble metaphysical problems to arise. They deal only with appearances. You have closed your eyes to true reality.

I shall not press the point. Let each of us undertake the experiment, let him give himself the direct vision of a change, of a movement: he will have a feeling of absolute indivisibility. I come then to the second point, closely allied to the first. *There are changes, but there are underneath the change no things which change: change has no need of a support. There are movements, but there is no inert or invariable object which moves: movement does not imply a mobile.*

It is difficult to picture things in this way, because the sense 'par excellence' is the sense of sight, and because the eye has developed the habit of separating, in the visual field, the relatively invariable figures which are then supposed to change place without changing form, movement is taken as super-added to the mobile as an accident. It is, in fact, useful to have to deal in daily life with objects which are stable and, as it were, responsible, to which one can address oneself as to persons. The sense of sight contrives to take things in this way: as an advance-guard for the sense of touch, it prepares our action upon the external world. But we already have less difficulty in perceiving movement and change as independent realities if we appeal to the sense of hearing. Let us listen to a melody, allowing ourselves to be lulled by it: do we not have the clear perception of a movement which is not attached to a mobile, of a change without anything changing? This change is enough, it is the thing itself. And even if it takes time, it is still indivisible; if the melody stopped sooner it would no longer be the same sonorous whole, it would be another, equally indivisible. We have, no doubt, a tendency to divide it and to picture, instead of the uninterrupted continuity of melody, a juxtaposition of distinct notes. But why? Because we are thinking of the discontinuous series of efforts we should be making to recompose approximately the sound heard if we were doing the singing, and also because our auditory perception has acquired the habit of absorbing visual images. We therefore listen to the melody through the vision which an orchestra-leader would have of it as he watched its score. We picture notes placed next to one another upon an imaginary piece of paper. We think of a keyboard upon which some one is playing, of the bow going up and down, of the musicians, each one playing his part along with the others. If we do not dwell on these spatial images, pure change remains, sufficient unto itself, in no way divided, in no way attached to a "thing" which changes.

Let us come back, then, to the sense of sight. In further concentrating our attention upon it we perceive that even here movement does not demand a vehicle nor change a substance in the ordinary meaning of the word. A suggestion of this vision of material things already comes to us from physical science. The more it progresses the more it resolves matter into actions moving through space, into movements dashing back and forth in a constant vibration so that mobility becomes reality itself. No doubt science begins by assigning a support to this mobility. But as it advances, the support recedes; masses are pulverized into molecules, molecules into atoms, atoms into electrons or corpuscles: finally, the support assigned to movement appears merely as a convenient schema—a simple concession on the part of the scholar to the habits of our visual imagination. But there is no need to go so far. What is the "mobile" to which our eye attaches movement as to a vehicle? Simply a colored spot which we know perfectly well amounts, in itself, to a series of extremely rapid vibrations. This alleged movement of a thing is in reality only a movement of movements.

But nowhere is the *substantiality* of change so visible, so palpable as in the domain of the inner life. Difficulties and contradictions of every kind to which the theories of personality have led come from our having imagined, on the one hand, a series of distinct psychological states, each one invariable, which would produce the variations of the ego by their very succession, and on the other hand an ego, no less invariable, which would serve as support for them. How could this unity and this multiplicity meet? How, without either of them having duration—the first because change is something superadded, the second because it is made up of elements which do not change—how could they constitute an ego which endures? But the truth is that there is neither a rigid, immovable substratum nor distinct states passing over it like actors on a stage. There is simply the continuous melody of our inner life—a melody which is going on and will go on, indivisible, from the beginning to the end of our conscious existence. Our personality is precisely that.

This indivisible continuity of change is precisely what constitutes true duration. I cannot here enter into the detailed examination of a question I have dealt with elsewhere. I shall confine myself therefore to saying, in reply to those for whom this "real duration" is something inexpressible and mysterious, that it is the clearest thing in the world: *real duration* is what we have always called *time,* but time perceived as indivisible. That time implies succession I do not deny. But that succession is first presented to our consciousness, like the distinction of a "before" and "after" set side by side, is what I cannot admit. When we listen to a melody we have the purest impression of succession we could possibly have—an impression as far removed as possible from that of simultaneity—and yet it is the very continuity of the melody and the impossibility of breaking it up which make that impression upon us. If we cut it up into distinct notes, into so many "befores" and "afters," we are bringing spatial images into it and impregnating the succession with simultaneity: in space, and only in space, is there a clear-cut distinction of parts external to one another. I recognize moreover that it is in spatialized time that we ordinarily place ourselves. We have no interest in listening to the uninterrupted humming of life's depths. And yet, that is where real duration is. Thanks to it, the more or less lengthy changes we witness within us and in the external world, take place in a single identical time.

Thus, whether it is a question of the internal or the external, of ourselves or of things, reality is mobility itself. That is what I was expressing when I said that there is change, but that there are not things which change.

Before the spectacle of this universal mobility there may be some who will be seized with dizziness. They are accustomed to terra firma; they cannot get used to the rolling and pitching. They must have "fixed" points to which they can attach thought and existence. They think that if everything passes, nothing exists; and that if reality is mobility, it has already ceased to exist at the moment one thinks it—it eludes thought. The material world, they say, is going to disintegrate, and the mind will drown in the torrent-like flow of things.—Let them be reassured! Change, if they consent to look directly at it without an interposed veil, will very quickly appear to them to be the most substantial and durable thing possible. Its solidity is infinitely superior to that of a fixity which is only an ephemeral arrangement between mobilities. I have come, in fact, to the third point to which I should like to draw your attention.

It is this: if change is real and even constitutive of reality, we must envisage the past quite differently from what we have been accustomed to doing through philosophy and language. We are inclined to think of our past as inexistent, and philosophers encourage this natural tendency in us. For them and for us the present alone exists by itself: if something of the past does survive it can only be because of help given it by the present, because of some act of charity on the part of the present, in short—to get away from metaphor—by the intervention of a certain particular function called memory, whose role is presumed to be to preserve certain parts of the past, for which exception is made, by storing them away in a kind of box.—This is a profound mistake! A useful one, I admit, perhaps necessary to action, but fatal to speculation. One could find in it, "in a nutshell" as you say, most of the illusions capable of vitiating philosophical thought.

Let us reflect for a moment on this "present" which alone is considered to have existence. What precisely is the present? If it is a question of the present instant— I mean, of a mathematical instant which would be to time what the mathematical point is to the line—it is clear that such an instant is a pure abstraction, an aspect of the mind; it cannot have real existence. You could never create time out of such instants any more than you could make a line out of mathematical points. Even if it does exist, how could there be an instant anterior to it? The two instants could not be separated by an interval of time since, by hypothesis, you reduce time to a juxtaposition of instants. Therefore they would not be separated by anything, and consequently they would be only one: two mathematical points which touch are identical. But let us put such subtleties aside. Our consciousness tells us that when we speak of our present we are thinking of a certain interval of duration. What duration? It is impossible to fix it exactly, as it is something rather elusive. My present, at this moment, is the sentence I am pronouncing. But it is so because I want to limit the field of my attention to my sentence. This attention is something that can be made longer or shorter, like the interval between the two points of a compass. For the moment, the points are just far enough apart to reach from the beginning to the end of my sentence; but if the fancy took me to spread them further my present would embrace, in addition to my last sentence, the one that preceded it: all I should have had to do is to adopt another punctuation. Let us go further: an attention which could be extended indefinitely would embrace, along with the preceding sentence, all the anterior phrases of the lecture and the events which preceded the lecture, and as large a portion of what we

call our past as desired. The distinction we make between our present and past is therefore, if not arbitrary,
at least relative to the extent of the field which our attention to life can embrace. The "present" occupies
exactly as much space as this effort. As soon as this particular attention drops any part of what it held beneath
its gaze, immediately that portion of the present thus
dropped becomes *ipso facto* a part of the past. In a word,
our present falls back into the past when we cease to attribute to it an immediate interest. What holds good for
the present of individuals holds also for the present of
of nations: an event belongs to the past, and enters into
history when it is no longer of any direct interest to the
politics of the day and can be neglected without the
affairs of the country being affected by it. As long as its
action makes itself felt, it adheres to the life of a nation
and remains present to it.

Consequently nothing prevents us from carrying back
as far as possible the line of separation between our
present and our past. An attention to life, sufficiently
powerful and sufficiently separated from all practical interest, would thus include in an undivided present the
entire past history of the conscious person—not as instantaneity, not like a cluster of simultaneous parts, but
as something continually present which would also be
something continually moving: such, I repeat, is the melody which one perceives as indivisible, and which constitutes, from one end to the other—if we wish to extend
the meaning of the word—a perpetual present, although
this perpetuity has nothing in common with immutability, or this indivisibility with instantaneity. What we
have is a present which endures.

That is not a hypothesis. It happens in exceptional
cases that the attention suddenly loses the interest it had
in life: immediately, as though by magic, the past once
more becomes present. In people who see the threat of
sudden death unexpectedly before them, in the mountain
climber falling down a precipice, in drowning men, in
men being hanged, it seems that a sharp conversion of

the attention can take place—something like a change
of orientation of the consciousness which, up until then
turned toward the future and absorbed by the necessities of action, suddenly loses all interest in them. That
is enough to call to mind a thousand different "forgotten" details and to unroll the whole history of the person before him in a moving panorama.

Memory therefore has no need of explanation. Or
rather, there is no special faculty whose role is to retain
quantities of past in order to pour it into the present.
The past preserves itself automatically. Of course, if
we shut our eyes to the indivisibility of change, to the
fact that our most distant past adheres to our present and
constitutes with it a single and identical uninterrupted
change, it seems that the past is normally what is abolished and that there is something extraordinary about
the preservation of the past: we think ourselves obliged
to conjure up an apparatus whose function would be to
record the parts of the past capable of reappearing in
our consciousness.

But if we take into consideration the continuity of the
inner life and consequently of its indivisibility, we no
longer have to explain the preservation of the past, but
rather its apparent abolition. We shall no longer have
to account for remembering, but for forgetting. The explanation moreover will be found in the structure of the
brain. Nature has invented a mechanism for canalizing
our attention in the direction of the future, in order to
turn it away from the past—I mean of that part of our
history which does not concern our present actions—
in order to bring to it at most, in the form of "memories," one simplification or another of anterior experience, destined to complete the experience of the moment;
it is in this that the function of the brain consists. We
cannot here undertake the discussion of that theory
which claims that the brain is useful for the preservation
of the past, that it stores up memories like so many
photographic plates from which we afterward develop
proofs, or like so many phonograms destined to become

sounds again. We have examined this thesis elsewhere. This doctrine was largely inspired by a certain metaphysics with which contemporary psychology and psycho-physiology are imbued, and which one accepts naturally: this accounts for its apparent clarity. But as we consider it more closely, we see what difficulties and impossibilities accumulate in it. Let us take the case most favorable to the thesis, that of a material object making an impression on the eye and leaving a visual memory in the mind. What can this memory possibly be, if it is really the result of the fixation in the brain of the impression received by the eye? The slightest movement on the part of the object or the eye and there would be not one image but ten, a hundred, a thousand images, as many and more than on a cinematographic film. Were the object merely considered for a certain time, or seen at various moments, the different images of that object could be counted by millions. And we have taken the simplest example! Let us suppose all those images are stored up; what good will they serve? which one shall we use? Let us grant that we have our reasons for choosing one of them, why, and how, shall we throw it back into the past when we perceive it? But to pass over these difficulties, how shall we explain the diseases of the memory? In those diseases which correspond to local lesions of the brain, that is in the various forms of aphasia, the psychological lesion consists less in an abolition of the memories than in an ability to recall them. An effort, an emotion, can bring suddenly to consciousness words believed definitely lost. These facts, with many others, unite to prove that in such cases the brain's function is to choose from the past, to diminish it, to simplify it, to utilize it, but not to preserve it. We should have no trouble in looking upon things from this angle if we had not acquired the habit of believing that the past is abolished. Then its partial reappearance creates the effect of an extraordinary event which demands an explanation. And that is why we imagine here and there in the brain, memory "pigeon-holes" for preserving frag-

ments of the past—the brain moreover, being self-pre-
serving. As though that were not postponing the difficulty and simply putting off the problem! As though, by
positing that cerebral matter is preserved through time,
or more generally that all matter endures, one did not
attribute to it precisely the memory one claimed to explain by it! Whatever we do, even if we imagine that the
brain stores up memories, we do not escape the conclusion that the past can preserve itself automatically.

This holds not only for our own past, but also for
the past of any change whatsoever, always providing that
it is a question of a single and therefore indivisible
change: the preservation of the past in the present is
nothing else than the indivisibility of change. It is true
that, with regard to the changes which take place outside
of us we almost never know whether we are dealing with
a single change or one composed of several movements
interspersed with stops (the stop never being anything
but relative). We would have to be inside beings and
things as we are inside ourselves before we could express
our opinion on this point. But that is not where the importance lies. It is enough to be convinced once and for
all that reality is change, that change is indivisible, and
that in an indivisible change the past is one with the
present.

Let us imbibe this truth and we shall see a good many
philosophical enigmas melt away and evaporate. Certain great problems such as that of substance, of change,
and of their relation to one another, will no longer arise.
All the difficulties raised around these points—difficulties which caused substance to recede little by little to the
regions of the unknowable—came from the fact that we
shut our eyes to the indivisibility of change. If change,
which is evidently constitutive of all our experience, is
the fleeting thing most philosophers have spoken of, if
we see in it only a multiplicity of states replacing other
states, we are obliged to re-establish the continuity
between these states by an artificial bond; but this immobile substratum of immobility, being incapable of pos-

sessing any of the attributes we know—since all are changes—recedes as we try to approach it: it is as elusive as the phantom of change it was called upon to fix. Let us, on the contrary, endeavor to perceive change as it is in its natural indivisibility: we see that it is the very substance of things, and neither does movement appear to us any longer under the vanishing form which rendered it elusive to thought, nor substance with the immutability which made it inaccessible to our experience. Radical instability and absolute immutability are therefore mere abstract views taken from outside of the continuity of real change, abstractions which the mind then hypostasizes into multiple *states* on the one hand, into *thing* or substance on the other. The difficulties raised by the ancients around the question of movement and by the moderns around the question of substance disappear, the former because movement and change are substantial, the latter because substance is movement and change.

At the same time that theoretical obscurities disappear we get a glimpse of the possible solution of more than one reputedly unsolvable problem. The discussions on the subject of free will would come to an end if we saw ourselves where we are really, in a concrete duration where the idea of necessary determination loses all significance, since in it the past becomes identical with the present and continuously creates with it—if only by the fact of being added to it—something absolutely new. And we could gradually acquire a deeper appreciation of the relation of man to the universe if we took into account the true nature of *states*, of *qualities*, in fact of everything which presents itself to us with the appearance of stability. In such a case the object and the subject should be, with regard to one another, in a situation analogous to that of the two trains we spoke of at the beginning: it is a certain regulating of mobility on mobility which produces the effect of immobility. Let us then become imbued with this idea, let us never lose sight of the particular relation of the object to the subject translated by a static vision of things: everything that experience teaches us of the one will increase the knowledge we had of the other, and the light the latter receives will in turn be able, by reflection, to illuminate the former.

But as I said in the beginning, pure speculation will not be the only thing to benefit by this vision of universal becoming. We shall be able to make it penetrate into our everyday life, and through it, obtain from philosophy satisfactions similar to those we receive from art, but more frequent, more continual and more accessible to the majority of men. Art enables us, no doubt, to discover in things more qualities and more shades than we naturally perceive. It dilates our perception, but on the surface rather than in depth. It enriches our present, but it scarcely enables us to go beyond it. Through philosophy we can accustom ourselves never to isolate the present from the past which it pulls along with it. Thanks to philosophy, all things acquire depth—more than depth, something like a fourth dimension which permits anterior perceptions to remain bound up with present perceptions, and the immediate future itself to become partly outlined in the present. Reality no longer appears then in the static state, in its manner of being; it affirms itself dynamically, in the continuity and variability of its tendency. What was immobile and frozen in our perception is warmed and set in motion. Everything comes to life around us, everything is revivified in us. A great impulse carries beings and things along. We feel ourselves uplifted, carried away, borne along by it. We are more fully alive and this increase of life brings with it the conviction that grave philosophical enigmas can be resolved or even perhaps that they need not be raised, since they arise from a frozen vision of the real and are only the translation, in terms of thought, of a certain artificial weakening of our vitality. In fact, the more we accustom ourselves to think and to perceive all things *sub specie durationis,* the more we plunge into real duration. And the more we immerse ourselves in it, the more we set ourselves back in the direction of the principle, though it be transcendent, in which we participate and whose eternity is not to be an eternity of immutability, but an eternity of life: how, otherwise, could we live and move in it? *In ea vivimus et movemur et sumus.*

VI

INTRODUCTION TO METAPHYSICS

If we compare the various ways of defining meta-physics and of conceiving the absolute, we shall find, despite apparent discrepancies, that philosophers agree in making a deep distinction between two ways of knowing a thing. The first implies going all around it, the second entering into it. The first depends on the viewpoint chosen and the symbols employed, while the second is taken from no viewpoint and rests on no symbol. Of the first kind of knowledge we shall say that it stops at the *relative;* of the second that, wher-ever possible, it attains the *absolute.*

Take, for example, the movement of an object in space. I perceive it differently according to the point of view from which I look at it, whether from that of mo-bility or of immobility. I express it differently, further-more as I relate it to the system of axes or reference points, that is to say, according to the symbols by which I translate it. And I call it *relative* for this double reason: in either case, I place myself outside the object itself. When I speak of an absolute movement, it means that I attribute to the mobile an inner being and, as it were, states of soul; it also means that I am in harmony with these states and enter into them by an effort of imagination. Therefore, according to whether the object is mobile or immobile, whether it adopts one movement or another, I shall not have the same feeling about it. And what I feel will depend neither on the point of view I adopt toward the object, since I am in the object itself, nor on the symbols by which I translate it, since I have renounced all translation in order to possess the original. In short, the movement will not be grasped from without and, as it were, from where I am, but from within, inside it, in what it is in itself. I shall have hold of an absolute.

Or again, take a character whose adventures make up the subject of a novel. The novelist may multiply traits of character, make his hero speak and act as much as he likes: all this has not the same value as the simple and indivisible feeling I should experience if I were to coincide for a single moment with the personage himself. The actions, gestures and words would then appear to flow naturally, as though from their source. They would no longer be accidents making up the idea I had of the character, constantly enriching this idea without ever succeeding in completing it. The character would be given to me all at once in its entirety, and the thousand and one incidents which make it manifest, instead of adding to the idea and enriching it, would, on the contrary, seem to me to fall away from it without in any way exhausting or impoverishing its essence. I get a different point of view regarding the person with every added detail I am given. All the traits which describe it to me, yet which can only enable me to know it by comparisons with persons or things I already know, are signs by which it is more or less symbolically expressed. Symbols and points of view then place me outside it; they give me only what it has in common with others and what does not belong properly to it. But what is properly itself, what constitutes its essence, cannot be perceived from without, being internal by definition, nor be expressed by symbols, being incommensurable with everything else. Description, history and analysis in this case leave me in the relative. Only by coinciding with the person itself would I possess the absolute.

It is in this sense, and in this sense alone, that *absolute* is synonymous with *perfection*. Though all the photographs of a city taken from all possible points of view indefinitely complete one another, they will never equal in value that dimensional object, the city along whose streets one walks. All the translations of a poem in all possible languages may add nuance to nuance and, by a kind of mutual retouching, by correcting one another, may give an increasingly faithful picture of the poem they translate, yet they will never give the inner meaning of the original. A representation taken from a certain point of view, a translation made with certain symbols still remain imperfect in comparison with the object whose picture has been taken or which the symbols seek to express. But the absolute is perfect in that it is perfectly what it is.

It is probably for the same reason that the *absolute* and the *infinite* are often taken as identical. If I wish to explain to someone who does not know Greek the simple impression that a line of Homer leaves upon me, I shall give the translation of the line, then comment on my translation, then I shall develop my commentary, and from explanation to explanation I shall get closer to what I wish to express; but I shall never quite reach it. When you lift your arm you accomplish a movement the simple perception of which you have inwardly; but outwardly, for me, the person who sees it, your arm passes through one point, then through another, and between these two points there will be still other points, so that if I begin to count them, the operation will continue indefinitely. Seen from within, an absolute is then a simple thing; but considered from without, that is to say relative to something else, it becomes, with relation to those signs which express it, the piece of gold for which one can never make up the change. Now what lends itself at the same time to an indivisible apprehension and to an inexhaustible enumeration is, by definition, an infinite.

It follows that an absolute can only be given in an *intuition,* while all the rest has to do with *analysis.* We call intuition here the *sympathy* by which one is transported into the interior of an object in order to coincide with what there is unique and consequently inexpressible in it. Analysis, on the contrary, is the operation which reduces the object to elements already known, that is, common to that object and to others. Analyzing then consists in expressing a thing in terms of what is not it. All analysis is thus a translation, a development into symbols, a representation taken from successive points of view from which are noted a corresponding number of contacts between the new object under consideration and others believed to be already known. In its eternally unsatisfied desire to embrace the object around which it is condemned to turn, analysis multiplies endlessly the points of view in order to complete the ever incomplete representation, varies interminably the symbols with the hope of perfecting the always imperfect translation. It is analysis ad infinitum. But intuition, if it is possible, is a simple act.

This being granted, it would be easy to see that for positive science analysis is its habitual function. It works above all with symbols. Even the most concrete of the sciences of nature, the sciences of life, confine themselves to the visible form of living beings, their organs, their anatomical elements. They compare these forms with one another, reduce the more complex to the more simple, in fact they study the functioning of life in what is, so to speak, its visual symbol. If there exists a means of possessing a reality absolutely, instead of knowing it relatively, of placing oneself within it instead of adopting points of view toward it, of having the intuition of it instead of making the analysis of it, in short, of grasping it over and above all expression, translation or symbolical representation, metaphysics is that very means. *Metaphysics is therefore the science which claims to dispense with symbols.*

* * *

There is at least one reality which we all seize from within, by intuition and not by simple analysis. It is our own person in its flowing through time, the self which endures. With no other thing can we sympathize intellectually, or if you like, spiritually. But one thing is sure: we sympathize with ourselves.

When, with the inner regard of my consciousness, I examine my person in its passivity, like some superficial encrustment, first I perceive all the perceptions which come to it from the material world. These perceptions are clear-cut, distinct, juxtaposed or mutually juxtaposable; they seek to group themselves into objects. Next I perceive memories more or less adherent to these perceptions and which serve to interpret them; these memories are, so to speak, as if detached from the depth of my person and drawn to the periphery by perceptions resembling them; they are fastened on me without being absolutely myself. And finally, I become aware of tendencies, motor habits, a crowd of virtual actions more or less solidly bound to those perceptions and these memories. All these elements with their well-defined forms appear to me to be all the more distinct from myself the more they are distinct from one another. Turned outwards from within, together they constitute the surface of a sphere which tends to expand and loose itself in the external world. But if I pull myself in from the periphery toward the center, if I seek deep down within me what is the most uniformly, the most constantly and durably myself, I find something altogether different.

What I find beneath these clear-cut crystals and this superficial congelation is a continuity of flow comparable to no other flowing I have ever seen. It is a succession of states each one of which announces what follows and contains what precedes. Strictly speaking they do not constitute multiple states until I have already got beyond them, and turn around to observe their trail. While I was experiencing them they were so solidly organized, so profoundly animated with a common life, that I could never have said where any one of them finished or the next one began. In reality, none of them do begin or end; they all dove-tail into one another.

It is, if you like, the unrolling of a spool, for there is no living being who does not feel himself coming little by little to the end of his span; and living consists in growing old. But it is just as much a continual winding, like that of thread into a ball, for our past follows us, becoming larger and larger with the present it picks up on its way; and consciousness means memory.

To tell the truth, it is neither a winding nor an unwinding, for these two images evoke the representation of lines or surfaces whose parts are homogeneous to and superposable on one another. Now, no two moments are identical in a conscious being. Take for example the simplest feeling, suppose it to be constant, absorb the whole personality in it: the consciousness which will accompany this feeling will not be able to remain identical with itself for two consecutive moments, since the following moment always contains, over and above the preceding one, the memory the latter has left it. A consciousness which had two identical moments would be a consciousness without memory. It would therefore die and be re-born continually. How otherwise can unconsciousness be described?

We must therefore evoke a spectrum of a thousand shades, with imperceptible gradations leading from one shade to another. A current of feeling running through the spectrum, becoming tinted with each of these shades in turn, would suffer gradual changes, each of which would announce the following and sum up within itself the preceding ones. Even then the successive shades of the spectrum will always remain external to each other. They are juxtaposed. They occupy space. On the contrary, what is pure duration excludes all idea of juxtaposition, reciprocal exteriority and extension.

Instead, let us imagine an infinitely small piece of elastic, contracted, if that were possible, to a mathematical point. Let us draw it out gradually in such a way as to bring out of the point a line which will grow progressively longer. Let us fix our attention not on the line as line, but on the action which traces it. Let us consider that this action, in spite of its duration, is indivisible if one supposes that it goes on without stopping; that, if we intercalate a stop in it, we make two actions of it instead of one and that each of these actions will then be the indivisible of which we speak; that it is not the moving act itself which is never indivisible, but the motionless line it lays down beneath it like a track in space. Let us take our mind off the space subtending the movement and concentrate solely on the movement itself, on the act of tension or extension, in short, on pure mobility. This time we shall have a more exact image of our development in duration.

And yet that image will still be incomplete, and all comparison furthermore will be inadequate, because the unrolling of our duration in certain aspects resembles the unity of a movement which progresses, in others, a multiplicity of states spreading out, and because no metaphor can express one of the two aspects without sacrificing the other. If I evoke a spectrum of a thousand shades, I have before me a complete thing, whereas duration is the state of completing itself. If I think of an elastic being stretched, of a spring being wound or unwound, I forget the wealth of coloring characteristic of duration as something lived and see only the simple movement by which consciousness goes from one shade to the other. The inner life is all that at once, variety of qualities, continuity of progress, unity of direction. It cannot be represented by images.

But still less could it be represented by *concepts*, that is, by abstract ideas, whether general or simple. Doubtless no image will quite answer to the original feeling I have of the flowing of myself. But neither is it necessary for me to try to express it. To him who is not capable of giving himself the intuition of the duration constitutive of his being, nothing will ever give it, neither concepts nor images. In this regard, the philosopher's sole aim should be to start up a certain effort which the utilitarian habits of mind of everyday life tend, in most men, to discourage. Now the image has at least the advantage of keeping us in the concrete. No image will replace the intuition of duration, but many different images, taken from quite different orders of things, will be able, through the convergence of their action, to direct the consciousness to the precise point where there is a certain intuition to seize on. By choosing images as dissimilar as possible, any one of them will be prevented from usurping the place of the intuition it is instructed to call forth, since it would then be driven out immediately by its rivals. By seeing that in spite of their differences in aspect they all demand of our mind the same kind of attention and, as it were, the same degree of tension, one will gradually accustom the consciousness to a particular and definitely determined disposition, precisely the one it will have to adopt in order to appear unveiled to itself. But even then the consciousness must acquiesce in this effort; for we shall have shown it nothing. We shall simply have placed it in the attitude it must take to produce the desired effort and, by itself, to arrive at the intuition. On the other hand the disadvantage of too simple concepts is that they are really symbols which take the place of the object they symbolize and which do not demand any effort on our part. Upon close examination one would see that each of them retains of the object only what is common to that object and to others. Each of them is seen to express, even more than does the image, a *comparison* between the object and those objects resembling it. But as the comparison has brought out a resemblance, and as the resemblance is a property of the object, and as a property seems very much as though it were a *part* of the object possessing it, we are easily persuaded that by juxtaposing concepts to concepts we shall recompose the whole of the object with its parts and obtain from it, so to speak, an intellectual equivalent. We shall in this way think we are forming a faithful representation of duration by lining up the concepts of unity, multiplicity, continuity, finite or infinite divisibility, etc. That is precisely the illusion. And that, also, is the danger. In so far as abstract ideas can render service to analysis, that is, to a scientific study of the object in its relations with all others, to that very extent are they incapable of replacing intuition, that is to say, the metaphysical investigation of the object in what essentially belongs to it. On the one hand, indeed, these concepts placed end to end will never give us anything more than an artificial recomposition of the object of which they can symbolize only certain general and, as it were, impersonal aspects: therefore it is vain to believe that through them one can grasp a reality when all they present is its shadow. But on the other hand, alongside the illusion, there is also a very grave danger. For the concept generalizes at the same time that it abstracts. The concept can symbolize a particular property only by making it common to an infinity of things. Therefore it always more or less distorts this property by the extension it gives to it. A property put back into the metaphysical object to which it belongs coincides with the object, at least molds itself on it, adopting the same contours. Extracted from the metaphysical object and represented in a concept, it extends itself indefinitely, surpassing the object since it must henceforth contain it along with others. The various concepts we form of the properties of a thing are so many much larger circles drawn round it, not one of which fits it exactly. And yet, in the thing itself, the properties coincided with it and therefore with each other. We have no alternative then but to resort to some artifice in order to re-establish the coincidence. We shall take any one of these concepts and with it try to rejoin the others. But the junction will be brought about in a different way, depending upon the concept we start from. According to whether we start, for example, from unity or from multiplicity, we shall form a different conception of the multiple unity of duration. Everything will depend on the weight we assign to this or that concept, and this weight will always be arbitrary, since the concept, extracted from the object, has no weight, being nothing more than the shadow of a body.

Thus a multiplicity of different *systems* will arise, as many systems as there are external viewpoints on the reality one is examining or as there are larger circles in which to enclose it. The simple concepts, therefore, not only have the disadvantage of dividing the concrete unity of the object into so many symbolical expressions; they also divide philosophy into distinct schools, each of which reserves its place, chooses its chips, and begins with the others a game that will never end. Either metaphysics is only this game of ideas, or else, if it is a serious occupation of the mind, it must transcend concepts to arrive at intuition. To be sure, concepts are indispensable to it, for all the other sciences ordinarily work with concepts, and metaphysics cannot get along without the other sciences. But it is strictly itself only when it goes beyond the concept, or at least when it frees itself of the inflexible and ready-made concepts and creates others very different from those we usually handle, I mean flexible, mobile, almost fluid representations, always ready to mold themselves on the fleeting forms of intuition. I shall come back to this important point a little later. It is enough for us to have shown that our duration can be presented to us directly in an intuition, that it can be suggested indirectly to us by images, but that it cannot—if we give to the word *concept* its proper meaning—be enclosed in a conceptual representation.

Let us for an instant try to break it up into parts. We must add that the terms of these parts, instead of being distinguished like those of any multiplicity, encroach upon one another; that we can, no doubt, by an effort of imagination, solidify this duration once it has passed by, divide it into pieces set side by side and count all the pieces; but that this operation is achieved on the fixed memory of the duration, on the immobile track the mobility of the duration leaves behind it, not on the duration itself. Let us therefore admit that, if there is a multiplicity here, this multiplicity resembles no other. Shall we say then that this duration has unity? Undoubtedly a continuity of elements prolonged into one another partakes of unity as much as it does of multiplicity, but this moving, changing, colored and living unity scarcely resembles the abstract unity, empty and motionless, which the concept of pure unity circumscribes. Are we to conclude from this that duration must be defined by both unity and multiplicity at the same time? But curiously enough, no matter how I manipulate the two concepts, apportion them, combine them in various ways, practice on them the most delicate operations of mental chemistry, I shall never obtain anything which resembles the simple intuition I have of duration; instead of which, if I place myself back in duration by an effort of intuition, I perceive immediately how it is unity, multiplicity and many other things besides. These various concepts were therefore just so many external points of view on duration. Neither separated nor reunited have they made us penetrate duration itself.

We penetrate it, nevertheless, and the only way possible is by an intuition. In this sense, an absolute internal knowledge of the duration of the self by the self is possible. But if metaphysics demands and can obtain here an intuition, science has no less need of an analysis. And it is because of a confusion between the roles of analysis and intuition that the dissensions between schools of thought and the conflicts between systems will arise.

Psychology, in fact, like the other sciences, proceeds by analysis. It resolves the self, first given to it in the form of a simple intuition, into sensations, feelings, images, etc. which it studies separately. It therefore substitutes for the self a series of elements which are the psychological facts. But these *elements,* are they *parts?* That is the whole question, and it is because we have evaded it that we have often stated in insoluble terms the problem of the human personality.

It is undeniable that any psychological state, by the sole fact that it belongs to a person, reflects the whole of a personality. There is no feeling, no matter how simple, which does not virtually contain the past and present of the being which experiences it, which can be separated from it and constitute a "state," other than by an effort of abstraction or analysis. But it is no less undeniable that without this effort of abstraction or analysis there would be no possible development of psychological science. Now, of what does the operation consist by which the psychologist detaches a psychological state in order to set it up as a more or less independent entity? He begins by disregarding the person's special coloration, which can be expressed only in common and known terms. He then strives to isolate, in the person thus already simplified, this or that aspect which lends itself to an interesting study. If, for example, it is a question of inclination, he will leave out of account the inexpressible shading which colors it and which brings it about that my inclination is not yours; he will then fix his attention on the movement by which our personality tends towards a certain object; he will isolate this attitude, and it is this special aspect of the person, this point of view on the mobility of the inner life, this "schema" of the concrete inclination which he will set up as an independent fact. In this there is a work analogous to that of an artist who, on a visit to Paris, would, for example, make a sketch of a tower of Notre Dame. The tower is an inseparable part of the edifice, which is no less inseparably a part of the soil, the surroundings, the whole of Paris, etc. He must begin by detaching it; he will focus only on a certain aspect of the whole, and that aspect is this tower of Notre Dame. Now the tower is in reality constituted of stones whose particular grouping is what gives it its form; but the sketcher is not interested in the stones, he only notices the silhouette of the tower. He substitutes for the real and internal organization of the thing an external and schematic reconstitution. So that his design corresponds, in short, to a certain point of view of the object and to the choice of a certain mode of representation. Now the same holds for the operation by which the psychologist extracts a psychological state from the whole person. This isolated psychological state is scarcely more than a sketch, the beginning of an artificial re-composition; it is the whole envisaged under a certain elementary aspect in which one has become especially interested and which one has taken care to note. It is not a part, but an element. It has not been obtained by fragmentation, but by analysis.

Now at the bottom of all the sketches made in Paris the stranger will probably write "Paris" by way of reminder. And as he has really seen Paris, he will be able, by descending from the original intuition of the whole, to place his sketches in it and thus arrange them in relation to one another. But there is no way of per-forming the opposite operation; even with an infinity of sketches as exact as you like, even with the word "Paris" to indicate that they must bear close connection, it is impossible to travel back to an intuition one has not had, and gain the impression of Paris if one has never seen Paris. The point is that we are not dealing here with parts of the whole, but with *notes* taken on the thing as a whole. To choose a more striking example, where the notation is more completely symbolical, let us sup-pose someone puts before me, all jumbled together, the letters which go to make up a poem, without my know-ing which poem it is. If the letters were *parts* of the poem, I could attempt to reconstruct it with them by trying various possible arrangements, as a child does with the pieces of a jigsaw puzzle. But I shall not for an instant think of attempting it, because the letters are not *component parts,* but *partial expressions,* which is quite another thing. That is why, if I know the poem, I put each one of the letters in its proper place and link them together without difficulty in one continuous chain, while the reverse operation is impossible. Even when I take into my head to try that reverse operation, even when I place the letters end to end, I begin by imagining a plausible meaning: I thus give myself an intuition, and it is from the intuition that I try to fall back on the elementary symbols which would re-create its expression. The very notion of reconstructing the thing by carrying out operations on symbolical elements alone implies such an absurdity that it would never occur to anyone if it were realized that he was not dealing with fragments of the thing, but in some sort with fragments of symbol.

That, however, is what philosophers undertake to do when they seek to recompose the person with psychological states, whether they confine themselves to these states or whether they add a thread for the purpose of tying the states to one another. Empiricists and rationalists alike are in this case dupes of the same illusion. Both take the *partial notions* for *real parts,* thus confusing the point of view of analysis and that of intuition, science and metaphysics.

The empiricists are right in saying that psychological analysis does not uncover in the person anything more than psychological states. And such is in fact the function, such is the very definition of analysis. The psychologist has nothing else to do but analyze the person, that is, take note of the states: at most he will place the rubic "Ego" on these states in saying that they are "states of ego," as the sketcher writes the word "Paris" on each of his sketches. Within the sphere in which the psychologist places himself and where he should place himself, the "Ego" is only a sign by which one recalls the primitive intuition (a very vague one at that) which furnished psychology with its object: it is only a word, and the great mistake is to think that one could, by staying in the same sphere, find a thing behind the word. That has been the mistake of those philosophers who have not been able to resign themselves to being simply psychologists in psychology, Taine and Stuart Mill, for example. Psychologists by the method they apply, they have remained metaphysicians by the object they have in view. Looking for an intuition, through a strange inconsistency they seek to get this intuition from its very negation, analysis. They are seeking the self (le moi), and claim to find it in the psychological states, even though it has been possible to obtain that diversity of psychological states only by transporting oneself outside of the self and taking a series of sketches of the person, a series of notes, of more or less schematic and symbolic representations. And so although they place states side by side with states, multiply their contacts, explore their intervening spaces, the self always escapes them, so that in the end they see nothing more in it than an empty phantom. One might just as well deny that the *Iliad* has a meaning, on the plea that one has looked in vain for this meaning in the spaces between the letters which go to make it up.

Philosophical empiricism, then, is here born of a confusion between the point of view of intuition and that of analysis. It consists in seeking the original in the translation where it naturally cannot be, and in denying the original on the plea that one does not find it in the translation. It necessarily ends in negations; but looking at it more closely, one perceives that these negations signify simply that analysis is not intuition, and this is self-evident. From the original and furthermore vague intuition which furnishes science with its object, science passes immediately to analysis, which multiplies indefinitely the points of view of that object. It is quickly persuaded that, by putting all the points of view together, it could reconstitute the object. Is it any wonder that, like the child who seeks to make a solid plaything of the shadows silhouetted along the wall, it too sees the object fleeing before it?

But rationalism is the dupe of the same illusion. It starts from the confusion empiricism made, and remains as powerless to reach the personality. Like empiricism, it takes the psychological states to be so many *fragments,* detached from an ego which supposedly holds them together. Like empiricism, it tries to bind these fragments to one another in order to reconstitute the unity of the person. Like empiricism, in short, it sees the unity of the person elude its grasp like a phantom each time it tries to lay hold of it. But while empiricism, tired of the struggle, in the end declares that there is nothing else than the multiplicity of psychological states, rationalism persists in affirming the unity of the person. It is true that, seeking this unity in the psychological states all the qualities or determinations it finds by analysis (since analysis, by definition, always ends in states), it is true that it has nothing left for the unity of the person but something purely negative, the absence of all determination. The psychological states having necessarily taken and kept for themselves in this analysis all that gives the slightest appearance of materiality, the "unity of the self" can be nothing more than a form without matter. It will be the absolute indeterminate and the absolute void. To the detached psychological states, to those shadows of the self the totality of which was, for the empiricists, the equivalent of the person, rationalism, to reconstitute the personality, adds something still more unreal, the vacuum in which these shadows move, one might say, the *locus* of the shadows. How could that "form," which is really formless, characterize a living, acting, concrete personality and distinguish Peter from Paul? Is it surprising that the philosophers who have isolated this "form" of the personality then find it powerless to determine a person, and that they are led by degrees to make of their empty Ego a bottomless receptacle which no more belongs to Paul than to Peter, and in which there will be place, as one sees fit, for the whole of humanity, or for God, or for existence in general? I see here between empiricism and rationalism this sole difference, that the first, seeking the unity of the self in the interstices, so to speak, of psychological states, is led to fill up these crannies with other states, and so on indefinitely, so that the self, confined in an interval which is continually contracting, tends towards Zero the further one pushes analysis; while rationalism, making the self the place where the states are lodged, is in the presence of an empty space that one has no more reason to limit here rather than there, which goes beyond each one of the succeeding limits we undertake to assign to it, which goes on expanding and tends to be lost, not in Zero this time, but in the Infinite.

Considerably less than is supposed, therefore, is the distance between a so-called "empiricism" like Taine's and the most transcendent speculations of certain German Pantheists. The method is analogous in the two cases: it consists in reasoning on the *elements* of the translation as though they were parts of the original. But a true empiricism is the one which purposes to keep as close to the original itself as possible, to probe more deeply into its life, and by a kind of spiritual *auscultation*, to feel its soul palpitate; and this true empiricism is the real metaphysics. The work is one of extreme difficulty, because not one of the ready-made conceptions that thought uses for its daily operations can be of any use here. Nothing is easier than to say that the ego is multiplicity, or that it is unity, or that it is the synthesis of both! Here unity and multiplicity are representations one need not cut according to the object, that one finds already made and that one has only to choose from the pile—ready-made garments which will suit Peter as well as Paul because they do not show off the figure of either of them. But an empiricism worthy of the name, an empiricism which works only according to measure, sees itself obliged to make an absolutely new effort for each new object it studies. It cuts for the object a concept appropriate to the object alone, a concept one can barely say is still a concept, since it applies only to that one thing. This empiricism does not proceed by combining ideas one already finds in stock, unity and multiplicity, for example; but the representation to which it leads us is, on the contrary, a simple, unique representation; and once it is formed one readily understands why it can be put into the frames unity, multiplicity, etc., all of which are much larger than itself. Finally, philosophy thus defined does not consist in choosing between concepts and taking sides with one school, but in seeking a unique intuition from which one can just as easily come down again to the various concepts, because one has placed oneself above the divisions of the schools.

That the personality has unity is certain; but such an affirmation does not teach me anything about the extraordinary nature of this unity which is the person. That our self is multiple I further agree, but there is in it a multiplicity which, it must be recognized, has nothing in common with any other. What really matters to philosophy is to know *what* unity, *what* multiplicity, *what* reality superior to the abstract one and the abstract multiple is the multiple unity of the person. And it will know this only if it once again grasps the simple intuition of the self by the self. Then, according to the slope it chooses to come down from the summit, it will arrive at unity or multiplicity or any one of the concepts by which we try to define the moving life of the person. But no mixing of these concepts among themselves, I repeat, would give anything resembling the person which endures.

If you put a solid cone before me, I see without difficulty how it narrows toward the peak and tends to become a mathematical point, how it also grows larger at its base into an indefinitely increasing circle. But neither the point nor the circle nor the juxtaposition of the two on a plane will give me the slightest idea of a cone. It is the same for the multiplicity and unity of the psychological life; the same for the Zero and the Infinite towards which empiricism and rationalism direct the personality.

These concepts, as we shall show elsewhere, ordinarily go by pairs and represent the two opposites. There is scarcely any concrete reality upon which one cannot take two opposing views at the same time and which is consequently not subsumed under the two antagonistic concepts. Hence a thesis and an antithesis that it would be vain for us to try logically to reconcile, for the simple reason that never, with concepts or points of view, will you make a thing. But from the object, seized by intuition, one passes without difficulty in a good many cases to the two contrary concepts, and because thesis and antithesis are seen to emerge from the reality, one grasps at the same time how this thesis and antithesis are opposed and how they are reconciled.

It is true that in order to do that one must institute a reversal of the habitual work of the intelligence. To think consists ordinarily in going from concepts to things, and not from things to concepts. To know a reality in the ordinary meaning of the word "to know," is to take ready-made concepts, apportion them, and combine them until one obtains a practical equivalent of the real. But it must not be forgotten that the normal work of the intelligence is far from being a disinterested work. We do not, in general, aim at knowing for the sake of knowing, but at knowing in order to take a stand, gain a profit, in fact to satisfy an interest. We try to find out up to what point the object to be known is *this* or *that,* into what known genus it fits, what kind of action, step or attitude it should suggest to us. These various possible actions and attitudes are so many *conceptual directions* of our thought, determined once and for all; nothing remains but for us to follow them; precisely in that consists the application of concepts to things. To try a concept on an object is to ask of the object what we have to do with it, what it can do for us. To label an object with a concept is to tell in precise terms the kind of action or attitude the object is to suggest to us. All knowledge properly so-called is, therefore, turned in a certain direction or taken from a certain point of view. It is true that our interest is often complex. And that is why we sometimes manage to turn our knowledge of the same object in several successive directions and to cause view-points concerning it to vary. This is what, in the ordinary meaning of these terms, a "wide" and "comprehensive" knowledge of the object consists in: the object, then, is led back, not to a unique concept, but to several concepts in which it is deemed to "participate." How it is to participate in all these concepts at once is a question of no practical importance and one that need not be asked. It is, therefore, natural and legitimate that we proceed by juxtaposition and apportioning of concepts in every-day life: no philosophical difficulties will be born of this since, by tacit consent, we shall abstain from philosophizing. But to transfer this *modus operandi* to philosophy, to go—here again—from concepts to the thing, to employ for the disinterested knowledge of an object one now aims at attaining in itself, a manner of knowing inspired by a definite interest and consisting by definition in a view taken of the object externally, is to turn one's back on the goal at which one was aiming; it is to condemn philosophy to an eternal friction between the schools and set up a contradiction in the very heart of the object and the method. Either there is no philosophy possible and all knowledge of things is a practical knowledge turned to the profit to be gained from them, or philosophizing consists in placing oneself within the object itself by an effort of intuition.

But in order to comprehend the nature of this intuition, to determine precisely where intuition ends and analysis begins, we must return to what was said above concerning the flow of duration.

It is to be observed that the concepts or schemas, to which analysis leads, have the essential characteristic of being immobile while under consideration. I have isolated from the whole of the inner life that psychological entity which I call a simple sensation. So long as I study it I suppose it to remain what it is. If I were to find some change in it, I should say that it was not a single sensation, but several successive sensations; and it is to each one of the succeeding sensations that I should then transfer the immutability at first attributed to the whole sensation. In any case I shall, by carrying analysis far enough, be able to arrive at elements I shall hold to be immovable. It is there, and there only, that I shall find the solid base of operations which science needs for its proper development.

There is no mood, however, no matter how simple, which does not change at every instant, since there is no consciousness without memory, no continuation of a state without the addition, to the present feeling, of the memory of past moments. That is what duration consists of. Inner duration is the continuous life of a memory which prolongs the past into the present, whether the present distinctly contains the ever-growing image of the past, or whether, by its continual changing of quality, it attests rather the increasingly heavy burden dragged along behind one the older one grows. Without that survival of the past in the present there would be no duration but only instantaneity.

It is true that if I am criticized for abstracting the psychological state from duration by the mere fact of analyzing it, I shall defend myself against the charge by saying that each of these elementary psychological states to which my analysis leads is a state which still occupies time. "My analysis," I shall say, "easily resolves the inner life into states each of which is homogeneous to itself; only, since the homogeneity spreads out over a definite number of minutes or seconds, the elementary psychological state does not cease to have duration, though it does not change."

But who does not see that the definite number of minutes and seconds I attribute to the elementary psychological state, has no more than the value of an indication meant to remind me that the psychological state, supposedly homogeneous, is in reality a state which changes and endures? The state, taken in itself, is a perpetual becoming. I have extracted from this becoming a certain mean of quality which I have supposed invariable: I have thus constituted a state which is stable, and by that very fact, schematic. Again, I have extracted becoming in general, the becoming that would no more be the becoming of this than of that, and this is what I have called the *time* this state occupies. Were I to examine it closely, I should see that this abstract time is as immobile for me as the state I localize in it, that it could flow only by a continual changing of quality and that, if it is without quality, a simple theater of change, it thus becomes an immobile milieu. I should see that the hypothesis of this homogeneous time is simply meant to facilitate the comparison between the various concrete durations, to permit us to count simultaneities and to measure one flowing of duration in relation to another. And finally, I should understand that in fastening to the representation of an elementary psychological state the indication of a definite number of minutes and seconds, I am merely recalling that the state has been detached from an ego which endures, and demarcating the place where it would have to be set in motion again in order to bring it, from the simple schema it has become, back to the concrete form it had at first. But I forget all that, having no use for it in analysis.

That is to say, analysis operates on immobility, while intuition is located in mobility or, what amounts to the same thing, in duration. That is the very clear line of demarcation between intuition and analysis. One recognizes the real, the actual, the concrete, by the fact that it is variability itself. One recognizes the element by the fact that it is invariable. And it is invariable by definition, being a schema, a simplified reconstruction, often a mere symbol, in any case, a view taken of the reality that flows.

But the mistake is to believe that with these schemas one could recompose the real. It cannot be too often repeated: from intuition one can pass on to analysis, but not from analysis to intuition.

With variability I shall make as many variations, as many qualities or modifications as I like because they are so many immobile views taken by analysis of the mobility given to intuition. But these modifications placed end to end will not produce anything resembling variability, because they were not parts of it but elements which is quite another thing.

Let us consider, for example, the variability nearest to homogeneity, movement in space. For the whole length of this movement I can imagine possible halts: they are what I call the positions of the mobile or the points through which the mobile passes. But with the positions, were they infinite in number, I shall not make movement. They are not parts of the movement; they are so many views taken of it; they are, we say, only halt suppositions. Never is the mobile really in any of these points; the most one can say is that it passes through them. But the passing, which is a movement, has nothing in common with a halt, which is immobility. A movement could not alight on an immobility for it would then coincide with it, which would be contradictory. The points are not *in* the movement as parts, nor even *under* the movement as places of the mobile. They are simply projected by us beneath the movement like so many places where, if it should stop, would be a mobile which by hypothesis does not stop. They are not, therefore, properly speaking, positions, but suppositions, views or mental viewpoints. How, with these points of view, could one construct a thing?

That, nevertheless, is what we try to do every time we reason about movement and also about time for which movement serves as representation. By an illusion deeply rooted in our mind, and because we cannot keep from considering analysis as equivalent to intuition, we begin by distinguishing, for the whole length of the movement, a certain number of possible halts or points which, willy-nilly, we make parts of the movement. Faced with our inability to recompose movement with these points we intercalate other points, in the belief that we are thus keeping closer to what mobility there is in movement. Then, as the mobility still escapes us, we substitute for a finite and definite number of points a number "infinitely increasing,"—trying thus, but vainly, through the movement of our thought, which indefinitely pursues the addition of points to points, to counterfeit the real and undivided movement of the mobile. Finally, we say that movement is made up of points, but that it comprises in addition the obscure, mysterious passing from one position to the next. As though the obscurity did not come wholly from the fact that we have assumed immobility to be clearer from mobility, the halt to precede movement! As though the mystery was not due to the fact that we claim to go from halts to movement by way of composition which is impossible, whereas we pass easily from movement to slowing down and to immobility! You have sought the meaning of a poem in the form of the letters which make it up, you have thought that in considering an increasing number of letters you would finally embrace the constantly fleeting meaning, and as a last resource, seeing that it was no use to seek a part of the meaning in each letter, you have assumed that between each letter and the one following was lodged the missing fragment of the mysterious meaning! But the letters, once more, are not parts of the thing, they are the elements of the symbol. The positions of the mobile are not parts of the movement: they are points of the space which is thought to subtend the movement. This empty and immobile space, simply *con*ceived, never *per*ceived, has exactly the value of a symbol. By manipulating symbols, how are you going to manufacture reality?

But in this case the symbol meets the demands of our most inveterate habits of thought. We install ourselves ordinarily in immobility, where we find a basis for practice, and with it we claim to recompose mobility. We obtain thus only a clumsy imitation, a counterfeit of real movement, but this imitation is of much greater use to us in life than the intuition of the thing itself would be. Now our mind has an irresistible tendency to consider the idea it most frequently uses to be the clearest. That is why immobility seems clearer to it than mobility, the halt preceding movement.

This explains the difficulties raised by the problem of movement from earliest antiquity. They are due to the fact that we claim to go from space to movement, from the trajectory to the flight, from immobile positions to mobility, and pass from one to the other by way of composition. But it is movement which precedes immobility, and between positions and a displacement there is not the relation of parts to the whole, but that of the diversity of possible viewpoints to the real indivisibility of the object.

Many other problems are born of the same illusion. What the immobile points are to the movement of a mobile, so are the concepts of various qualities to the qualitative change of an object. The different concepts into which a variation is resolved are therefore so many stable visions of the instability of the real. And to think an object, in the usual sense of the word "think," is to take one or several of these immobile views of its mobility. It is, in short, to ask oneself from time to time just where it is, in order to know what to do with it. Nothing is more legitimate than this method of procedure, as long as it is only a question of practical knowledge of reality. Knowledge, in so far as it is directed toward the practical, has only to enumerate the possible principal attitudes of the thing in relation to us, as also our best possible attitudes in respect to it. That is the ordinary role of ready-made concepts, those stations with which we mark out the passage of the becoming. But to desire, with them, to penetrate to the innermost nature of things, is to apply to the mobility of the real a method designed to give of it immobile points of view. It is to forget that if metaphysics is possible, it can only be an effort to re-ascend the slope natural to the work of thought, to place oneself immediately, through a dilation of the mind, in the thing one is studying, in short, to go from reality to concepts and not from concepts to reality. Is it surprising that philosophers so often see the object they claim to embrace recede from them, like children trying to catch smoke by closing their fists? A good many quarrels are thus perpetuated between the schools, in which each one accuses the others of having let the real escape them.

But if metaphysics is to proceed by intuition, if intuition has as its object the mobility of duration, and if duration is psychological in essence, are we not going to shut the philosopher up in exclusive self-contemplation? Will not philosophy consist simply in watching oneself live, "as a dozing shepherd watches the running water"? To speak in this fashion would be to return to the error I have not ceased to emphasize from the very beginning of this study. It would be to fail to recognize the particular nature of duration and at the same time the essentially active character of metaphysical intuition. It would be to fail to see that only the method of which we are speaking allows one to pass beyond idealism as well as realism, to affirm the existence of objects both inferior and superior to us, though nevertheless in a certain sense inferior to us, to make them coexistent without difficulty, and progressively to dispel the obscurities that analysis accumulates around great problems. Without taking up the study of these different points here, let us confine ourselves to showing how the intuition we are discussing is not a single act but an indefinite series of acts, all doubtless of the same genus but each one of a very particular species, and how this variety of acts corresponds to the degrees of being.

If I try to *analyze* duration, that is, to resolve it into ready-made concepts, I am certainly obliged by the very nature of the concept and the analysis, to take two opposing views of *duration in general,* views with which I shall then claim to recompose it. This combination can present neither a diversity of degrees nor a variety of forms: it is or it is not. I shall say, for example, that there is, on the one hand, a *multiplicity* of successive states of consciousness and, on the other hand, a *unity* which binds them together. Duration will be the "synthesis" of this unity and multiplicity, but how this mys-

terious operation can admit of shades or degrees—I repeat—is not quite clear. In this hypothesis there is,
there can only be, a single duration, that in which our
consciousness habitually operates. To make certain of
what we mean, if we take duration under the simple aspect of a movement being accomplished in space and if
we try to reduce to concepts movement considered as representative of time, we shall have on the one hand any
desired number of points of the trajectory, and on the
other hand an abstract unity joining them, like a thread
holding together the beads of a necklace. Between this
abstract multiplicity and this abstract unity their combination, once assumed to be possible, is some strange
thing in which we shall find no more shadings than the
addition of given numbers in arithmetic would allow.
But if, instead of claiming to analyze duration (that
is, in reality, to make a synthesis of it with concepts),
one first installs oneself in it by an effort of intuition, one
has the feeling of a certain well-defined *tension,* whose
very definiteness seems like a choice between an infinity
of possible durations. This being so one perceives any
number of durations, all very different from one another, even though each one of them, reduced to concepts, that is to say, considered externally from two
opposite points of view, is always brought back to the
indefinable combination of the multiple and the one.

Let us express the same idea more precisely. If I
consider duration as a multiplicity of moments bound to
one another by a unity which runs through them like
a thread, these moments, no matter how short the
chosen duration, are unlimited in number. I can imagine
them as close together as I like; there will always be,
between these mathematical points, other mathematical points, and so on, ad infinitum. Considered from
the standpoint of multiplicity, duration will therefore
disappear in a dust of moments not one of which has
duration, each one being instantaneous. If on the other
hand I consider the unity binding the moments together,

it is evident that it cannot have duration either since, by hypothesis, everything that is changing and really durable in duration has been put to the account of the multiplicity of the moments. This unity, as I examine its essence, will then appear to me as an immobile substratum of the moving reality, like some intemporal essence of time: that is what I shall call eternity—the eternity of death, since it is nothing else than movement emptied of the mobility which made up its life. Examining closely the opinions of the schools antagonistic to the subject of duration, one would see that they differ simply in attributing to one or the other of these two concepts a capital importance. Certain of them are drawn to the point of view of the multiple; they set up as concrete reality the distance moments of a time which they have, so to speak, pulverized; they consider as being far more artificial the unity which makes a powder of these grains. The others, on the contrary, set up the unity of duration as concrete reality. They place themselves in the eternal. But as their eternity nevertheless remains abstract, being empty, as it is the eternity of a concept which by hypothesis excludes the opposite concept, one cannot see how this eternity could allow an indefinite multiplicity of moments to co-exist with it. In the first hypothesis one has a world suspended in mid-air which would have to end and begin again by itself each instant. In the second, one has an infinitely abstract eternity of which one can say that it is especially difficult to understand why it does not remain enveloped in itself and how it allows things to co-exist with it. But in either case, and no matter which one of the two metaphysics is chosen, time appears from the psychological point of view as a mixture of two abstractions neither one of which admits of either degrees or shadings. In either system, there is only a single duration which carries everything along with it, a river without bottom and without banks and flowing without assignable forces in a direction one cannot define. Even then it is a river and the river flows only because reality obtains this sacrifice from the two doctrines, taking advantage of an inadvertence in their logic. As soon as they regain possession of themselves, they congeal this flowing either into an immense solid sheet, or into an infinity of crystallized needles, but always in a *thing* which necessarily participates in the immobility of a *point of view.*

It is altogether different if one places oneself directly, by an effort of intuition, in the concrete flowing of duration. To be sure, we shall find no logical reason for positing multiple and diverse durations. Strictly speaking, there might exist no other duration than our own, as there might be no other color in the world than orange, for example. But just as a consciousness of color, which would harmonize inwardly with orange instead of perceiving it outwardly, would feel itself caught between red and yellow, would perhaps even have, beneath the latter color, a presentiment of a whole spectrum in which is naturally prolonged the continuity which goes from red to yellow, so the intuition of our duration, far from leaving us suspended in the void as pure analysis would do, puts us in contact with a whole continuity of durations which we should try to follow either downwardly or upwardly: in both cases we can dilate ourselves indefinitely by a more and more vigorous effort, in both cases transcend ourselves. In the first case, we advance toward a duration more and more scattered, whose palpitations, more rapid than ours, dividing our simple sensation, dilute its quality into quantity: at the limit would be the pure homogeneous, the pure *repetition* by which we shall define materiality. In advancing in the other direction, we go toward a duration which stretches, tightens, and becomes more and more intensified: at the limit would be eternity. This time not only conceptual eternity, which is an eternity of death, but an eternity of life. It would be a living and consequently still moving eternity where our own duration would find itself like the vibrations in light, and which would be the concretion of all duration as materiality is its dispersion. Between these two extreme limits moves intuition, and this movement is metaphysics itself.

*   *   *

We cannot stop here to outline the various stages of this movement. But after having presented a general view of the method and made a first application of it, it will perhaps be not without point to formulate in as precise terms as possible the principles upon which it rests. Of the propositions I am about to set forth, most have received in the present work a beginning of proof. I hope to demonstrate them more completely when we attack other problems.

I. *There is an external reality which is given immediately to our mind.* Common sense is right on this point against the idealism and realism of the philosophers.

II. This reality is mobility. There do not exist *things* made, but only things in the making, not *states* that remain fixed, but only states in process of change. Rest is never anything but apparent, or rather, relative. The consciousness we have of our own person in its continual flowing, introduces us to the interior of a reality on whose model we must imagine the others. *All reality is, therefore, tendency, if we agree to call tendency a nascent change of direction.*

III. Our mind, which seeks solid bases of operation, (point d'aper çu) has as its principal function, in the ordinary course of life, to imagine *states* and *things*. Now and then it takes quasi-instantaneous views of the undivided mobility of the real. It thus obtains *sensations* and *ideas*. By that means it substitutes for the continuous the discontinuous, for mobility stability, for the tendency in process of change it substitutes fixed points which mark a direction of change and tendency. This substitution is necessary to common sense, to language, to practical life, and even, to a certain extent which we shall try to determine, to positive science. *Our intelli-*

*gence, when it follows its natural inclination, proceeds by
solid perceptions on the one hand, and by stable conceptions on the other.* It starts from the immobile and conceives and expresses movement only in terms of immobility. It places itself in ready-made concepts and tries
to catch in them, as in a net, something of the passing
reality. It does not do so in order to obtain an internal
and metaphysical knowledge of the real. It is simply to
make use of them, each concept (like each sensation)
being a *practical question* which our activity asks of
reality and to which reality will answer, as is proper
in things, by a yes or a no. But in so doing it allows what
is the very essence of the real to escape.

IV. The difficulties inherent in metaphysics, the antinomies it raises, the contradictions into which it falls,
the division into opposing schools and the irreducible oppositions between systems, are due in large part to the
fact that we apply to the disinterested knowledge of the
real the procedures we use currently with practical utility as the aim. They are due principally to the fact that
we place ourselves in the immobile to watch for the moving reality as it passes instead of putting ourselves back
into the moving reality to traverse with it the immobile
positions. They come from the fact that we claim to reconstitute reality, which is tendency and consequently
mobility, with the percepts and concepts which have as
their function to immobilize it. One will never create
mobility with halts, however numerous: if one begins
with mobility, one can draw from it through thought as
many halts as one wishes. In other words, *it is understood that fixed concepts can be extracted by our thought
from the mobile reality; but there is no means whatever
of reconstituting with the fixity of concepts the mobility
of the real.* Dogmatism, as the constructor of systems, has
nevertheless always attempted this reconstitution.

V. It was bound to fail. This is the impotence, and
this alone, pointed out by the skeptical, idealistic and
critical doctrines, all those doctrines, in fact, which question our mind's ability to attain the absolute. But it does

not follow from the fact that we fail to reconstitute living reality with concepts that are rigid and ready-made, that we could not grasp it in any other manner. *The demonstrations which have been given of the relativity of our knowledge are therefore tainted with an original vice: they assume, like the dogmatism they attack, that all knowledge must necessarily start from rigidly defined concepts in order to grasp by their means the flowing reality.*

VI. But the truth is that our mind is able to follow the reverse procedure. It can be installed in the mobile reality, adopt its ceaselessly changing direction, in short, grasp it intuitively. But to do that, it must do itself violence, reverse the direction of the operation by which it ordinarily thinks, continually upsetting its categories, or rather, recasting them. In so doing it will arrrive at fluid concepts, capable of following reality in all its windings and of adopting the very movement of the inner life of things. Only in that way will a progressive philosophy be constituted, freed from the disputes which arise between the schools, capable of resolving problems naturally because it will be rid of the artificial terms chosen in stating them. *To philosophize means to reverse the normal direction of the workings of thought.*

VII. This reversal has never been practiced in a methodical manner; but a careful study of the history of human thought would show that to it we owe the greatest accomplishments in the sciences, as well as whatever living quality there is in metaphysics. The most powerful method of investigation known to the mind, infinitesimal calculus, was born of that very reversal. Modern mathematics is precisely an effort to substitute for the *ready-made* what is in process of *becoming,* to follow the growth of magnitudes, to seize movement no longer from outside and in its manifest result, but from within and in its tendency towards change, in short, to adopt the mobile continuity of the pattern of things. It is true that it contents itself with the pattern, being but the science of magnitudes. It is also true that it has been able to realize these marvelous applications only through the invention of certain symbols, and that, if the intuition we have just mentioned is at the origin of the invention, it is the symbol alone which intervenes in the application. But metaphysics, which does not aim at any application, can and for the most part ought to abstain from converting intuition into symbol. Exempt from the obligation of arriving at results useful from a practical standpoint, it will indefinitely enlarge the domain of its investigations. What it will have lost with regard to science, in utility and occurrence, it will regain in scope and range. If mathematics is only the science of magnitudes, if mathematical procedures only apply to quantities, it must not be forgotten that quantity is always nascent quality: it is, one might say, its limiting case. It is therefore natural that metaphysics should adopt the generative idea of our mathematics in order to extend it to all qualities, that is, to reality in general. In so doing, it will in no way proceed to universal mathematics, that chimera of modern philosophy. Quite the contrary, as it makes more headway, it will meet with objects less and less translatable into symbols. But it will at least have begun by making contact with the continuity and mobility of the real exactly where this contact happens to be the most utilizable. It will have looked at itself in a mirror which sends back an image of itself no doubt very reduced, but also very luminous. It will have seen with a superior clarity what mathematical procedures borrow from concrete reality, and it will continue in the direction of concrete reality, not of mathematical methods. Let us say, then, with all due qualifications to what might seem either too modest or too ambitious in this formula, that *one of the objects of metaphysics is to operate differentiations and qualitative integrations.*

VIII. What has caused this object to be lost sight of, and misled science itself about the origin of certain methods it employs, is that intuition once grasped must find a mode of expression and application which conforms to our habits of thought and which furnishes us, in well-defined concepts, the solid basis (point d'aper çu) we so greatly need. That is the condition of what we call strictness, precision, and indefinite extension of a general method to particular cases. Now this extension and this work of logical perfectioning can be carried on for centuries, while the generative act of the method lasts only an instant. That is why we so often take the logical apparatus of science for science itself, forgetting the intuition from which the rest was able to ensue.

All that has been said by the philosophers and by scientists themselves about the "relativity" of scientific knowledge is due to forgetting this intuition. *Relative is symbolic knowledge through pre-existing concepts, which goes from the fixed to the moving, but not so intuitive knowledge which establishes itself in the moving reality and adopts the life itself of things.* This intuition attains the absolute.

Science and metaphysics then meet in intuition. A truly intuitive philosophy would realize the union so greatly desired, of metaphysics and science. At the same time that it constituted metaphysics in positive science— I mean progressive and indefinitely perfectible—it would lead the positive sciences, properly speaking, to become conscious of their true bearing, which is often very superior to what they suppose. It would put more of science into metaphysics and more of metaphysics into science. Its result would be to re-establish the continuity between the intuitions which the various positive sciences have obtained at intervals in the course of their history, and which they have obtained only by strokes of genius.

IX. That there are not two different ways of knowing things thoroughly, that the various sciences have their roots in metaphysics, is what the philosophers of antiquity, in general, believed. Not in that lay their error. It consisted in adopting the belief so natural to the human mind, that a variation can only express and develop invariabilities. The result of this was that Action was a weakened Contemplation, duration a false, deceptive and mobile image of immobile eternity, the Soul a fall of the

Idea. The whole of that philosophy which begins with Plato and ends with Plotinus is the development of a principle that we should formulate thus: "There is more in the immutable than in the moving, and one passes from the stable to the unstable by a simple diminution." Now the contrary is the truth.

Modern science dates from the day when mobility was set up as an independent reality. It dates from the day when Galileo, rolling a ball down an inclined plane, made the firm resolution to study this movement from high to low for itself, in itself, instead of seeking its principle in the concepts of the *high* and the *low*, two immobilities by which Aristotle thought he sufficiently explained its mobility. And that is not an isolated fact in the history of science. I take the view that several of the great discoveries, of those at least which have transformed the positive sciences or created new ones, have been so many soundings made in pure duration. The more living was the reality touched, the more profound had been the sounding.

But the sounding made on the sea floor brings up a fluid mass which the sun very quickly dries into solid and discontinuous grains of sand. And the intuition of duration, when exposed to the rays of the understanding, also quickly congeals into fixed, distinct and immobile concepts. In the living mobility of things, the understanding undertakes to mark out real or virtual stations, it notes arrivals and departures; that is all that is important to the thought of man in its natural exercise. But philosophy should be an effort to go beyond the human state.

On the concepts with which they have blazed the trail of intuition scholars have preferred to fix their glance. The more they considered these residua which have reached the state of symbols, the more they attributed to all science a symbolic character. And the more they believed in the symbolic character of science, the more they effected it and emphasized it. It was not long before they noticed no difference, in positive science, between the data of immediate intuition and the immense work of analysis that the understanding pursues around intuition. Thus they prepared the way for a doctrine which affirms the relativity of all our forms of knowledge.

But metaphysics has also worked toward that.

Why did the masters of modern philosophy, who were renovators of science in addition to being metaphysicians, not have the feeling of the mobile continuity of the real? Why did they not place themselves in what we call concrete duration? They did so more than they thought, and much more than they said they did. If any attempt is made to connect by continuous links the intuitions around which systems are organized, one finds, along with several other convergent or divergent lines, a well-determined direction of thought and feeling. What is this latent thought? How is this feeling to be expressed? To borrow once more the language of the Platonists, and stripping the words of their psychological meaning, by calling Idea a certain *assurance of easy intelligibility* and Soul a certain *preoccupation* with life, we shall say that an invisible current makes modern philosophy tend to lift the Soul above the Idea. In this, as in modern science and even more so, it tends to move in the opposite direction from ancient thought.

But this metaphysics, like this science, has deployed around its inner life a rich tissue of symbols, occasionally forgetting that if science needs symbols in its analytical development, the principal justification for metaphysics is a break with symbols. Here again the understanding has pursued its work of fixing, dividing, reconstructing. True, it has pursued it under a somewhat different form. Without emphasizing a point I propose to develop elsewhere, let me confine myself to saying that the understanding, whose role is to operate on stable elements, can seek stability either in *relations* or in *things*. In so far as it works on relational concepts, it ends in *scientific* symbolism. In so far as it operates on concepts of things, it ends in *metaphysical* symbolism. But in either case the arrangement comes from it. It would willingly believe itself independent. Rather than recognizing at once what it owes to the deep intuition of reality, it is exposed to what is only seen in all its work, to an artificial arrangement of symbols. With the result that if one keeps to the letter of what metaphysicians and scholars say, as well as to the content of what they do, one might believe that the first have dug a deep tunnel under reality, while the others have thrown over it an elegant bridge, but that the moving river of things passes between these two works of art without touching them.

One of the principal tricks of Kantian criticism consisted in taking the metaphysician and the scholar at their word, in pushing metaphysics and science to the utmost possible limit of symbolism, where, in any case, they lead of their own accord the moment the understanding lays claim to an independence full of dangers. Once the relation of science and metaphysics with "intellectual intuition" is misunderstood, Kant has no difficulty in showing that our science is entirely relative and our metaphysics wholly artificial. Because he strained the independence of the understanding in both cases, because he relieved metaphysics and science of the "intellectual intuition" which gave them their inner weight, science with its relations presents to him only an outer wrapping of form, and metaphysics with its things, an outer wrapping of matter. Is it surprising, then, that the first shows him only frameworks within frameworks, and the second phantoms pursuing phantoms?

He struck our science and metaphysics such rude blows that they have not yet entirely recovered from their shock. Our mind would willingly resign itself to see in science a wholly relative knowledge and in metaphysics an empty speculation. It seems to us even today that Kantian criticism applies to all metaphysics and to all science. In reality it applies especially to the philosophy of the ancients, as well as to the form—still ancient—that the moderns have given most often to their thought. It is valid against a metaphysics which claims to give us a *unique* and ready-made system of things, against a science which would be a *unique* system of relations, finally against a science and a metaphysics which present themselves with the architectural simplicity of the Platonic theory of Ideas, or of a Greek temple. If metaphysics claims to be made up of concepts we possessed prior to it, if it consists in an ingenious arrangement of pre-existing ideas which we utilize like the materials of construction for a building, in short, if it is something other than the constant dilation of our mind, the constantly renewed effort to go beyond our actual ideas and perhaps our simple logic as well, it is too evident that it becomes artificial like all works of pure understanding. And if science is wholly the work of analysis or of conceptual representation, if experience is only to serve as the verification of "clear ideas," if instead of starting from multiple and varied intuitions inserted into the movement proper to each reality but not always fitting into one another, it claims to be an immense mathematics, a single system of relations which imprisons the totality of the real in a mesh prepared for it, it becomes a knowledge purely relative to the human understanding.

A close reading of the *Critique of Pure Reason* will show that for Kant this kind of *universal mathematics* is science, and this barely modified Platonism, metaphysics. To tell the truth, the dream of a universal mathematics is itself only a survival of Platonism. Universal mathematics is what the world of Ideas becomes when one assumes that the Idea consists in a relation or a law, and no longer in a thing. Kant took for a reality this dream of certain modern philosophers: much more, he thought that all scientific knowledge was only a detached fragment, or rather a projecting stone of universal mathematics. The main task of the *Critique*, therefore, was to lay the foundations of this mathematics, that is, to determine what the intelligence should be and what should be the object in order that an unbroken mathematics might bind them together. And it follows that if all possible experience is thus assured of admittance into the rigid and already constituted frameworks of our understanding (unless we assume a pre-established harmony), our understanding itself organizes nature and finds itself reflected in it as in a mirror. Whence the possibility of science, which owes all its effectiveness to its relativity—and the impossibility of metaphysics, since the latter will find nothing more to do than to parody, on the phantoms of things, the work of conceptual arrangement which science pursues seriously on relations. In short, *the whole* Critique of Pure Reason *leads to establishing the fact that Platonism, illegitimate if Ideas are things, becomes legitimate if ideas are relations, and that the ready-made idea, once thus brought down from heaven to earth, is indeed as Plato wished, the common basis of thought and nature. But the whole* Critique of Pure Reason *rests also upon the postulate that our thought is incapable of anything but Platonizing,* that is, of pouring the whole of possible experience into pre-existing molds.

That is the whole question. If scientific knowledge is indeed what Kant insisted it was, there is a simple science pre-formed and even pre-formulated in nature, as Aristotle believed: from this logic immanent in things the great discoveries only illuminate point by point the line traced in advance, as, on a festival night, a string of bulbs flick on, one by one, to give the outline of a monument. And if metaphysical knowledge is indeed what Kant intended, it is reduced to the equal possibility of two opposed attitudes of mind toward all the great problems; its manifestations are so many arbitrary choices, always ephemeral, between two solutions virtually formulated from all eternity: it lives and dies from antinomies. But the truth is that neither does the science of modern times present this unilinear simplicity, nor the metaphysics of the moderns these irreducible oppositions.

Modern science is neither one nor simple. It rests, I readily agree, upon ideas one ultimately finds clear; but these ideas, when they are profound, become progressively clear by the use made of them; they owe then the best part of their luminosity to the light cast back upon them, through reflection, by the facts and applications to which they have led, the clarity of a concept being little else, accordingly, than the assurance, once it is acquired, of manipulating it to advantage. At the start, more than one of them must have appeared obscure, difficult to reconcile with the ideas already accepted by science, and bordering on the absurd. That is to say that science does not proceed by the regular nesting of concepts predestined to fit neatly inside one another. Profound and fruitful ideas are so many points of contact with currents of reality which do not necessarily converge on a same point. It is true that the concepts in which they lodge always manage somehow or other, in rounding off their corners by reciprocal friction, to makeshift among themselves.

On the other hand, the metaphysics of the moderns is not made of solutions so radical that they can lead to irreducible oppositions. This would no doubt be so if there were no means of accepting at the same time and in the same field the thesis and antithesis of the antinomies. But to philosophize consists precisely in placing oneself, by an effort of intuition, inside this concrete reality on which from the outside the *Critique* takes the two opposing views, thesis and antithesis. I shall never imagine how black and white intermingle if I have not seen grey, but I have no difficulty in understanding, once I have seen grey, how one can envisage it from the double viewpoints of black and white. Doctrines which have a basis of intuition escape Kantian criticism to the exact extent that they are intuitive; and these doctrines are the whole of metaphysics, provided one does not take the metaphysics congealed and dead in *theses,* but living in *philosophers.* To be sure, these divergences are striking between the schools, that is to say, in short, between the groups of disciples formed around certain of the great masters. But would one find them as clear-cut between the masters themselves? Something here dominates the diversity of systems, something, I repeat, simple and definite like a sounding of which one feels that it has more or less reached the bottom of a same ocean, even though it brings each time to the surface very different materials. It is on these materials that disciples normally work: in that is the role of analysis. And the master, in so far as he formulates, develops, translates into abstract ideas what he brings, is already, as it were, his own disciple. But the simple act which has set analysis in motion and which hides behind analysis, emanates from a faculty quite different from that of analyzing. This is by very definition intuition.

Let it be said, in conclusion, that there is nothing mysterious about this faculty. Whoever has worked successfully at literary composition well knows that when the subject has been studied at great length, all the documents gathered together, all notes taken, something more is necessary to get down to the work of composition itself: an effort, often painful, immediately to place oneself in the very heart of the subject and to seek as deeply as possible an impulsion which, as soon as found, carries one forward of itself. This impulsion, once received, sets the mind off on a road where it finds both the information it had gathered and other details as well; it develops, analyzes itself in terms whose enumeration follows on without limit; the farther one goes the more is disclosed about it; never will one manage to say everything: and yet, if one turns around suddenly to seize the impulsion felt, it slips away; for it was not a thing but an urge to movement, and although indefinitely extensible, it is simplicity itself. Metaphysical intuition seems to be something of the same kind. What in this case matches the notes and documents of the literary composition, is the collection of observations and experiences gathered by positive science and above all by a reflection of the mind on the mind. For one does not obtain from reality an intuition, that is to say, a spiritual harmony with its innermost quality if one has not gained its confidence by a long comradeship with its superficial manifestations. And it is not a question simply of assimilating the oustanding facts; it is necessary to accumulate and fuse such an enormous mass of them that one may be assured, in this fusion, of neutralizing by one another all the preconceived and premature ideas observers may have deposited unknowingly in their observations. Only thus does the raw material of the known facts emerge. Even in the simple and privileged case which served us as an example, even for the direct contact of the self with the self, the definitive effort of distinct intuition would be impossible for anyone who had gathered and collated a very great number of psychological analyses. The masters of modern philosophy have been men who had assimilated all the material of the science of their time. And the partial eclipse of metaphysics since the last half century has been caused more than anything else by the extraordinary difficulty the philosopher experiences today in making contact with a science already much too scattered. But metaphysical intuition, although one can achieve it only by means of material knowledge, is an entirely different thing from the summary or synthesis of this knowledge. It is as distinct from it as the motor impulsion is distinct from the path traced by the moving object, as the tension of the spring is distinct from the visible movements in the clock. In this sense, metaphysics has nothing in common with a generalization of experience, and yet it could be defined as the whole of experience (*l'expérience intégrale*).

VII

THE PHILOSOPHY OF CLAUDE BERNARD

What philosophy owes above all to Claude Bernard is the theory of the experimental method. Modern science has regulated itself upon experience; but as it began with mechanics and astronomy, as it contemplated at first, in matter, only what was most general and nearest to mathematics, for a long time it asked of experience only to furnish it with a point of departure for its calculations and to verify them on their arrival. The laboratory sciences, those which follow experiment in all its sinuosities without ever losing contact with it, date from the XIXth century. To these more concrete forms of research Claude Bernard was to bring the formula of their method, as Descartes once did to the abstract sciences of matter. In this sense, the *Introduction to Experimental Medicine* is for us a little like the *Discourse on Method* was for the XVII and XVIII centuries. In each case we find ourselves in the presence of a man of genius who began by making great discoveries, and then asked himself how one would have to go about it to make them: a course paradoxical to all appearances and yet the only natural one, since the opposite method of procedure had been tried much more frequently and had never succeeded. Only twice in the history of modern science and for the two main forms that our knowledge of nature took, the spirit of invention retired within itself to analyze itself and thus to determine the general conditions of scientific discovery. This happy combination of spontaneity and reflection, of science and philosophy, happened both times in France.

The constant thought of Claude Bernard in his *Introduction* was to show us how fact and idea collaborate in experimental research. The fact, more or less clearly perceived, suggests the idea of an explanation; this idea the scholar asks experiment to confirm; but all the time his experiment is going on he should be ready to abandon his hypothesis or change it on the basis of the facts. Scientific research is therefore a dialogue between mind and nature. Nature rouses our curiosity; we ask it questions; its answers give an unexpected turn to the conversation, starting new questions to which nature replies by suggesting new ideas, and so on indefinitely. When Claude Bernard describes this method, when he gives examples of it, when he recalls what applications he has made of it, everything he sets forth seems to us so simple and natural that it was hardly necessary for him to have said it: we feel we have always known it. In the same way the portrait painted by a great master can give us the illusion of having known the model.

Claude Bernard's method, nevertheless, even today is far from being always understood and put into practice as it should be. For fifty years we have known his work; we have never stopped reading and admiring it: but have we learned from it all that it has to teach?

One of the most evident results of that analysis should be to teach us that there is no difference between an observation well-taken and a well-founded generalization. We are still inclined to imagine experience as intended to present us with bare facts; the intelligence (so we imagine), taking possession of these facts, putting them one beside another, thus rises to higher and higher laws. Generalizing would then be one function, observing would be another. Nothing is more false than that conception of how synthesis works, nothing more dangerous for science and philosophy. It led to the belief that there was a scientific interest in assembling facts for no reason in particular, for the mere fun of it, in recording them lazily and even passively, while awaiting the arrival of a mind capable of dominating them and submitting them to laws. As though a scientific observation were not always an answer to a question, be it precise or hazy! As though observations, recorded passively one after another, were anything but disconnected answers to questions asked at random! As though the work of generalization consisted in finding, after the event, a plausible meaning in this incoherent discourse! The truth is that the discourse should have a meaning immediately evident, or it will never have one. Its signification may change as one goes more deeply into the facts, but it must first have a signification. Generalization is not the utilization, in view of some process of condensation or other, of facts already assembled, already recorded: synthesis is an entirely different thing. It is less a special operation than a certain power of thought, the capacity for penetrating into the interior of a fact whose significance one has divined and in which one will find the explanation of an indefinite number of facts. In a word, the spirit of synthesis is only the spirit of analysis raised to a higher power.

This conception of the work of scientific research singularly reduces the distance between master and apprentice. It no longer permits us to distinguish two categories of research workers, one made up of routine workers, the other of those whose mission is to invent. Invention should be everywhere, even in the humblest research, even to the simplest experiment. Wherever there is no personal and even original effort there is not even the beginning of science. Such is the great pedagogical maxim revealed in the work of Claude Bernard.

To the eyes of the philosopher it contains something more: a certain conception of the truth, and consequently, a philosophy.

When I speak of the philosophy of Claude Bernard I am not alluding to that metaphysics of life people thought they found in his writings and which was perhaps quite far from his thought. True, it has been widely discussed. Some, quoting the passages in which Claude Bernard criticizes the hypothesis of a "vital principle," claimed that he saw nothing more in life than a collection of physical and chemical phenomena.

Others, referring to that "organizing and creative idea" which, according to the author, presides over vital phenomena, insist that he has made a radical distinction between living matter and inorganic matter, thus attributing to life an independent cause. And finally, according to some, Claude Bernard is supposed to have wavered between the two conceptions, or else to have started off with the first and by progressive stages arrived at the second. Read the master's work over again very carefully: you will find in it, I believe, neither that affirmation, nor that negation, nor that contradiction. To be sure, Claude Bernard protested a great many times against the hypothesis of a "vital principle"; but wherever he does so he is aiming purposely at the superficial vitalism of those doctors and psychologists who affirm the existence, in the living being, of a force capable of battling against the physical forces and thwarting their action. It was at the time when it was currently thought that the same cause, operating in the same conditions on the same living being, did not always produce the same effect. One had to take into account, they said, the capricious character of life. Even Magendie himself, who contributed so much toward making physiology a science, believed in a certain indetermination of the vital phenomenon. To all those who voice such opinions Claude Bernard answers that physiological facts are submitted to an inflexible determination as rigorous as that of physical or chemical facts: he even says that among the operations which take place in the animal machine there is not a single one which will not some day be explained by physics and chemistry. So much for the vital principle. But now let us turn to a consideration of the organizing and creative idea. We shall find that wherever it is a question of this idea Claude Bernard attacks those who refuse to see in physiology a special science distinct from physics and chemistry. The qualities, or rather the dispositions of mind, which make the physiologist are not the same, according to him, as those which make the chemist and physicist. He is not a physiologist who has not the organizing sense, that is to say, the sense of that special coordination of the parts to the whole characteristic of the vital phenomenon. In a living being things take place as though a certain "idea" stepped in, which took into account the order in which the elements are grouped. This idea, furthermore, is not a force but simply a principle of explanation: if it worked effectively, if it could, in anything whatever, thwart the play of physical and chemical forces, there would be no experimental physiology. The physiologist should not only take into consideration that organizing idea in instituting the study of the phenomena of life: he must further remember, according to Claude Bernard, that the facts he is concerned with have as the theater of their operations an already constructed organism and that the construction of this organism or, as he says, the "creation," is an operation of an entirely different order. Certainly, in insisting on the very clear distinction established by Claude Bernard between the construction of the machine and its destruction or wear, between the machine and what happens inside it, one would doubtless end by restoring in another form the vitalism he attacked; but he did not go that far and he preferred not to declare himself on the nature of life, any more than he expressed his opinion on the constitution of matter; he thus reserves the question of the relation of the one to the other. To tell the truth, whether he attacks the hypothesis of the "vital principle" or whether he evokes the "directing idea," in either case he is preoccupied exclusively in determining the conditions of experimental physiology. He seeks less to define life than to define the science of life. He defends physiology both against those who believe the physiological fact to be too elusive to lend itself to experimentation and against those who, while judging it to be accessible to our experiments, would not distinguish these experiments from those of physics or chemistry. To the first group he answers that the physiological fact is governed by an absolute determinism and that physiology is consequently a rigorous science; to the second, that physiology has its proper laws and proper methods, distinct from those of physics and chemistry, and that physiology is in consequence an independent science.

But if Claude Bernard did not give us and did not wish to give us a metaphysics of life, there is, present in the whole of his work, a certain general philosophy whose influence will probably be more lasting and more profound than that of any particular theory could have been.

For a long time, in fact, philosophers considered reality as a systematic whole, as a great edifice which we could, in a pinch, reconstruct by thought with the resources of reasoning alone, although we should, as a matter of fact, call observation and experiment to our assistance. Nature would thus be a collection of laws inserted one into the other according to the principles of human logic; and these laws would be there, ready-made, internal to things; scientific and philosophical effort would consist in bringing them out by scraping off, one by one, the facts which cover them, as one lays bare an Egyptian monument by removing by shovelfuls the sand of the desert. The entire work of Claude Bernard is a protest against this conception of facts and laws. Long before the philosophers had insisted on the extent to which human science can be conventional and symbolical, he perceived, he measured the difference between man's logic and the logic of nature. If, according to him, we can never bring too much prudence to bear upon the verification of a hypothesis, we shall never have exercised sufficient audacity in inventing it. What is absurd in our eyes is not necessarily so in the eyes of nature: let us try the experiment and if the hypothesis is verified it will of necessity become clearer and more intelligible the more the facts constrain us to become familiar with it. But let us also remember that an idea, no matter how flexible we may have made it, will never have the same flexibility as a thing. Let us therefore be ready to abandon it for another, which will fit the experiment still more closely. "Our ideas," said Claude Bernard, "are only intellectual instruments which serve to let us penetrate phenomena; they must be changed when they have played their part, as one changes a blunted lancet when it has served long enough." And he added, "That exaggerated faith in reasoning which leads a physiologist to a false simplification of things is due to the absence of the feeling for the complexity of natural phenomena." He said: "When we make a general theory in our sciences, the only thing of which we are certain is that all these theories are false, absolutely speaking. They are only partial and temporary truths, which are necessary to us as the degrees on which we rely to advance in our investigation." And he came back to this point when he spoke of his own theories: "They will be replaced later by others which will represent a more advanced state of the question, and so on. Theories are like successive steps climbed by science as it widens its horizon." But there is nothing more significant than the opening words of one of the last paragraphs in his *Introduction to Experimental Medicine:* "One of the greatest obstacles encountered in this general and free progression of human knowledge is the tendency which leads the various forms of knowledge to become individualized into systems. . . . Systems tend to enslave the human mind. . . . We must try to break the fetters of philosophical and scientific systems. . . . Philosophy and science should not be systematic." Philosophy should not be systematic! It was a paradox of the time in which Claude Bernard was writing and in which people, either in order to justify the existence of philosophy or to proscribe it, were inclined to identify the philosophical mind with the *esprit de système.* It is nevertheless the truth, and a truth with which one will become more and more imbued as a philosophy is developed, capable of following concrete reality in all its sinuosities. We shall no longer witness a succession of doctrines each one of which, to be chosen or discarded at will, claims to embrace the totality of things in simple formulas. We shall have a single philosophy, an edifice which will, little by little, be built up alongside science, and to which all those who think will bring their stone. We shall no longer say, "Nature is one, and we are going to seek among the ideas we already possess the one into which we can put it." We shall say, "Nature is what it is, and as our intelligence, which is a part of it, is less vast than nature, it is doubtful whether any one of our present ideas is large enough to embrace it. Let us then work to expand our thought: let us strain our understanding: break, if need be, all our frameworks; but let us not claim to shrink reality to the measure of our ideas, when it is for our ideas, as they grow larger, to mould themselves upon reality." That is what we shall say and what we shall try to do. But in advancing farther and farther down the road along which we are starting out, we must always remember that Claude Bernard helped to open it. That is why we can never be sufficiently grateful for what he has done for us. And that is why we are come to pay our respects, alongside the physiologist of genius who was one of the greatest experimentors of all times, to the philosopher in him, who was perhaps one of the masters of contemporary thought.

VIII

ON THE PRAGMATISM OF WILLIAM JAMES. TRUTH AND REALITY

To talk about pragmatism after William James might well seem superfluous. And indeed what is there for me to say about it that has not already been said, and much better, in the fascinating and delightful book for which we now have an excellent translation? I should in fact refrain from saying anything were it not that James's thought is frequently impoverished and falsified by the way in which it is interpreted. There are many ideas in circulation which threaten to come between the reader and the book and to cast an artificial obscurity over a work which is clarity itself.

One would have a mistaken idea of James's pragmatism if one did not begin by modifying the idea usually held of reality in general. We speak of the "world" or the "cosmos"; and these words, according to their origin, designate something simple or at least well composed. We say "universe" and the word makes us think of a possible unification of things. One can be a spiritualist, a materialist, a pantheist, just as one can be indifferent to philosophy and satisfied with common sense: the fact remains that one always conceives of one or several simple principles by which the whole of material and moral things might be explained.

This is because our intelligence loves simplicity. It seeks to reduce effort, and insists that nature was arranged in such a way as to demand of us, in order to be thought, the least possible labor. It therefore provides itself with the exact minimum of elements and principles with which to recompose the indefinite series of objects and events.

But if instead of reconstructing things ideally for the greater satisfaction of our reason we confine ourselves purely and simply to what is given us by experience, we should think and express ourselves in quite another way. While our intelligence with its habits of economy imagines effects as strictly proportioned to their causes, nature, in its extravagance, puts into the cause much more than is required to produce the effect. While our motto is *Exactly what is necessary,* nature's motto is *More than is necessary*—too much of this, too much of that, too much of everything. Reality, as James sees it, is redundant and superabundant. Between this reality and the one constructed by the philosophers, I believe he would have established the same relation as between the life we live every day and the life which actors portray in the evening on the stage. On the stage, each actor says and does only what has to be said and done; the scenes are clear-cut; the play has a beginning, a middle and an end; and everything is worked out as economically as possible with a view to an ending which will be happy or tragic. But in life, a multitude of useless things are said, many superfluous gestures made, there are no sharply-drawn situations; nothing happens as simply or as completely or as nicely as we should like; the scenes overlap; things neither begin nor end; there is no perfectly satisfying ending, nor absolutely decisive gesture, none of those telling words which give us pause: all the effects are spoiled. Such is human life. And such, no doubt, in James's eyes, is reality in general.

To be sure, our experience is not incoherent. At the same time as it presents us with things and facts it shows us relationships between the things and connections between the facts: these relations are as real, as directly observable, according to William James, as the things and facts themselves. But the relations are fluctuating and the things fluid. This is vastly different from that dry universe constructed by the philosophers with elements that are clear-cut and well-arranged, where each part is not only linked to another part, as experience shows us, but also, as our reason would have it, is coordinated to the whole.

The "pluralism" of William James means little else than this. Antiquity had imagined a world shut off, arrested, finite: it is a hypothesis which answers certain demands of our reason. The moderns think rather of an infinite: it is another hypothesis which satisfies other needs of our reason. From the point of view taken by James, which is that of pure experience or of "radical empiricism," reality no longer appears as finite or as infinite, but simply as indefinite. It flows without our being able to say whether it is in a single direction, or even whether it is always and throughout the same river flowing.

Our reason is less satisfied. It feels less at ease in a world where it no longer finds, as in a mirror, its own image. And certainly the importance of human reason is diminished. But the importance of man himself—the whole of man, will and sensibility quite as much as intelligence—will thereby be immeasurably enhanced!

The universe our reason conceives is, in fact, a universe which extends infinitely beyond human experience, the characteristic of reason being to prolong the data of experience, to extend them by way of generalization, in order to make us conceive many more things than we shall ever perceive. In such a universe man is expected to do very little and to occupy very little space: what he gives to his intelligence he takes away from his will. Above all, having attributed to his thought the power of embracing everything, he is obliged to imagine all things in terms of thought; of his aspirations, his desires, his enthusiasms he cannot ask enlightenment in a world in which everything accessible to him has been first considered by him as translatable into pure ideas. His sensibility cannot enlighten his intelligence, for it is with his intelligence that he has made what light there is.

Most philosophies, therefore, restrict our experience on the side of feeling and will as at the same time they indefinitely prolong it on the side of thought. What

James asks of us is not to add too much to experience through hypothetical considerations, and also not to mutilate it in its solid elements. We are absolutely sure only of what experience gives us; but we should accept experience wholly, and our feelings are a part of it by the same right as our perceptions, consequently, by the same right as "things." In the eyes of William James, the whole man counts.

In fact, he counts for a great deal in a world which no longer overwhelms him with its immensity. Considerable surprise has been expressed at the importance James attributes, in one of his books, to the curious theory of Fechner which makes of the Earth an independent being, endowed with a divine soul. He did so because he saw in it a convenient means of symbolizing—perhaps even of expressing—his own thought. The things and facts which make up our experience constitute for us a *human* world, no doubt connected with others, but so far removed from them and so close to us that we must consider it, in practice, as sufficient for man and sufficient unto itself. We are an integral part of these things and these events—we, that is to say, all that we are conscious of being, all that we experience. The powerful feelings which stir the soul at certain special moments are forces as real as those that interest the physicist; man does not create them any more than he creates heat or light. According to James, we bathe in an atmosphere traversed by great spiritual currents. If many of us resist, others allow themselves to be carried along. And there are certain souls which open wide to the beneficent breeze. Those are the mystical souls. We know with what sympathy James studied them. When his book *Religious Experience* appeared, many saw in it only a series of very vivid descriptions and very penetrating analyses—a psychology, they said, of religious feeling. This was a complete misinterpretation of the author's thought. The truth is that James leaned out upon the mystic soul as, on a spring day, we lean out to feel the caress of the breeze on our cheek, or as, at the sea-side, we watch the coming and going of sail-boats to know how the wind blows. Souls filled with religious enthusiasm are truly uplifted and carried away: why could they not enable us to experience directly, as in a scientific experiment, this uplifting and exalting force? That is undoubtedly the origin, the inspiring idea of the "pragmatism" of William James. For him those truths it is most important for us to know, are truths which have been felt and experienced before being thought.

It has at all times been said that there are truths which have to do with feeling as much as with reason; and that along with those truths we find already made there are also others we assist in the making, which depend in part on our will. But it must be said that in James this idea takes on a new strength and significance. Thanks to his particular conception of reality it blossoms into a general theory of truth.

What constitutes a true judgment? If an affirmation agrees with reality we say that it is true. But in what does this agreement consist? Our inclination is to see in it something like the resemblance of a portrait to the model: the true affirmation would be the one which would *copy* reality. Upon reflection, however, we shall see that it is only in rare and exceptional cases that this definition of the true finds its application. What is real is any determined fact taking place at any point in space and time, it is singular—it is changing. On the contrary, most of our affirmations are general and imply a certain stability on the part of their object. Let us take a truth as close to experience as possible, for instance: "heat expands bodies." Of what model is this truth a copy? It is possible, in a certain sense, to copy the expansion of a specific body at particular moments, by photographing it in its various stages. Even by metaphor I can still say that the affirmation, "that iron bar is expanding," is the copy of what happens when I watch the expansion of the iron bar. But a truth which is applied to all bodies without concerning any one in particular that I have seen, copies nothing, reproduces nothing. We insist however that it copy something and as far back as one can go philosophy has always sought to give us satisfaction on this point. For the ancient philosophers there was, above time and space, a world in which were located from all eternity all possible truths: the truth of human affirmations was measured by the degree of faithfulness with which they copied these eternal truths. Modern philosophers have brought truth from heaven down to earth; but they still see in it something which is pre-existent to our affirmations. According to them, truth is lodged in things and facts: our science seeks it in them, draws it from its hiding-place and exposes it to the light of day. An affirmation, such as "heat expands bodies," would then be a law governing facts, which is enthroned if not above them, at least in their midst, a law veritably contained in our experience; all we should have to do would be to extract it therefrom. Even a philosophy like that of Kant, which insists that all scientific truth is relative to the human mind, considers true affirmations as given in advance in human experience: once that experience is organized by human thought in general, all the work of science consists, so to speak, in piercing the resisting envelope of the facts inside which the truth is lodged, like a nut in its shell.

This conception of truth is natural to our mind and natural also to philosophy, because it is natural to picture reality as a perfectly coherent and systematized whole sustained by a logical armature. This armature would be truth itself; all that our science does is to rediscover it. But experience pure and simple tells us nothing of the kind, and James confines himself to experience. Experience presents us a flow of phenomena: if a certain affirmation relating to one of them enables us to master those which follow or even simply to foresee them, we say of this affirmation that it is true. A proposition such as "heat expands bodies," a proposition suggested by seeing a certain body expand, means that we foresee how other bodies will act when exposed to heat; it helps us to proceed from a past experience to new experiences; it is a clue conducting to what will happen, nothing more. Reality flows; we flow with it; and we call true any affirmation which, in guiding us through moving reality, gives us a grip upon it and places us under more favorable conditions for acting.

The difference between this conception of the truth and the traditional one is plain to see. We ordinarily define the true by its conformity to what already exists; James defines it by its relation to what does not yet exist. The true, according to William James, does not copy something which has been or which is: it announces what will be, or rather it prepares our action upon what is going to be. Philosophy has a natural tendency to have truth look backward: for James, it looks ahead.

More precisely, other doctrines make of truth something anterior to the clearly-determined act of the man who formulates it for the first time. He was the first to see it, we say, but it was waiting for him, just as America was waiting for Christopher Columbus. Something hid it from view and, so to speak, covered it up: he uncovered it.—Quite different is William James's conception. He does not deny that reality is independent, at least to a great extent, of what we say or think of it; but the truth, which can be attached only to what we affirm about reality, is, for him, created by our affirmation. We invent the truth to utilize reality, as we create mechanical devices to utilize the forces of nature. It seems to me one could sum up all that is essential in the pragmatic conception of truth in a formula such as this: *while for other doctrines a new truth is a discovery, for pragmatism it is an invention.*

It does not follow, of course, that the truth is arbitrary. The value of a mechanical invention lies solely in its practical usefulness. In the same way an affirmation, because it is true, should increase our mastery over things. It is no less the creation of a certain individual mind, and it was no more pre-existent to the effort of that mind than the phonograph, for example, existed before Edison. No doubt the inventor of the phonograph had to study the properties of sound, which is a reality. But his invention was superadded to that reality as a thing absolutely new, which might never have been produced had he not existed. Thus a truth, if it is to endure, should have its roots in realities; but these realities are only the ground in which that truth grows, and other flowers could just as well have grown there if the wind had brought other seeds.

Truth, according to pragmatism, has come little by little into being, thanks to the individual contributions of a great number of inventors. If these inventors had not existed, if there had been others in their place, we should have had an entirely different body of truths. Reality would evidently have remained what it is, or approximately the same; but quite different would have been the paths we should have traced in reality, for our convenience in finding our way about it. And this has to do not only with scientific truths. We cannot construct a sentence, we cannot even today pronounce a word, without accepting certain hypotheses which were created by our ancestors and which might have been very different from what they are. When I say: "My pencil has just fallen under the table," I am certainly not enunciating a fact of experience, for what sight and touch show me is simply that my hand opened and let fall what it held: the baby tied in his high-chair, who sees his plaything fall, probably does not imagine that this object continues to exist; or rather he has not the clear idea of an "object," that is to say, of something which subsists, invariable and independent, through the diversity and mobility of the appearances which pass before him. The first to venture to believe in this invariability and independence made a hypothesis: it is that hypothesis which we currently adopt every time we use a substantive, every time we speak. Our grammar would have been different, the articulations of our thought would have been other than what they are, had humanity in the course of its evolution preferred to adopt hypotheses of another kind.

The structure of our mind is therefore to a great extent our work, or at least the work of some of us. That, it seems to me, is the most important thesis of pragmatism, even though it has not been explicitly stated. It is in this way that pragmatism continues Kantianism. Kant had said that truth depends upon the general structure of the human mind. Pragmatism adds, or at least implies, that the structure of the human mind is the effect of the free initiative of a certain number of individual minds.

That, again, does not mean that truth depends upon each one of us: we might as well believe that each of us could invent the phonograph. But it does mean that of the various kinds of truth, the one which most nearly coincides with its object is not scientific truth, nor is it the truth of common sense, nor more generally truth of an intellectual order. Every truth is a path traced through reality: but among these paths there are some to which we could have given an entirely different turn if our attention had been orientated in a different direction or if we had aimed at another kind of utility; there are some, on the contrary, whose direction is marked out by reality itself: there are some, one might say, which correspond to currents of reality. Doubtless these also depend upon us to a certain extent, for we are free to go against the current or to follow it, and even if we follow it, we can variously divert it, being at the same time associated with and submitted to the force manifest within it. Nevertheless these currents are not created by us; they are part and parcel of reality. Pragmatism thus results in a reversal of the order in which we are accustomed to place the various kinds of truth. Apart from the truths which translate mere sensations, it is, according to pragmatism, the truths of feeling which would push their roots deepest into reality. If we agree to say that all truth is an invention, I believe we must, if we wish to remain faithful to the thought of William James, establish between the truths of feeling and the scientific truths the same kind of difference as there is,

for example, between the sail-boat and the steamer:
both are human inventions; but the first makes only
slight use of artificial means—it takes the direction of
the wind and makes the natural force it utilizes perceptible to the eye; on the contrary, in the second the
artificial mechanism holds the most important place; it
covers the force it puts into play and assigns to it a
direction which we ourselves have chosen.

The definition that James gives to truth therefore, is
an integral part of his conception of reality. If reality
is not that economic and systematic universe our logic
likes to imagine, if it is not sustained by a framework of
intellectuality, intellectual truth is a human invention
whose effect is to utilize reality rather than to enable us
to penetrate it. And if reality does not form a single
whole, if it is multiple and mobile, made up of cross-
currents, truth which arises from contact with one of
these currents—truth felt before being conceived—is
more capable of seizing and storing up reality than truth
merely thought.

Therefore it is, in fact, with this theory of reality
that a critique of pragmatism should first grapple. One
may raise objections to it—and I myself should make
certain reservations concerning it: but no one will challenge its depth and originality. Neither will anyone,
after having closely examined the conception of truth
allied with it, fail to recognize its high moral value.
People have said that the pragmatism of James was only
a form of skepticism, that it lowered truth, that it subordinated truth to material utility, that it advised against
and discouraged disinterested scientific research. Such
an interpretation will never enter the heads of those who
read his work attentively. And it will greatly astonish
those who have had the pleasure of knowing the man.
No one loved truth with a more ardent love. No one
sought it with greater passion. He was stirred by an
immense unrest, and went from science to science, from
anatomy and physiology to psychology, from psychology
to philosophy, tense over great problems, heedless of

anything else, forgetful of himself. All his life he observed, experimented, meditated. And as if he had not done enough, he still dreamed, as he fell into his last slumber, of extraordinary experiments and super-human efforts by which he could continue even beyond death to work with us for the greater good of science, and the greater glory of truth.

IX

THE LIFE AND WORK OF RAVAISSON

Jean-Gaspard-Félix Laché Ravaisson was born the twenty-third of October, 1813, at Namur, then a French city, administrative center of the department of Sambre-et-Meuse. His father, the city treasurer, came originally from the south of France; Ravaisson is the name of a little territory situated in the environs of Caylus, not far from Montauban. The child was scarcely a year old when the events of 1814 forced his family to leave Namur. Shortly after that he lost his father. His early education was supervised by his mother and also by his maternal uncle, Gaspard-Théodore Mollien, whose name he later took. In a letter dated 1821, Mollien wrote of his little eight-year-old nephew: "Félix is a complete mathematician, an antiquary, an historian, everything, in fact." The child already gave evidence of exceptional facility, only one of the many intellectual qualities he was later to develop.

For his secondary education he went to Rollin College. I should like to have traced his progress there from class to class, but the college archives have kept no record of that period. The honors list informs us, however, that the young Ravaisson entered the sixth form in 1825, that he left the college in 1832, and that he was, from first to last, a brilliant student. He carried off several prizes in the general competition in 1832, in particular the honor prize in philosophy. His professor of philosophy was M. Poret, a distinguished master, disciple of the Scottish philosophers, certain of whose works he translated; he was highly esteemed by Cousin, who took him as his deputy at the Sorbonne. Ravaisson remained always attached to his former master. I have been able to read some of the essays, piously preserved in the Poret family, which the student Ravaisson wrote the year he took his philosophy; I have had access, at the Sorbonne, to the dissertation on "method in philosophy" which obtained the honor prize in 1832. They are the works of a docile and intelligent student who has followed a well-organized course of lectures. Those who would seek in them the characteristic stamp of Ravaisson and the early indications of a budding philosophical vocation would experience a certain disappointment. Everything leads us to suppose that young Ravaisson left college without any decided preference for philosophy, without having a clear idea of the road he was to take. Your Academy it was which showed it to him.

The royal statute of October twenty-sixth, 1832, had just re-established the Académie des Sciences morals et politiques. At the suggestion of Cousin, the Academy had announced a competition, the subject to be the study of Aristotle's *Metaphysics*. "The competitors," ran the program, "will be required to explain this work in an extensive analysis, and set out its plan—give its history, show its influence on later systems—seek out and discuss the parts of error and of truth found in it, which of its ideas still hold good today, and those which might advantageously come into the philosophy of our century." It was probably on the advice of his former professor of philosophy that Ravaisson decided to compete. We know how this competition, the first to be opened by the reconstituted Academy, gave the most brilliant results, how nine dissertations were presented, most of which had a certain degree of merit and three of which were judged very highly, how the Academy awarded the prize to Ravaisson and asked the minister to give a supplementary prize for the philosopher Michelet, of Berlin; how Ravaisson re-cast his dissertation, extended, broadened and deepened it, and made it into an admirable book. The first volume of the *Essay on the Metaphysics of Aristotle* appeared as early as 1837, the second was not published until nine years later. Two other volumes were announced but never appeared; but such as we have it the work is a complete exposition of Aristotle's metaphysics and the influence it had on Greek philosophy.

Aristotle, a systematic genius if ever there was one, did not build up a system at all. He proceeded by analysis of concepts rather than by synthesis. His method consists in taking the ideas stored up in the language, in adjusting or renewing them, in circumscribing them in a definition, in cutting out their extension and comprehension according to their natural articulations, in pushing their development to its farthest possible limits. Yet he rarely accomplishes this development all at once: he comes back to it again and again, in different treatises on the same subject, following over again the same road, always advancing a little further. What are the elements implied in thought or existence? What are matter, form, causality, time, place, movement? On all these points and a hundred others he dug up the ground; from each one of them he starts a sort of subterranean gallery which he pushes out ahead, like an engineer who digs a huge tunnel by starting it simultaneously at many points. And indeed we feel that the measurements were made and the calculations performed so that everything should fit; but the junction is not always completed and often, between points which seem to us about to touch, when we flatter ourselves that all we have to do is to remove a few more shovelfuls of sand, we strike bedrock. Ravaisson did not stop at any obstacle. The metaphysics he sets forth at the end of his first volume is Aristotle's doctrine unified and reorganized. He expounds it in a language he created for it, where the fluidity of the images allows the naked idea to show through, where the abstractions come alive and live as they lived in Aristotle's thought. It has been possible to dispute the material correctness of some of his translations; doubts have been raised concerning certain of his interpretations; especially have we asked if the historian's role was really to push the unification of a doctrine further than

the master wished to do, and if, by readjusting the
pieces so perfectly and drawing the gears so tightly, we
are not in danger of distorting some of them. It is none
the less true that our mind demands that unification,
that the undertaking had to be attempted, and that
no one after Ravaisson has dared to repeat it.

Bolder still is the second volume of the *Essay*. In the
comparison he introduces between Aristotle's doctrine
and Greek thought in general, it is the very soul of Aristotelianism that Ravaisson tries to bring out.

Greek philosophy, he says, first explained all things
by a material element, water, air, fire or some undefined
matter. Dominated by sensation, as human intelligence
is to begin with, it did not know any intuition other
than sensible intuition, any aspect of things other
than their materiality. Then came the Pythagoreans and
the Platonists, who pointed out the insufficiency of ex-
planations based on matter alone, and took as their
principles Numbers and Ideas. But the progress was more
apparent than real. With the Pythagorean numbers,
with the Platonist ideas one is in abstraction, and no
matter how erudite the manipulation to which one
submits these elements, one still remains in the abstract.
The intelligence, amazed at the simplification it brings to
the study of things by grouping them under general
ideas, fancies no doubt that through them it will penetrate to the very substance of which things are made.
The farther it goes in the series of generalities the
higher it feels it is rising in the scale of realities. But
what it takes to be a higher spirituality is only the increasing rarefaction of the air it breathes. It does not
see that the more an idea is general, the more it is
abstract and empty, and that from abstraction to abstraction, from generality to generality one proceeds to
pure nothingness. One might as well have clung to the
sense data which no doubt only gave us one side of
reality, but which left us at least on the solid ground
of the real. But perhaps there is another course open.
This would be to extend the vision of the eye by a

vision of the mind: without leaving the domain of intuition, that is, the intuition of things real, individual and concrete, to seek an intellectual intuition beneath the sensible intuition. To do that would be to pierce by a powerful effort of mental vision the material wrapping of things and to read the formula, invisible to the eye, which their materiality unrolls and manifests. Then, gathering itself into its own substance, would appear the unity joining beings to one another, the unity of a thought that we see, from inorganic matter to the plant, from plant to animal, from animal to man, until from concentration to concentration we should end in divine thought, which thinks all things in thinking itself. Such was the doctrine of Aristotle. Such is the intellectual discipline whose rule and example he produced. In that sense Aristotle is the founder of metaphysics and the initiator of a certain method of thinking which is philosophy itself.

It is a great idea and an important one! Doubtless one could challenge, from the historical viewpoint, some of the developments the author gives it. Perhaps Ravaisson looks at Aristotle occasionally through the Alexandrians, themselves so highly colored with Aristotelianism. He may also perhaps have pushed a bit far, even to the point of converting it into a radical opposition, the frequently light and superficial, if not to say verbal, difference separating Aristotle from Plato. But if Ravaisson had fully satisfied the historians of philosophy on these points, we should doubtless have lost what is most original and profound in his doctrine. For the opposition he established here between Plato and Aristotle is the distinction he never ceases to make during his whole life between the philosophical method he considers definitive and the one which according to him is only its counterfeit. The idea he puts at the bottom of Aristotelianism is the very one which inspired most of his meditations. Throughout his whole work rings the affirmation that instead of diluting his thought in the general, the philosopher should concentrate it on the individual.

Let us imagine, for example, all the colors of the rainbow, violet and blue, green, yellow and red. I do not feel I am betraying the governing idea of Ravaisson by saying that there are two ways of determining what they have in common and consequently of philosophizing on them. The first consists simply in saying that they are colors. The abstract and general idea of color thus becomes the unity to which the variety of shades is reduced. But we obtain this general idea of color only by removing from the red that which makes it red, from the blue what makes it blue, from the green what makes it green; we can define it only by saying that it does not represent either red, or blue, or green; it is an affirmation made up of negations, a form circumscribing vacuum. The philosopher who remains in the abstract stops at that. He thinks he can proceed to the unification of things by way of increasing generalization: he really proceeds by gradual extinction of the light which brought out the differences between the colors, and ends by blending them together into a common obscurity. Quite different is the method of true unification. In this case it consists in taking the thousand and one different shades, of blue, violet, green, yellow and red, and, by having them pass through a convergent lens, bringing them to a single point. Then appears in all its radiance the pure white light which, perceived here below in the shades which disperse it, enclosed above, in its undivided unity, the indefinite variety of multi-colored rays. Then would also be revealed, even to each shade taken individually, what the eye did not notice at first, the white light in which it participates, the common illumination from which it draws its own coloring. Such is no doubt the kind of vision that, according to M. Ravaisson, we must ask of metaphysics. From the contemplation of an antique marble can spring more concentrated truth, in the eyes of a real philosopher, than is to be found in the diffused state, in a whole philosophical treatise. The object of metaphysics is to recapture in individual existences and to follow even to the source from which it emanates the particular ray which, while it confers on each one its own particular shade, attaches it by that means to the universal light.

How, at what moment, and under what influences was the philosophy whose first outlines we have here, formed in the mind of Ravaisson? I have found no trace of it in the thesis crowned by your Academy and whose manuscript is lodged in your archives. Between this manuscript thesis and the published work there is, furthermore, such a divergence of fundamentals and form that one would scarcely think they were by the same author. In the manuscript, the *Metaphysics* of Aristotle is simply analyzed book by book; it is not a question of reconstructing the system. In the published work the earlier analysis, with alterations, appears to have been preserved only to serve as a substruction to the edifice, now reconstituted, of Aristotelian philosophy. In the manuscript, Aristotle and Plato are on about the same level. The author considers that he must give Plato his share, and Aristotle his, and blend them together into a philosophy which goes beyond them both. In the published work, Aristotle is distinctly opposed to Plato and his doctrine is presented to us as the source from which all philosophy draws its substance. In fact, the form of the manuscript is correct but impersonal whereas the book already speaks an original language, a mixture of highly colored images and clearly-outlined abstractions, the language of a philosopher who knew how to paint and how to sculpture. Certainly the treatise of 1835 deserved the eulogy Cousin gave it in his report, and the prize the Academy awarded him. No one will deny that it is a piece of work very well done. But it is only work well done. The author has remained outside his work. He studies, analyzes and comments on Aristotle with sagacity, he does not breathe new life into him doubtless because he himself does not yet have a sufficiently intense inner life. It is from 1835 to 1837, in the two years that passed between the writing of the thesis and the appearance of the first volume, it is especially from

1837 to 1846, between the publication of the first volume and that of the second, that Ravaisson became conscious of what he was and, so to speak, was revealed to himself.

No doubt many external influences stimulated the development of his latent energies and the awakening of his personality. It must not be forgotten that the period from 1830 to 1848 was one of intense intellectual life. The Sorbonne still vibrated with the words of people like the Guizots, the Cousins, the Villemains, Geoffroy Saint-Hilaire; Quinet and Michelet were teaching at the Collège de France. Ravaisson knew most of them, especially the last named, whom he served for some time as secretary. In an unpublished letter from Michelet to Jules Quicherat is this sentence: "I have known in France only four critical minds (few people know all that this word implies): Letronne, Burnouf, Ravaisson and yourself." Ravaisson was, therefore, in touch with famous masters at a time when higher education shone with a brilliant luster. It must be added that the same epoch saw a greater intimacy achieved between political men, artists, writers, scholars, all those in fact who might be said to constitute, in a society democratic in tendency, an intellectual aristocracy. This élite met in a number of drawing-rooms privileged to receive them. Ravaisson loved society. While he was still young and as yet little-known, many doors were open to him, thanks to his relationship to the former minister Mollien. We know that he was a frequent visitor at the home of the Princess Belgiojoso where he must have met Mignet, Thiers, and especially, Alfred de Musset; he visited Madame Récamier, already well along in years but still gracious and collecting about her men like Villemain, Ampère, Balzac and Lamartine: it was probably in Madame Récamier's salon that he made the acquaintance of Chateaubriand. Frequent contact with so many superior men must have acted as a stimulant to the intellect.

We must also mention a few weeks spent by Ravaisson in Germany where he visited Schelling in Munich.

There is more than one page in Ravaisson's works which might be compared, for the direction of its thought as well as for its style, to the best writings of the German philosopher. Schelling's influence must not on that account be exaggerated. Perhaps it was not so much a matter of influence as of natural affinity, community of inspiration and, if one may say so, pre-established harmony between two minds both of which were traveling on a lofty plane, and met each other on certain peaks. Conversation, furthermore, was rather difficult between the two philosophers as the one knew very little French and the other scarcely any more German.

Travel, conversations, social intercourse must have aroused Ravaisson's curiosity and stimulated his mind to express itself outwardly. But the causes which led him to retire within himself lay deeper.

First and foremost must be a prolonged contact with the philosophy of Aristotle. The treatise which won the Academy award already bore witness to a close and penetrating study of the texts. But in the published work we find more than textual knowledge, more even than the comprehension of the doctrine: we find an adherence of the heart and of the mind, something like a permeation of the whole soul. It sometimes happens that the ability of men of superior intelligence becomes more and more evident the more intimate they become with the work of a revered master. As scattered particles of iron filings are attracted toward the poles by the force of the magnetic bar and compose themselves in harmonious curves, so, at the call of a genius it loves, the virtualities slumbering here and there in a soul awaken, join and work together with a common action in view. Now it is through this concentration of all the powers of mind and heart on a single point that a personality is constituted.

But aside from Aristotle another influence never ceased to make itself felt, accompanying Ravaisson through life like a familiar demon.

From early childhood Ravaisson had shown an aptitude for the arts in general and for painting in particular. His mother, a talented artist, dreamed perhaps of making an artist of him. She placed him in the hands of the painter Broc, and possibly the artist Chassériau who was a frequent visitor at the house. Both men were pupils of David. If Ravaisson did not actually hear the voice of the master, he at least caught its echo. It was not simply for amusement that he learned to paint. On several occasions he exhibited at the Salon, under the name of Laché, portraits which received favorable notice. He was especially gifted in drawing, and his sketches had an exquisite grace. Ingres used to tell him: "You have charm." Just when did his predilection for Italian painting manifest itself? Probably at an early age, for he began to make copies of Titian when he was sixteen or seventeen years old. But there seems to be no doubt that from the period between 1835 and 1845 dates his most profound study of Italian Renaissance art. And it is to the same period that we must trace the influence assumed over him and retained by the master who never ceased to be, in his eyes, the very personification of art, Leonardo da Vinci.

There is, in Leonardo da Vinci's *Treatise on Painting*, a page that Ravaisson loved to quote. It is the one where the author says that the living being is characterized by the undulous or serpentine line, that each being has its own way of undulating, and that the object of art is to render this undulation distinctive. "The secret of the art of drawing is to discover in each object the particular way in which a certain flexuous line which is, so to speak, its generating axis, is directed through its whole extent, like one main wave which spreads out in little surface waves." It is possible, moreover, that this line is not any one of the visible lines of the figure. It is not in one place any more than in another, but it gives the key to the whole. It is less perceived through the eye than thought by the mind. "Painting," said Leonardo da Vinci, "is a mental thing." And he added that it is the soul which creates the body in its image. The whole work of the master could serve as a commentary on this assertion. Let us look for a moment at the portrait of Mona Lisa or even at the picture of Lucrezia Crivelli: does it not seem to us that the visible lines of the figure rise toward a virtual center, located behind the canvas, where would be revealed all at once, gathered into a single word, the secret we shall never have finished reading, phrase by phrase, in the enigmatic physiognomy? That is where the painter has placed himself. It is in developing a mental vision, simple and direct, concentrated on this point, that he found, trait for trait, the model he had before his eyes, reproducing in his own way the generating effort of nature.

For Leonardo da Vinci, then, the painter's art does not consist in taking in detail each trait of the model, in order to transfer it to the canvas and reproduce, portion by portion, its materiality. Neither does it consist in picturing some impersonal and abstract type, where the model one sees and touches is dissolved into a vague ideality. True art aims at portraying the individuality of the model and to that end it will seek behind the lines one sees the movement the eye does not see, behind the movement itself something even more secret, the original intention, the fundamental aspiration of the person: a simple thought equivalent to all the indefinite richness of form and color.

How can one help being struck by the resemblance between the aesthetics of Leonardo da Vinci and the metaphysics of Aristotle as interpreted by Ravaisson? When he contrasts Aristotle with the physicists, who saw in things only their material mechanism, and with the Platonists, who absorbed the whole of reality into general types, when he shows us in Aristotle the master who sought in the heart of individual beings, by an intuition of the mind, the characteristic thought impelling them, does he not make of Aristotelianism the very philosophy of that art conceived and practiced by Leonardo da Vinci, an art which neither emphasizes the material contours of the model, nor tones them down to the advantage of an abstract ideal, but simply centers them around the latent thought and generative soul? The whole philosophy of Ravaisson springs from the idea that art is a figured metaphysics, that metaphysics is a reflection of art, and that it is the same intuition, variously applied, which makes the profound philosopher and the great artist. Ravaisson took possession of himself, became master of his thought and his pen the day that this identity revealed itself clearly to his mind. The identification occurred the moment the two distinct currents carrying him toward art and philosophy merged in him. And the junction took place when the two geniuses who, in his eyes, represented what was most profound in philosophy and highest in art, Aristotle and Leonardo da Vinci, seemed to him to interpenetrate and be animated with a common life.

Ravaisson's doctoral thesis, sustained about that period (1838), is a first application of method. It bears a modest title: *De l'habitude*. But it is a whole philosophy of nature that the author sets forth in it. What is nature? How is one to imagine its inner workings? What does it conceal under the regular succession of cause and effect? Does it really conceal something, or is it not perhaps reduced, in short, to an entirely superficial deployment of movements mechanically enmeshed in one another? In conformity with his principle, Ravaisson seeks the solution of this very general problem in a very concrete intuition; the one we have of our own particular condition when we contract a habit. For motor habit, once contracted, is a mechanism, a series of movements which determine one another: it is that part of us which is inserted into nature and which coincides with nature; it is nature itself. Now, our inner experience shows us in habit an activity which has passed, by imperceptible degrees, from consciousness to unconsciousness and from will to automatism. Should we not then imagine nature, in this form, as an obscured consciousness and a dormant will? Habit thus gives us the living demonstration of this truth, that mechanism is not sufficient to itself: it is, so to speak, only the fossilized residue of a spiritual activity.

These ideas, like many we owe to Ravaisson, have become classic. They have so thoroughly permeated our philosophy, a whole generation has been imbued with them to such a point, that we have some difficulty today in reconstructing them in their original form. They impressed his contemporaries. The thesis on *Habit,* and likewise the *Essay on the Metaphysics of Aristotle,* created an ever deepening effect on the philosophical world. The author, still quite young, was already a master. He appeared to be headed for a professorship in higher education, either at the Sorbonne or at the Collège de France, where he desired, where he almost got the post as substitute for Jouffroy. His career was already marked out. It would have developed in precise terms, on decisive points, the still somewhat vague principles of his philosophy. The necessity of setting forth his doctrines orally, of testing them on various problems, of applying them concretely to the questions raised by science and life, would have made him come down sometimes from those heights he loved to frequent. The flower of our youth, always ready to become inflamed with noble ideas expressed in beautiful language, would have crowded to hear him. Soon, doubtless, your Academy would have opened its doors to him. A school would have been created which would not have been prevented by its Aristotelian origin from being very modern, any more than its sympathies toward art would have alienated it from positive science. But fate decided otherwise. Ravaisson did not become a member of the Académie des Sciences morales until forty years later, and he never occupied a chair of philosophy.

It was, in fact, the time when Victor Cousin, from the heights of his seat on the royal council, exercised undisputed authority over the teaching of philosophy. To be sure, he had been the first to encourage the early efforts of Ravaisson. With his customary glance, he had seen what promise the thesis presented to the Academy contained. Full of esteem for the young philosopher, he admitted him for a time to those philosophical discussions which began with long walks in the Luxembourg and finished in the evening with dinner at some restaurant in the neighborhood—a delightful eclecticism that prolonged the peripatetic discussion into a Platonic symposium. Furthermore, looking at it from outside, everything seemed as though it would draw Ravaisson and Cousin together. Had not the two philosophers the same love of ancient philosophy, the same aversion for the sensualism of the XVIIIth century, the same respect for the tradition of the great masters, the same solicitude in rejuvenating that traditional philosophy, the same confidence in internal observation, the same general views on the relationship between the true and the beautiful, philosophy and art? Without the slightest doubt; but the thing that creates harmony between two minds is less a similarity of opinion than a certain affinity of intellectual temperament.

With Cousin thought led almost entirely to speech, and speech to action. He had to dominate, to conquer, to organize. He was fond of speaking of his philosophy as "my colors," of the professors of philosophy as "my regiment"; and he marched at their head, not forgetting on occasion to give a sonorous blast of the bugle. He was not, however, actuated by vanity or ambition, but by a sincere love of philosophy. Only, he loved it in his own way, as a man of action. He judged that the time had come for it to create a stir in the world. He wanted it to be powerful, catching hold of the child at school, directing the man through the course of his life, providing him, in his moral, social and political difficulties, with a law of conduct marked exclusively with the seal of reason. He began to realize his dream when he solidly installed in our University a disciplined philosophy: a skilful organizer, a sagacious politician, a matchless speaker, a stirring professor in whom perhaps the only thing lacking to make him fully worthy of being called a philosopher was the ability to stand being face to face, sometimes, with his own thought.

It was pure ideas to which Ravaisson was attached. He lived for them and with them, in an invisible temple where he surrounded them with a silent adoration. One felt him to be detached from everything else, and as though absent from the realities of life. His whole person exuded that extreme discretion which is the supreme distinction. Restrained in gesture, sparing in speech, delicate in the expression of an idea, never over-emphasizing, speaking softly as though he feared to frighten by too much noise the winged thoughts which settled around him, he probably thought that in order to make oneself heard afar it was unnecessary to raise one's voice very much when one gave out only the purest of sounds. Never did a man seek less to influence others than did that man. But never was mind more naturally, more tranquilly, more invincibly rebellious to the authority of others: it eluded by its immateriality all attempts to come to grips with it. He was one of those who offer so little resistance that no one can flatter himself that he has ever seen them yield. Cousin, if he ever attempted anything of the sort, quickly perceived that he was losing his time and his trouble.

And so these two minds, after a contact which revealed their incompatibility, naturally drifted apart. Forty years later, old and seriously ill, just before leaving for Cannes where he was to die, Cousin made known his desire for a reconciliation: at the station, as the train was ready to start, he held out his hand to Ravaisson; they exchanged a few words fraught with emotion. But it remains none the less true that it was Cousin's attitude toward him that discouraged Ravaisson from becoming, if one may so express it, a philosopher by profession, and which made him decide to follow a different career.

M. de Salvandy, at that time Minister of Public Instruction, was personally acquainted with Ravaisson. He took him as his principal private secretary. Shortly afterwards he put him in charge (only as a matter of form, for Ravaisson never occupied the post) of a course on the Faculty at Rennes. Finally, in 1839, he entrusted him with the newly created position of Inspector of Libraries. Ravaisson thus found himself committed to a way of life quite foreign to the one he had intended. He remained Inspector of Libraries until the day he became Inspector General of Higher Education, that is, for about fifteen years. On diverse occasions he published important works on the service in his charge: in 1841, a *Report on the Libraries of the Western Departments;* in 1846 a *Catalogue of the Manuscripts in the Library of Laon;* in 1862, a *Report on the Archives of the Empire and on the Organization of the Imperial Library.* Scholarly research had always attracted him, and on the other hand, the thorough knowledge of antiquity revealed in the *Essay on the Metaphysics of Aristotle,* was to make him the natural choice for the Académie des Inscriptions. He was elected a member of this Academy in 1849, replacing Letronne.

One cannot avoid a feeling of regret when one thinks that the philosopher who so young, had produced in so little time two masterly works, then went twenty years without contributing anything of importance to philosophy: the excellent memoir on Stoicism, read at the Acadèmie des Inscriptions in 1849 and 1851, published in 1857, must have been composed of material gathered for the *Essay on the Metaphysics of Aristotle.* Did Ravaisson drop his philosophical pursuits during this long interval? Certainly not, but he was one of those people who only make up their minds to write when led to do so by some external pressure, or by their professional pursuits. He wrote his *Essay* for an academic competitive examination; for his doctoral examination, the dissertation on *Habit.* Nothing in his new occupations incited him to produce. And perhaps he would never have formulated the conclusions to which twenty additional years of reflection had led him had he not been officially invited to do so.

The imperial government had decided that on the occasion of the Exposition of 1867 a collection of reports should be edited on the progress of the sciences, and of letters and the arts in France during the XIXth century. Duruy was at that time Minister of Public Instruction. He was well acquainted with Ravaisson, having been his fellow-student at Rollin. Already, in 1863, on the re-establishment of the examinations for the "agrégation" in philosophy, he had made Ravaisson president of the board of examiners. Whom should he ask to write the report on the progress of philosophy? More than one eminent philosopher on the staff of the University might have laid claim to that honor. Duruy preferred to approach Ravaisson, who was a philosopher not on the regular staff. And this minister, who had so many fine inspirations during his all-too-short tenure of office, never had a better one than on that day.

Ravaisson might have been content to review the most notable philosophical works of the century. Probably nothing more than that was asked of him. But he had a different conception of his task. Without paying any attention to opinion which some thinkers consider worthy of attention and others negligible, he read everything, as a man who knows what sincere reflection is capable of and how, by the sole force of that instrument, the humblest workers have extracted from the basest metal some particles of gold. After he had read everything, he then took upon himself the mastery of the whole. What he was looking for, through all the hesitations and deviations of a thought which has not always been fully conscious of what it wanted or what it was doing, was the point, situated perhaps in the distant future, to which our philosophy is tending.

Taking up and broadening the governing idea of his *Essay*, he distinguished two different ways of philosophizing. The first proceeds by analysis; it resolves things into their inert elements; from simplification to simplification it passes to what is most abstract and empty. Furthermore, it matters little whether this work of abstraction is effected by a physicist that we may call a mechanist or by a logician who professes to be an idealist: in either case it is materialism. The other method not only takes into account the elements but their order, their mutual agreement and their common direction. It no longer explains the living by the dead, but, seeing life everywhere, it defines the most elementary forms by their aspiration toward a higher form of life. It no longer brings the higher down to the lower, but on the contrary, the lower to the higher. It is, in the real sense of the word, spiritualism.

Now, if one examines the French philosophy of the XIXth century, not only with regard to the metaphysicians but also those scholars who have worked out the philosophy of their science, here, according to Ravaisson, is what one finds. It is not unusual for the mind to turn first in the direction of materialism and even to imagine it is persisting in that direction. It seeks quite naturally a mechanical or geometrical explanation of what it sees. But the habit of remaining in that attitude is only a survival from preceding centuries. It dates back to an epoch in which science was almost exclusively geometry. What characterizes the science of the XIXth century, the new undertaking it attempted, is the more concentrated study of living beings. Now, once on this ground, one can, if one sees fit, still continue to speak of pure mechanics; yet one is thinking of something else.

Let us open the first volume of the *Cours de philosophie positive* of Auguste Comte. In it we read that the phenomena observable in living beings are of the same nature as inorganic facts. Eight years later, in the second volume, he expresses the same ideas on the subject of plant-life, but only plant-life; he is already putting animal life off by itself. Finally, in his last volume, it is the whole of the phenomena of life that he completely isolates from physical and chemical facts. The more he considers the manifestations of life, the more he tends to establish between the various orders of facts, a distinction of rank or value and not simply of complication. Now, in following this direction, one arrives at spiritualism.

Claude Bernard at first speaks as though the play of mechanical forces gave us all the elements of a universal explanation. But when he leaves generalities and concentrates on describing in greater detail those phenomena of life on which his works have thrown such light, he reaches the hypothesis of the "directing" and even "creative idea," which would be the true cause of the organization.

All those, philosophers or scholars, who give careful study to the nature of life, display, according to Ravaisson, the same tendency, the same progress. One can foresee that the more the sciences of life develop, the more they will feel the necessity for reintegrating thought into the heart of nature.

Under what form, and in what way, what kind of operation? If life is a creation, we must represent it by analogy with the creations it is given us to observe, that is to say, with those we ourselves achieve. Now, in artistic creation, for example, it seems that the materials we have to work with, words and images for the poet, forms and colors for the painter, rhythms and harmonies for the musician, range themselves spontaneously under the idea they are to express, drawn, as it were, by the charm of a superior ideality. Is it not a similar movement, is it not also a state of fascination we should attribute to material elements when they are organized into living beings? In Ravaisson's eyes, the originative force of life was of the same nature as that of persuasion.

But whence come the materials which have come under this spell? This most important of all questions, Ravaisson answers by showing us, in the original production of matter, a movement opposite to the one accomplished when matter organizes itself. If the organization is, as it were, an awakening of matter, matter can only be a slumber of the mind. It is the last degree, it is the shadow of an existence which has diminished and, so to speak, emptied itself of all its contents. If matter is the "base of natural existence, a base on which, by this continuous progress that is the order of nature, from degree to degree, from kingdom to kingdom, everything comes back to the unity of mind," then conversely we should imagine at the beginning a *distention* of mind, a diffusion into space and time, constituting materiality. Infinite Thought "has annulled something of the plenitude of its being, in order to draw from it, by a kind of awakening and resurrection, all that exists."

Such is the doctrine set forth in the last part of the *Report.* The visible universe is presented to us as the external aspect of a reality which, seen from within and grasped in itself, would appear to us as a gratuitous gift, as a great act of liberality and love. No analysis can give an idea of these admirable pages. Twenty generations of students have learned them by heart. They have counted for a great deal in the influence exercised by the *Report* on philosophy as studied in the universities, an influence whose precise limits cannot be determined, nor whose depth be plumbed, nor whose nature be exactly described, any more than one can convey the inexpressible coloring which a great enthusiasm of early youth sometimes diffuses over the whole life of a man. May I add that by their dazzling brilliance they have slightly eclipsed the most original idea of the book? That the serious study of the phenomena of life must lead positive science to widen its framework, and go beyond the pure mechanism in which it has been enclosed for the last three centuries, is an eventuality we are beginning to consider today, even though most of us refuse to admit it. But when Ravaisson was writing, it took a veritable effort of divination to assign this term to a movement of ideas which seemed to be going in the opposite direction.

What are the facts, what are the reasons which led Ravaisson to judge that the phenomena of life, instead of being explained wholly by physical and chemical forces, could, on the contrary, throw some light on them? All the elements of the theory are already found in the *Essay on the Metaphysics of Aristotle* and in the thesis on *Habit*. But in the more precise form it assumes in the *Report*, I think it is connected with certain very special reflections Ravaisson made during this period on art, and in particular on an art whose theory and practice he knew, the art of drawing.

The Minister of Public Instruction had, in 1852, gone into the question of the teaching of drawing in the lycées. The twenty-first of June, 1853, a decree instructed a commission to present to the minister a plan of organization for teaching this subject. The commission included such men as Delacroix, Ingres and Flandrin; Ravaisson was its chairman. It was Ravaisson, too, who directed the report. He had won acceptance of his views, and had elaborated the ruling that a decree of December twenty-ninth, 1853, put into force in the State schools. It was a radical reform of the method in use until then in the teaching of drawing. The theoretical considerations which had inspired the reform occupy but little space in the report addressed to the minister; but Ravaisson took them up again later and set them forth more fully in the two articles *Art* and *Dessin* he contributed to the *Dictionnaire pédagogique*. Written in 1882, when the author was in full possession of his philosophy, these articles give us Ravaisson's ideas about drawing in a metaphysical form they did not, in the beginning, possess. (One can easily be convinced of this by reading the report of 1853.) At least they bring out with precision the latent metaphysics that these views implied from the outset. They show us how the leading ideas of the philosophy we have just summarized are connected, in Ravaisson's thought, with an art he had never ceased to practice. And they also confirm a law we consider general, namely, that in philosophy really viable ideas are those which have previously been lived by their author—lived, that is to say, applied by him, every day, to a work he loves, and modeled by him in the course of time, on that particular technique.

The method then used for the teaching of drawing was inspired by the ideas of Pestalozzi. In the arts pertaining to design as well as in everything else, they said, one must go from the simple to the complex. The pupil will, therefore, at first trace straight lines, then triangles, rectangles, squares; from there he will go on to the circle. Later he will reach the point where he draws the outlines of living forms: even so, he will have to give his drawing, as far as possible, an underpinning of straight lines and geometric curves, whether it be by drawing around the model (supposedly flat) an imaginary rectilinear figure upon which he will provide himself with guide marks (*points de repère*) or by temporarily replacing the curves of the model by geometric curves which he will then go back over in order to make the necessary retouchings.

This method, according to Ravaisson, cannot produce any result. For, in fact, either one wishes to learn only how to draw geometrical figures, in which case one might just as well make use of the appropriate instruments and apply the rules established by geometry; or else it is art properly so-called one is claiming to teach, but in that case experience shows us that the application of mechanical processes to the imitation of living forms only succeeds in having them badly understood and badly reproduced. What counts above all in these circumstances is, in fact, the "good judgment of the eye." The student who begins by providing himself with guide marks, who then links them together by means of a continuous line, drawing his inspiration as far as possible from geometric curves, can only learn to see falsely. He never grasps the characteristic movement of the form to be drawn. "The spirit of the form" always eludes him. The result is entirely different when one begins with the characteristic curves of life. The simplest of these will be, not what is most closely allied to geometry, but what appeals most to the intelligence, what is most expressive: the animal will be easier to understand than the plant, man will be easier than the animal, the Apollo Belvedere easier than a model picked at random off the street. Let us then begin by having the child draw the most perfect of human figures, the models furnished by Greek statuary. If we are doubtful about his difficulties with perspective, let us at first replace the models by photographic reproductions. We shall see that all the rest will come, over and above. By starting from geometry one can go as far as one wishes in the direction of complication without ever drawing any closer to the curves by which life expresses itself. On the contrary, if one begins with these curves, one perceives, the moment one attempts the geometric curves, that one has them already in hand.

Here, then, we have the first of the two theses developed in the *Report on Philosophy in France:* from mechanics one cannot pass to the living by way of composition; rather it is life which furnishes the key to the inorganic world. This metaphysics is implied, foreshadowed and even felt in the concrete effort by which the hand practices reproducing the characteristic movements of figures.

In its turn, the consideration of these movements and of the connection between them and the figure they draw, gives a special meaning to the second thesis of Ravaisson, to the views he develops on the origin of things and on the act of "condescension," as he calls it, of which the universe is the manifestation.

If we consider, from our point of view, the things of nature, the thing we find most striking about them is their beauty. That beauty, furthermore, is more and more accentuated as nature goes from the inorganic up to the organic, from the plant to the animal, and from the animal to man. Therefore, the more intense the work of nature, the more beautiful is its product. That is to say that, if beauty were to reveal to us its secret, we should penetrate through it into the very intimacy of nature's work. But will it reveal it? Perhaps—that is, if we consider that beauty itself is only an effect, and if we go back to the cause. Beauty belongs to form, and all form has its origin in a movement which outlines it: form is only recorded movement. Now, if we ask ourselves which are the movements that describe *beautiful* forms, we find that they are the graceful movements: beauty, said Leonardo da Vinci, is arrested grace. The question then is to know what constitutes grace. But this problem is more easily resolved, for in everything that is graceful we see, we feel, we divine a kind of abandon, as it were, a condescension. Thus, for him who contemplates the universe with the eye of an artist, it is grace that is apprehended through the veil of beauty, and beneath grace it is goodness which shines through. Each thing manifests, in the movement recorded by its form, the infinite generosity of a principle which gives itself. And it is not by mistake that we call by the same name the charm we see in movement, and the act of liberality characteristic of the divine goodness: the two meanings of the word *grace* were identical for Ravaisson.

He remained faithful to his method in seeking the most lofty metaphysical truths in a concrete vision of things, in passing by imperceptible transitions from aesthetics to metaphysics and even to theology. There is nothing more instructive, in that regard, than the study he published in 1887, in the *Revue des Deux Mondes* on the philosophy of Pascal. In it is evident his preoccupation with linking Christianity up to ancient philosophy and art, without, however, failing to recognize what Christianity brought that was new to the world. This preoccupation fills the whole latter part of Ravaisson's life.

In this latter period, Ravaisson had the satisfaction of seeing his ideas spread, his philosophy penetrate into education, a whole movement take shape in favor of a doctrine which made spiritual activity the very foundation of reality. The *Report* of 1867 had given rise to a change of orientation in philosophy in the university: Ravaisson's influence succeeded the influence of Cousin. As Boutroux put it in the splendid pages he dedicated to his memory: "M. Ravaisson never sought influence, but in the end he exercised it after the manner of the divine song which, according to the ancient fable, led submissive material to arrange itself, of its own accord, into walls and turrets." As chairman of the examining committee for the agrégation he brought a benevolent impartiality to those functions, being concerned solely in distinguishing talent and effort wherever they were encountered. In 1880, your Academy called him to take his place among its members, replacing M. Peisse. One of the first lectures he presented before your company was an important report on skepticism, on the occasion of a competition in which your future colleague, Brochard, so brilliantly carried off the prize. In 1899, the Académie des Inscriptions et Belles-Lettres celebrated the fiftieth anniversary of his election. He himself, still young, still smiling, went from one Academy to the other, gave a memoir on some point in Greek archeology here, spoke on morality or education there, presided at the distribution of prizes or, in familiar conversation, expressed the most abstract truths in the most delightful form. During those last thirty years of his life, Ravaisson never ceased to pursue the development of a thought whose principal stages had been marked by the *Essay on the Metaphysics of Aristotle,* the thesis on *Habit* and the *Report* of 1867. But this new effort, having led to no finished work, is less known. Furthermore, what results he did publish were of such a nature as to cause a slight surprise, I might almost say bewilderment, in those very disciples who followed him with the closest attention. These were, first, a series of reports and articles on the Venus de Milo; many people were surprised at the insistence with which he kept coming back to so particular a subject. Next were works on funeral monuments of antiquity. Finally, there were considerations on the moral or pedagogical problems which confront us today.

The relation between such varied preoccupations was not immediately apparent. The truth is that his hypotheses on the masterpieces of Greek sculpture, his attempts at reconstructing the group of Milo, his interpretations of funeral bas-reliefs, his views on morality and education, all formed a perfectly coherent whole, all linked up, in Ravaisson's thought, with a new development of his metaphysical doctrine. We find a preliminary sketch of his latest philosophy in an article entitled *Métaphysique et morale* which appeared in 1893 as the introduction to the review by that name. We should have had the definitive formula of it in the book Ravaisson was writing when death overtook him. The fragments of this work, collected by reverent hands, have been published under the title *Testament philosophique*. They give us what is probably a sufficient idea of what the book would have been. But if we wish to follow Ravaisson's thought to its final stage, we must go back beyond 1870, even beyond the *Report* of 1867, and betake ourselves to the time when Ravaisson first directed his attention to the works of ancient statuary.

It was his own reflections on the teaching of drawing which led him to become interested in the ancients. If the study of drawing must begin by the imitation of the human figure, and beauty in its most perfect manifestation, one must seek one's models among antique statuary, since it brought the human figure to its greatest degree of perfection. Furthermore, in order to spare the child the difficulties of perspective, the statues themselves, we said, will be replaced by their photographic reproductions. Ravaisson was thus led first to build up a collection of photographs; then, a thing even more important, to have casts made of the masterpieces of Greek art. These casts, first placed in the Campana collection, later became the beginning of the Charles Ravaisson-Mollien collection of antique plasters in the Louvre. By a natural development, Ravaisson then came to envisage the plastic arts from a new angle. Having until then devoted himself to modern painting, he then began to concentrate on antique sculpture. And, faithful to the idea that one must know the technique of an art in order to enter into its spirit, he took up the roughing-chisel, practiced modeling, and by dint of hard work achieved real skill in it. The opportunity soon presented itself for him to turn it to the advantage of art and even, by an imperceptible transition, of philosophy.

The emperor Napoleon III, who had several opportunities of forming his own personal opinion of Ravaisson's worth, notably at the installation of the Campana museum, appointed him curator of antiques and of modern sculpture at the Louvre in June, 1870. Several weeks later war broke out, the enemy was at the gates of Paris, the bombardment was imminent and Ravaisson, after having proposed that the Académie des Inscriptions should launch a protest to the civilized world against the violence menacing art treasures, attended to having the most valuable pieces in the museum of antiques carried to a deep underground cavern to protect them from any possible fire. When the Venus de Milo was being moved, he noticed that the two blocks of which the statue is made had been badly put together at the time of its original installation, and that the wooden wedges interposed between them had thrown the original attitude out of line. He himself settled anew the relative positions of the two blocks: he personally directed the correction. Some years later, he carried out on the Winged Victory a task of the same nature, but even more important. In the first restoration of that statue it had been impossible to adjust the wings that we now find have so powerful an effect. Ravaisson recast in plaster a piece that was lacking on the right side, as well as the whole of the left side, of the chest: from that moment the wings found their proper connection and the goddess appeared as we see her today on the stair-case of the Louvre, a body without arms, without a head, where only the swelling of the draperies and the spreading wings make visible to the eye a gust of enthusiasm passing over a soul.

Now, as Ravaisson became more familiar with antique statuary, an idea formed in his mind which applied to the whole of Greek sculpture, but which had its most concrete significance for the work to which circumstances had especially directed his attention, the Venus de Milo.

It seemed to him that the art of statuary, in the time of Phidias, had modeled great and noble figures, whose standard had from then on gone down and down, and that this decline must have been due to the deterioration of the classical conception of divinity as it became popularized. "Greece, in its early days, worshipped in Venus a goddess it called Urania. . . . The Venus of that day was the sovereign ruler of worlds. . . . She was a Providence, supreme power and at the same time supreme benevolence, whose ordinary symbol was a dove signifying that it was by love and gentleness that she reigned. . . . These old conceptions changed: an Athenian legislator, indulgent to the populace, established for it, alongside of the cult of the celestial Venus, the cult of an inferior Venus, called the Venus of the people. The ancient and sublime poem changed by degrees into a novel interwoven with frivolous adventures."

Back to this antique poem the Venus de Milo leads us. The work of Lysippus or one of his pupils, this Venus, according to Ravaisson, is only a variation of a Venus by Phidias. Originally she was not alone; she was part of a group. It is this group that Ravaisson worked so hard to restore. People smiled to see him model and remodel the arm of the goddess. Did they know that what Ravaisson was really trying to recapture in that rebellious clay was the very soul of Greece, and that the philosopher remained true to the spirit of his doctrine in seeking the fundamental aspirations of pagan antiquity not only in the abstract and general formulas of philosophy, but in a concrete figure, the very one that, in the hey-day of Athens, the greatest of artists sculptured, aiming at the highest possible expression of beauty?

It is not our place to evaluate, from the archeological

point of view, the conclusions Ravaisson reached. Suffice it to say that he placed beside the original Venus a god who might have been Mars, or a hero who could have been Theseus. From induction to induction he succeeded in seeing in this group the symbol of a triumph of persuasion over brute force. It is of this victory that Greek mythology sang its epic poem. Hero-worship had been only the grateful worship dedicated by Greece to those who, being the strongest, desired also to be the best, and used their strength only to help suffering humanity. The religion of the ancients was thus an homage paid to pity. Above everything, at the very origin of everything, it placed generosity, magnanimity, and, in the highest sense of the word, love.

Thus, by a strange deviation, Greek sculpture brought Ravaisson back to the central idea of his philosophy. Had he not said in his *Report* that the universe is the manifestation of a principle which gives itself through liberality, condescension and love? But this idea, rediscovered among the ancients, seen through Greek sculpture, now took shape in his mind in a more ample and simple form. Ravaisson was able to give us only an incomplete sketch of this new form; but his *Testament philosophique* gives us its broad general outlines.

He said in it that a great philosophy had appeared at the dawning of human thought and had continued through the vicissitudes of history: the heroic philosophy, the philosophy of the magnanimous, the strong, the generous. This philosophy, even before being thought by superior intelligences, had been lived by the noblest hearts. It was at all times the philosophy of truly royal souls, born for the whole world and not for themselves, who remained faithful to the original impulse, in tune with the unison of the fundamental note of the universe, a note of generosity and love. Those who first practiced it were the heroes Greece worshipped. Those who later taught it were the thinkers who, from Thales to Socrates, from Socrates to Plato and Aristotle, from Aristotle to Descartes and Leibnitz, extend in a single long line. All of them, foreshadowing or developing Christianity, thought and practiced a philosophy which is wholly contained in a state of soul; and this state of soul is the one our Descartes called by the beautiful name of "generosity."

From this new point of view Ravaisson took up, in his *Testament philosophique,* the principal theses of his *Report.* He found them in the great philosophers of all times. He verified them by examples; he animated them with a new spirit by giving to feeling a larger part in the search for the truth, and to enthusiasm a greater share in the creation of the beautiful. He stressed the highest of all arts, the very art of life, which molds the soul. He summarized it in the precept of Saint Augustine: "Love, and do what you wish to do." And he added that love thus understood is at the core of every one of us, that it is natural, that we do not have to create it, that it blossoms of its own accord when we put from us the obstacle our will opposes to it: the adoration of ourselves.

He would have liked to have our system of education tend to give full play to the feeling of generosity. "The evil we suffer from," he wrote as early as 1887, "does not reside in the inequality of social conditions— extreme though these may sometimes be—as much as in the unfortunate sentiments connected with it. . . ." "The remedy for this evil should be sought principally in a moral reform, which establishes reciprocal harmony and sympathy between the classes, a reform which is especially a matter of education. . . ." He set little store by book-learning. In a few words he outlined the program for a truly liberal education, to free the soul of all its limitations, especially egoism, the worst of them: "Society," he said, "should rest on generosity, that is to say, on the disposition to consider itself as being of a noble race, of a race heroic and even divine." "Social divisions arise from the fact that there are, on the one hand, wealthy people who are wealthy for their own sakes and not for the common cause; and on the other hand are the poor who, being able to count on nothing but their own efforts, look upon the wealthy only as objects of envy." It rests with the wealthy, with the upper classes, to modify the state of soul of the working classes. "Amid their sufferings and their shortcomings the people, always ready to help, have conserved much of that disinterestedness and generosity which were qualities of the early ages. . . . Let some sign come down from heaven to point out, in the midst of our obscurities, the path to follow to re-establish magnanimity in its former sovereign rule: nowhere will it receive quicker response than among the people. 'The people,' said Adam Smith, 'admires and reveres so much that nothing appeals to it as much as austerity.' "

At the same time that he set forth generosity as a natural sentiment in which we become conscious of the nobility of our origin, Ravaisson pointed out, in our belief in immortality, a no less natural presentiment of our future destiny. In fact, he found that belief all through classical antiquity. He read it on Grecian funeral steles, in those pictures where, according to his interpretation, the dead man returns to announce to the members of his family, still in the land of the living, that he is enjoying unalloyed bliss in the abode of the blessèd. He said that the feeling of the ancients had not misled them on that point, that we should find in the beyond those we had cherished here below, and that he who had once loved would always love. He added that the immortality promised by religion was an eternity of happiness, that one could not, one should not conceive it otherwise, else generosity would not have the last word. "In the name of justice," he wrote, "a theology foreign to the spirit of mercy which is the very spirit of Christianity, misusing the word 'eternity' which often signifies only a long duration, condemns to endless misery sinners who die unrepentant, that is to say, almost the whole of humanity. What idea, then, are we to have as to the felicity of a God listening, throughout eternity, to the moaning of so many voices? . . . We find in the land where Christianity was born, an allegorical fable inspired by an entirely different thought, the fable of Cupid and Psyche, or the soul. Love becomes enamoured of Psyche. The latter becomes guilty, like the Eve of the Bible, of an unholy curiosity to know, otherwise than through God, how to tell good from evil, and thus, how to deny divine grace. Love imposes on her expiatory punishment, but only in order that she may anew be worthy of his choice, and he does not do so without regret. A bas-relief represents him holding a butterfly in one hand (soul and butterfly, the symbol of resurrection, have always been synonymous); with the other hand he is burning it with the flame of his torch; but he is turning away his head, as though full of pity."

Such were the theories, and such the allegories, that Ravaisson set down in the last few pages of his *Testament philosophique,* a few days before his death. Between those lofty thoughts and those graceful images, as though along an avenue bordered by superb trees and sweet-scented flowers, he made his way until the last moment, careless of the night approaching, intent only on looking straight ahead at the sun on the far horizon, —the sun which showed its form the better in the softening of its light. A short illness in which he neglected to look after himself, carried him off in a few days. With his family at his bedside, he died, on the eighteenth of May, 1900, having kept to the very end all the lucidity of his great intelligence.

The history of philosophy shows us the constantly renewed efforts on the part of a reflection which labors to lessen difficulties, to resolve contradictions, to measure with increasing approximation a reality incommensurate with our thought. But now and then a soul looms up which seems to triumph over these complications by sheer force of simplicity, the soul of an artist or a poet, that has remained close to its origin, reconciling in a harmony sensitive to the heart, terms perhaps irreconcilable to the intelligence. The language it speaks when it lends its voice to philosophy is not understood in the same way by everyone. Some think it vague, and so it is in what it expresses. Others feel it precise, because they experience everything it suggests. To many ears it brings only the echo of a by-gone past; but others already hear in it, as in a dream, the joyous song of the future. The work of Ravaisson will leave behind it these very different impressions, like all philosophy which addresses itself to feeling as much as to reason. That its form may be a little vague, no one will deny: it is the form of an inspiration; but the inspiration comes from above, and clear is its direction. That in parts it utilized ancient materials furnished in particular by the philosophy of Aristotle, Ravaisson was fond of repeating: but the spirit which quickens it is a new spirit, and the future will perhaps tell that the ideal it proposed to our knowledge and activity was, on more than one point, ahead of our own. Is there anything more daring, anything newer than to announce to physicists that the inert will be explained by the living, to biologists that life will only be understood through thought, to philosophers that generalities are not philosophical, to teachers that the whole must be taught before its elements, to students that one must begin by perfection, to man, more than ever given over to egoism and hatred, that the natural driving power of man is generosity?